Directe Post-Dampfschiffahrt

Agenturen.

Agenturen.

Hamburg:
August Bolten,
William Miller's Nachfolger.
37. Admiralitätsstrasse.

London:
Smith, Sundius & Co.
17. Gracechurch Street.

Southampton:
Smith, Sundius & Co.
4. Oriental Place.

New-York:
Kunhardt & Co.
45. Exchange Place.

C. B. Richard & Boas.
6. Barclay Street.

New-Orleans:
Williams Roperti & Co.

Hâvre:
W. Dunran.
31. Quai d'Orleans.

Paris:
A. Chateauneuf jeune.
8. Boulevard Montmartre.

der

Hamburg-Amerikanischen Packetfahrt-Actien-Gesellschaft

zwischen

Hamburg & New-York

eventuell Southampton anlaufend.

unter Direction der Herren

Adolph Godeffroy, H. J. Merck & Co., Joh⁸ Schuback & Söhne, Albrecht & Dill, C. Woermann,

vermittelst der prachtvollen, auf das Solideste construirten und rühmlichst bekannten grossen Post-Dampfschiffe

Hammonia, (neu)	**Cimbria,** (neu)	**Allemannia,**	**Germania,**
Capt. Ehlers.	Capt. Trautmann.	Capt. Meier.	Capt. Schwensen.
Saxonia,	**Bavaria,**	**Teutonia,**	**Borussia,**
Capt. Haack	Capt. J. Meyer.	Capt. Bardua	Capt. Franzen.

Die Expeditionen von Hamburg nach New-York finden Statt wie folgt:

alle 14 Tage Sonnabends	alle 8 Tage Sonnabends, von Mitte März bis Ende October					alle 14 Tage Sonnabends
5. Januar,	16. März,	27. April,	15. Juni,	3. August,	21. September,	9. November.
19. Januar,	23. März,	4. Mai,	22. Juni,	10. August,	28. September,	23. November,
2. Februar,	30. März,	11. Mai,	29. Juni,	17. August,	5. October.	7. December,
16. Februar,	6. April,	18. Mai,	6. Juli,	24. August,	12. October,	21. December.
2. März,	13. April,	25. Mai,	13. Juli,	31. August,	19. October,	
	20. April,	1. Juni,	20. Juli,	7. September,	26. October.	
		8. Juni,	27. Juli,	14. September,		

Auch zwischen

Hamburg & New-Orleans

wird die Gesellschaft mit diesem Jahre eine Dampfschiff-Verbindung eröffnen und demzufolge vorläufig zwei Expeditionen, nämlich

von **Hamburg** am **1. October** und **1. November,**
„ **New-Orleans** „ **15. November** , **15. December**

Statt finden lassen.

Passage-Preise, einschliesslich vollständiger Beköstigung, jedoch ohne Wein &c.:

Nach **New-York:** Erste Kajüte oberer Salon Pr. Crt. Thlr. 165. — Erste Kajüte unterer Salon Pr. Crt. Thlr. 115. — Zwischendeck Pr. Crt. Thlr. 60.
„ **New-Orleans:** „ „ „ 200. „ „ „ 150. „ „ 60.

Kinder unter 10 Jahren zahlen auf allen Plätzen die Hälfte. — Für Säuglinge unter 1 Jahr sind Pr. Crt. Thlr. 3 auf allen Plätzen zu entrichten.

An Reisegepäck hat ein jeder Passagier frei: 20 Cubicf., Kinder 10 Cubicf. Alles Reisegepäck ist mit dem vollen Namen des Passagiers zu bezeichnen.

Nähere Auskunft ertheilt auf portofreie Anfragen:

HAMBURG, Januar 1867.

August Bolten, William Miller's Nachfolger.
37 Admiralitätsstrasse.

DESTINATION AMERICA

DESTINATION AMERICA

MALDWYN A. JONES

Weidenfeld and Nicolson   London

Designed by Tim Higgins for
George Weidenfeld and Nicolson Ltd,
11 St John's Hill London SW11

Printed in Great Britain by
Butler & Tanner Ltd,
Frome and London

ISBN 0 297 77076 4

CONTENTS

PREFACE

DESTINATION AMERICA tells the story of the greatest mass migration in history – the movement of millions of Europeans to the United States in the past century and a half. The book was written to accompany the television series of the same name, but although it covers ground similar to that of the television programmes it does not follow them rigidly. I have tried to amplify the themes of the programmes, and also to add complementary material with a view to providing a general introductory account of the Atlantic migration.

I have not attempted to be comprehensive but instead have concentrated on the peoples who contributed the greatest numbers to the confluent tides of immigration: the Irish, British, Germans, Scandinavians, Italians and east-European Jews. That other groups have been virtually or entirely ignored is not because I do not acknowledge their importance but because of the constraints imposed by a small book on a vast topic. The book focuses mainly on the century between 1815 and 1914, but it also deals with the period since mass migration came to an end. It should be realized, however, that the story is necessarily incomplete since emigration to America is still going on, though on a greatly reduced scale.

Most of the book deals with what befell the immigrants after they struggled down the gangplank at Castle Garden or Ellis Island to begin a new life. But considerable space is allotted to the ordeals they passed through in crossing the Atlantic as well as to the forces that led them to leave their homes in the first place. Indeed the European background is all-important. To understand the problems immigrants faced – and created – in the new world it is essential to bear in mind what they brought with them from the old.

One recurrent theme is why America became such a magnet for so many millions of the uprooted. Another is the impact of a huge and variegated army of newcomers upon a young and rapidly-expanding country. But what the book seeks above all to convey is what it meant to disrupt one's life and travel to an unknown future in a far-off land. It tries to bring generalizations about immigration to life by relating them to the experience of individual men and women. Wherever possible I have allowed the immigrants to speak for themselves. I have been able to make use of the interviews with immigrants and their descendants which were recorded for the television series but not used in full in the programmes.

I have tried, however, not to idealize the immigrant, recognizing that those who travelled steerage were neither more nor less lovable than the rest of humanity. Nor have I depicted immigration as the simple success story of American popular tradition. In the end the promise of America was generally fulfilled but the story was not invariably one of a steady rise to fame and fortune. The emphasis of this book is rather upon the variety, indeed the ambivalence, of the immigrant experience.

I have been given a great deal of help. Alison Wade of Thames Television has offered welcome advice and suggestions about a whole variety of problems. Richard S. Barnes of Chicago has kept me up-to-date by supplying material about recent developments. The production staff involved in making the television series, and especially Isobel Hinshelwood, Peter Tiffin, Jerome Kuehl and Tom Steel, the producer, have generously shared with me their ideas and discoveries. Liz Neeson gave invaluable help in choosing illustrations. Christine Bernard greatly improved the manuscript by her masterly editing and the book has benefited from the sympathetic interpretation of the designer, Tim Higgins, and from the editorial skill of Hilary Lloyd Jones. My daughter, Caroline, turned an almost illegible manuscript into an almost legible typescript with remarkable speed. My wife has attempted, not wholly successfully, to cure me of my stylistic bad habits. Finally, I must acknowledge my debt to those historians on whose specialized studies, listed in Further Reading, any general account must necessarily depend. To all who helped I offer my grateful thanks but I must be held solely accountable for the book and its shortcomings.

M.A.J.

NOTE ON CURRENCY

In some cases I have given dollar equivalents for sterling and vice versa. To do so in all cases would have been cumbersome and unnecessary but the reader should note that for the bulk of the period covered in this book the exchange rate was approximately £1=$5.

1
THE GOLDEN DOOR

Steerage passengers gaze joyfully at the Statue of Liberty from the deck of an incoming vessel. Such prints helped to popularize the notion that the Statue of Liberty was a symbol of welcome to the 'huddled masses' of the old world.

ON A SMALL ISLAND IN NEW YORK HARBOUR stands one of the most familiar landmarks in the world – the Statue of Liberty. Designed by the French sculptor, Bartholdi, it was a gift to America from the people of France, commemorating the centenary of the War of Independence, when France had been America's ally. The statue was unveiled on 28 October 1886 by President Grover Cleveland. Today, few people know why it was erected, or that it was intended to represent the ideal of American liberty, radiating outwards to the world. Instead, the uplifted torch has been seen as a welcoming beacon to those millions who crossed the Atlantic in search of a better life.

A poem, 'The New Colossus', is inscribed on the base of the statue. Written in 1883 by Emma Lazarus, a scholarly member of a wealthy New York family, it has enjoyed an enormous vogue in recent decades, probably because it manages to define the American ethos in terms that unite as well as inspire:

> *Not like the brazen giant of Greek fame*
> *With conquering limbs astride from land to land,*
> *Here at our sea-washed, sunset gates shall stand*
> *A mighty woman with a torch, whose flame*
> *Is the imprisoned lightning, and her name*
> *Mother of Exiles. From her beacon-hand*
> *Glows world-wide welcome; her mild eyes command*
> *The air-bridged harbor that twin cities frame.*
> *'Keep, ancient lands, your storied pomp!' cries she*
> *With silent lips. 'Give me your tired, your poor,*
> *Your huddled masses yearning to breathe free*
> *The wretched refuse of your teeming shore.*
> *Send these, the homeless, tempest-tost to me,*
> *I lift my lamp beside the golden door!'*

The poem also reminds Americans of their common condition, namely of being immigrants from foreign shores, or their descendants. Admittedly, the indigenous Indians and the Negroes were forcibly incorporated into American society and can hardly be described as immigrants. The Indians – mistakenly described as such by Columbus – were in America since pre-historic times. The Negroes are descendants of African slaves transported involuntarily over a period of two and a half centuries. But the 800,000 Indians and twenty-two million Negroes together account for only about eleven per cent of the present population. The remainder is of immigrant origin and the history of immigration spans the history of America.

In the period before the American colonies became independent, newcomers from Europe were known as colonists or settlers. The word 'immigrant' was coined only in 1787, eleven years after the Declaration of Independence. It has been argued that the change was significant in itself and that there is a fundamental difference between those who settle in a wilderness and establish a new society, and those foreigners who arrive only when the country's laws, customs and language are fixed. The first, runs the argument, should be called colonists, the second immigrants. This division has appealed to organizations like the Daughters of the American Revolution who regard 'immigrant' as a pejorative term, believing firmly that their own ancestors, who arrived before 1776, were a superior breed to later-comers.

Such a distinction has little basis in historical reality, as Franklin D. Roosevelt recognized when he addressed the Daughters of the American Revolution as 'fellow immigrants'. Colonists and immigrants were drawn from the same social classes and emigrated for the same mixture of motives. It is wrong to assume that all who settled in America before 1776 entered a wilderness and that later-comers entered a fully settled country. The experience of those who crossed the Atlantic in the seventeenth and eighteenth centuries was basically the same as that of their nineteenth- and twentieth-century successors: that is, they had to adjust to a society very different from the one they had left. For though many of the white inhabitants of the American colonies were English, the population included large numbers from Germany and Ireland and sprinklings of Scots, Swedes, Dutchmen, French Huguenots and Jews. In Pennsylvania the English constituted no more than a third of the population. Already by 1776, therefore, Americans had some claim to being a cosmopolitan people.

It is not known exactly how many people emigrated to the American colonies during this early period, but it is clear that the number was never more than a fraction of what it later became. The so-called Puritan Great Migration to Massachusetts between 1628 and 1640 totalled only 20,000 people and though the pace of migration quickened in the eighteenth century, it did not approach a mass movement; it is doubtful whether the annual arrivals ever rose above 10,000. Indeed the total emigration to the American colonies in the eighteenth century has been put at only 450,000. For about thirty years after independence the number of arrivals did not increase much. Then, at the close of the Napoleonic Wars a mass movement began which was to persist until it was checked by the restrictive immigration laws of the 1920s. In a period of little more than a century a total of thirty-five million people entered the United States – the largest human migration in recorded history.

They came in three distinct waves, each more powerful than its predecessor: the first reached its peak in the 1850s, the second in the 1880s, the last in the decade immediately preceding the outbreak of the First World War, when immigrants were entering the United States at the rate of a million a year. Despite their huge numbers immigrants have never threatened to swamp older Americans. Whereas there have been times when the foreign-born have accounted for more than a fifth of Canada's population and nearly a third of Argentina's, they have never exceeded more than a seventh of the population of the United States, though in some Middle Western States, like Wisconsin, the proportion rose at times to a quarter.

The Golden Door

Immigration had its greatest impact in the cities. At the time of the Civil War more than half the residents of New York and Chicago were foreign-born. Thereafter the proportion dwindled because of the native Americans' drift to the cities. Nevertheless, by the beginning of the twentieth century immigrants and their children were in the majority in every large American city and in many smaller ones as well. In 1910 three-quarters of the population of New York, Chicago, Cleveland, Detroit and Boston consisted of first- and second-generation immigrants.

More remarkable even than the size of America's immigrant population is its diversity. The contrast with other immigrant-receiving countries is striking. More than two-thirds of Argentina's immigrants have come from Italy and Spain; more than three-quarters of those who entered Brazil have been Portuguese, Italian and Spanish. Canada and Australia, until very recently, have recruited largely from the British Isles. Nearly all of South Africa's immigrants have been Dutch or British. The United States, however, has drawn heavily on a much wider range of countries. Between 1820 and 1950 she admitted six million immigrants from Germany, nearly five million from Italy, four and a half million from Ireland, and nearly four million from Great Britain. Another four million – Poles, Hungarians, Czechs, Croats, Slovenes, Serbs, Ruthenes and Slovaks – came from the Austro-Hungarian Empire and its successor states. More than three million entered from Russia, chiefly Jews, but with substantial numbers of Poles, Ukrainians and Lithuanians. A further two million came from the Scandinavian countries, half a million from Greece and a quarter of a million from the Netherlands. Indeed, except for France and Spain, there was no country in Europe, hardly even a province or town, which did not contribute considerably to the peopling of America. Asia sent 400,000 Chinese and 280,000 Japanese, as well as numbers of Syrians, Lebanese and Armenians. And from within the western hemisphere came three million Canadians, one million Mexicans, and half a million West Indians. Thus the population of the United States presents a truly extraordinary variety of nationalities, races, cultures and religions.

The great size of this folk movement made it a unique phenomenon; nevertheless it was in fact only part of a still larger pattern, for America was not the only magnet for dislocated Europeans. Nineteenth-century Europe was a continent on the move. People moved from countryside to town, from province to province, across boundaries and within them, overland and across oceans. Five and a half million Europeans went to Argentina, four and a half million to Canada, four million to Brazil, and sizeable numbers to Australia, New Zealand and South Africa. Millions more changed their location without leaving Europe. Irishmen emigrated to England and Scotland, Italians, Spaniards and Poles to France, the motley peoples of Austria-Hungary to Germany, Russian *moujiks* to the steppes of Siberia. Many European countries were consequently countries of immigration as well as emigration.

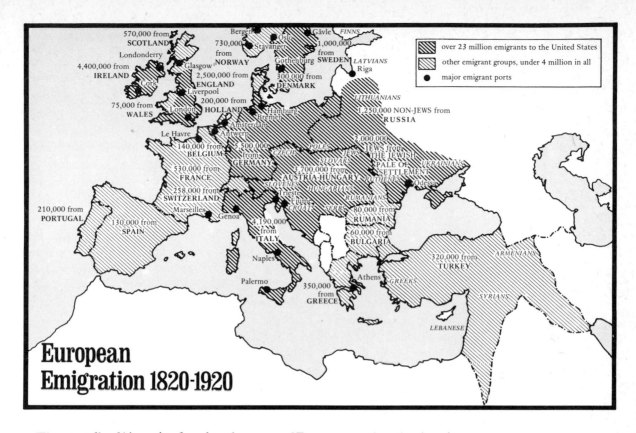

European Emigration 1820-1920

Thus to talk of 'America fever' as the cause of European emigration is naive. There was not merely one westward-setting tide but a whole series of cross-currents which carried people to different destinations and indeed brought them back again; perhaps as many as one-third of those who emigrated to the United States eventually went back to Europe. To believe therefore that it was only the lure of American freedom that set people in motion is simplistic. The reality was more complex and more prosaic. To be sure, an Irish peasant might end up in Boston, but he might just as readily go to Dublin or Liverpool. An Italian peasant might move to Milan or Buenos Aires or Philadelphia – or to all three successively, and not necessarily in that order.

It is clear, then, that the causes of mass emigration must be sought in Europe rather than in America. People were uprooted from their homes largely because of hardship, itself the result of far-reaching economic changes. A massive increase in population, the collapse of the old agricultural order, the industrial revolution – these were the factors that forced people out of their accustomed places and compelled them to move elsewhere. Sometimes special local conditions gave an extra impetus to emigration: a famine, an earthquake or a blight. But such events merely intensified the long-term pressure of numbers on the means of subsistence. These changes appeared first in the north and west of the continent and only later in the south and east. Up to 1880 or so immigrants were drawn overwhelmingly from the British Isles, Germany and Scandinavia.

Thereafter the centre of gravity of emigration moved steadily southward and eastward. By the end of the century the bulk of America's immigrants mainly consisted of Slavs, Italians, Greeks, Hungarians and east-European Jews. That shift, as we shall see, produced a profound change in American attitudes towards immigration.

In the seventeenth and eighteenth centuries governments had been keen to keep their citizens at home. They saw population as a form of wealth, emigration as a drain on national strength. Hence they discouraged – some positively forbade – emigration. But the spectre of overpopulation produced a change of heart. After 1815 governments came increasingly to see emigration as a remedy for distress and a safety-valve for discontent. Some even tried to use the United States as a dumping-ground for convicts, paupers and other undesirables. The United Kingdom was the first country to grant absolute freedom of movement to its subjects, largely out of fear that, unless the Irish poor were allowed to go elsewhere, they would in the words of a Parliamentary committee in 1826, 'deluge Great Britain with poverty and wretchedness'. Other governments, more or less grudgingly, followed suit, though there were some that attempted, not very successfully, to ensure that no one left without fulfilling his military service obligations and discharging his debts. By the end of the nineteenth century the right of emigration had been formally granted by every European country except Russia and Turkey. Even in those countries restrictions were largely ignored. At all events both the Russian and Turkish authorities were prepared in practice to allow the departure of those people they did not want to keep: Jews, Poles and Lithuanians in the first case, Syrians and Armenians in the second.

As if in answer to society's new needs, the industrial age brought a revolution in transport which gave Europe's teeming populations an unprecedented mobility. Speed, it has been well said, now became an 'exhilarating new factor in man's experience'. It accelerated movement, reduced distances and opened up new horizons. Journeys which had taken months or weeks could now be made in days, or even hours. The prime agent of this revolution was steam-power. The introduction of steamboats on Europe's rivers and lakes and the construction of a massive railway network enabled people to move about within the continental land mass more easily and more cheaply than ever before. The same thing happened across the Atlantic; it was the transport revolution that opened up the American West for settlement – and for that matter the Canadian prairies and the Argentine *pampas*. At the same time the development of ocean steam-navigation facilitated movement between continents. It would be several decades before the Atlantic crossing could be made in safety and reasonable comfort. But even before steam supplanted sail the expansion of transatlantic commerce had reduced the price of passage to a level that all but the very poorest could afford. By 1860 it was possible to reach New York from Liverpool or Hamburg for £3 ($15) or £4.

The chief characteristic of the transatlantic exodus, apart from its astonishing volume, was that it was unplanned. Colonization societies played little part in organizing it; governments none at all. This was in great contrast to emigration to other countries: a large part of the emigration to Australia, for instance, was government-financed. Emigrant aid societies, like the St Raphaels Verein and the Hebrew Immigrant Aid Society, did sometimes help the sick and destitute on their way, but only a tiny minority benefited. The movement to America was essentially one of individuals rather than of groups, of people paying their own way, making their own decisions, settling wherever their inclinations took them. Each nationality, as we shall see, had its own distinctive pattern of settlement, but the tendency was to congregate in the north of the United States, especially in the industrial north-east. Relatively few immigrants became frontier farmers and almost all avoided the South, not so much because of an aversion to slavery, or indeed to the Negro, but because that region offered fewer opportunities of the kind they were seeking.

The lure of America is evident enough, but it remains difficult to define in universal terms. Certainly, immigrants must have responded to the idea of 'freedom' that America offered, but freedom is a many-sided concept. To some it meant religious or political liberty; to others freedom from conscription or from heavy taxation; to others again, the chance to improve their economic and social status. Each of these elements played a part in drawing people to America. When Emma Lazarus wrote in 1883 of Europe's 'huddled masses, yearning to breathe free', she was thinking of the Jewish refugees then fleeing from Tsarist persecution. For them, and for others so placed, the right to worship as they pleased was paramount. For others, political considerations were uppermost. Each revolutionary upheaval in Europe produced its political refugees, but they constituted only a small proportion of the total exodus. The great mass of immigrants was inspired by different considerations. Once in America, they were quick to appreciate its free atmosphere, but religion and politics played little part in their decision to leave home. All the evidence suggests that the vast majority went to improve their economic condition.

For many the empty West, with its abundance of cheap or free land, was a great attraction – particularly so during the first half of the nineteenth century, when the United States was predominantly an agricultural country. Even then, however, the prospect of becoming an American farmer attracted only a minority of newcomers. For many Europeans, as indeed for many Americans, the West had a purely symbolic significance. Andrew Carnegie, the Scots immigrant boy who became a millionaire industrialist, recalled in old age a well-known emigration ballad his father had sung:

> *To the West, to the West, to the land of the free,*
> *Where the mighty Missouri rolls down to the sea;*
> *Where a man is a man even though he must toil*
> *And the poorest may gather the fruits of the soil.*

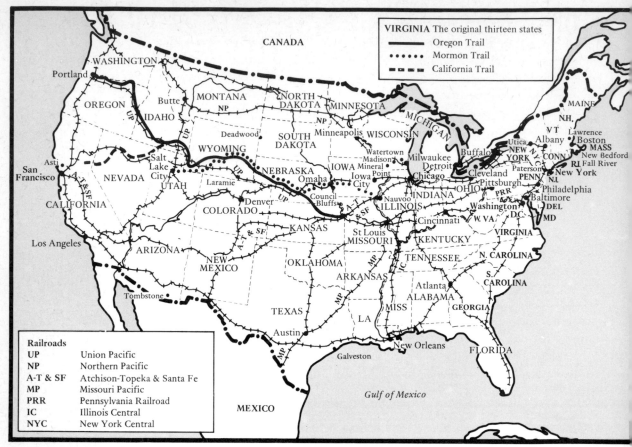

VIRGINIA The original thirteen states
——— Oregon Trail
••••• Mormon Trail
– – – California Trail

CANADA

WASHINGTON
Portland
OREGON
Butte
IDAHO
MONTANA
NP
NORTH DAKOTA
NP
MINNESOTA
MICHIGAN
MAINE
N.H.
VT
Deadwood
SOUTH DAKOTA
Minneapolis
WISCONSIN
Lawrence
Albany
Boston
Utica
MASS
Buffalo
NEW YORK
CONN
New Bedford
WYOMING
Watertown
Madison
Milwaukee
Cleveland
Paterson
Fall River
RI
Salt Lake City
San Francisco
NEBRASKA
Iowa City
IOWA
Mineral Point
Chicago
Detroit
Pittsburgh
PENN
New York
N.J.
Philadelphia
NEVADA
UTAH
Laramie
Omaha
Council Bluffs
Nauvoo
INDIANA
OHIO
PRR
Baltimore
DEL
Asti
CALIFORNIA
UP
Denver
A-T & SF
ILLINOIS
Cincinnati
Washington D.C.
W. VA.
MD
Los Angeles
COLORADO
KANSAS
St Louis
MISSOURI
KENTUCKY
VIRGINIA
ARIZONA
NEW MEXICO
OKLAHOMA
MP
IC
TENNESSEE
N. CAROLINA
S. CAROLINA
Tombstone
ARKANSAS
Atlanta
ALABAMA
GEORGIA
TEXAS
Austin
MISS
LA
MP
New Orleans
FLORIDA
Galveston
MEXICO
Gulf of Mexico

Railroads
UP   Union Pacific
NP   Northern Pacific
A-T & SF Atchison-Topeka & Santa Fe
MP   Missouri Pacific
PRR   Pennsylvania Railroad
IC   Illinois Central
NYC   New York Central

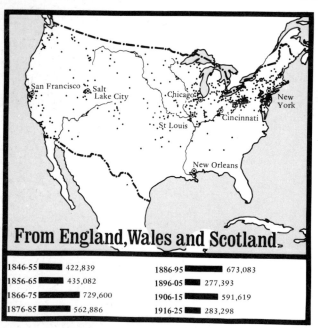

From England, Wales and Scotland

1846-55	422,839	1886-95	673,083
1856-65	435,082	1896-05	277,393
1866-75	729,600	1906-15	591,619
1876-85	562,886	1916-25	283,298

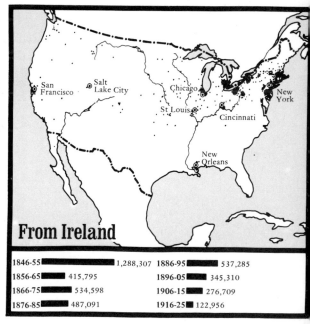

From Ireland

1846-55	1,288,307	1886-95	537,285
1856-65	415,795	1896-05	345,310
1866-75	534,598	1906-15	276,709
1876-85	487,091	1916-25	122,956

Immigration in the United States by 1920

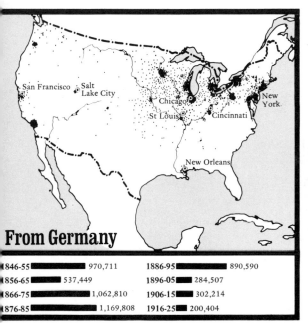

From Germany

1846-55	970,711	1886-95	890,590
1856-65	537,449	1896-05	284,507
1866-75	1,062,810	1906-15	302,214
1876-85	1,169,808	1916-25	200,404

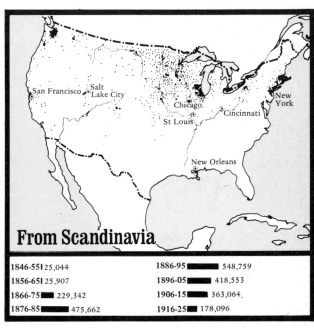

From Scandinavia

1846-55	25,044	1886-95	548,759
1856-65	25,907	1896-05	418,553
1866-75	229,342	1906-15	363,064
1876-85	475,662	1916-25	178,096

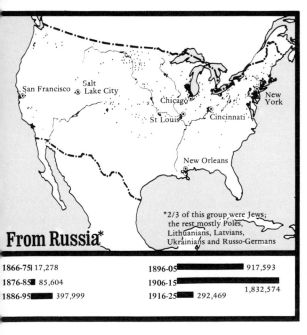

From Russia*

*2/3 of this group were Jews; the rest mostly Poles, Lithuanians, Latvians, Ukrainians and Russo-Germans

1866-75	17,278	1896-05	917,593
1876-85	85,604	1906-15	1,832,574
1886-95	397,999	1916-25	292,469

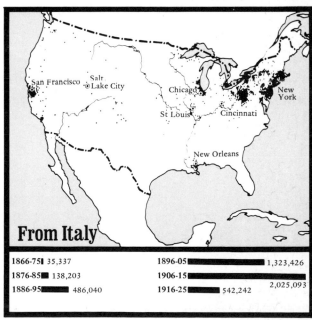

From Italy

1866-75	35,337	1896-05	1,323,426
1876-85	138,203	1906-15	2,025,093
1886-95	486,040	1916-25	542,242

The Golden Door

But the Carnegie family never saw an American farm, on the banks of the Missouri or anywhere else; they settled in Pittsburgh. Even in the 1840s, when the Carnegies emigrated, it was high wages – anything from one to three dollars (between four and twelve shillings) a day, about five times more than in Europe – that constituted America's main appeal. This became even more the case after the Civil War, when the area of unoccupied land rapidly dwindled and the United States experienced a phenomenal boom which was to make it by 1900 the most powerful industrial nation on earth. The apparently inexhaustible demand for labour in industrial America was probably the main reason why immigrants went there in preference to other destinations.

Awareness of American opportunity was sharpened in a variety of ways: newspapers, travel accounts, and guidebooks provided Europeans with an abundance of information about America. More influential still was the letter from a relative or friend who had already emigrated. The returned emigrant, too, was visible proof of the opportunity that awaited the industrious in the young republic across the Atlantic. In such ways the image of America as the 'best poor man's country in the world' was created.

It has been said that America's immigrants consisted largely of the poor. But while poverty may have stimulated the desire to emigrate, it could also diminish the capacity to do so. The most impoverished elements in the European population simply lacked the means to move, though this handicap was greatly lessened during the nineteenth century by the growth of the prepaid passage system. Many travelled on passage tickets sent by relatives or friends who had emigrated earlier. But there was a further obstacle: the American poor laws. From the seventeenth century onwards American communities sought to protect themselves against the burden of imported pauperism by requiring ships' captains to give bonds for any passengers they brought who seemed likely to become public charges. Thus, while Tocqueville was right when he remarked that 'the happy and powerful do not go into exile', those who had plumbed the depths of destitution were not always able to do so either.

It has sometimes been suggested that those who emigrated to America were united, not by their economic condition, but by the possession of certain distinctive qualities. The Puritan founders of New England never doubted that they were, in a quite special way, God's chosen people. One of their leaders spoke of God's having 'sifted a whole nation' in order to find the instruments which were to work out his purposes in the new world. In the twentieth century Darwin's theory of natural selection has taken over from the hand of God. In 1943, General George S. Patton, addressing American troops who were about to invade Hitler's Europe, informed them that victory was assured because, among other reasons, emigration had transferred to America the most virile and courageous, as well as the most enterprising, elements in the European population. This remarkable statement may have been good for the morale of the troops, but there is no evidence to support it – or to refute it, if it comes

OPPOSITE The hopes, fears and weariness of all new immigrants are captured in the face of this young Russian Jewish girl at Ellis Island, 1905. The great majority of immigrants were young – usually between fifteen and thirty-five years old.

to that. It is in fact no more persuasive than the wild complaints that the United States was being swamped by the scum of Europe, voiced by Americans who had wanted to restrict immigration fifty years earlier.

The truth is that no simple formula can characterize those who emigrated to the United States. In their ranks were to be found the restless, the enterprising, the unfortunate, the ambitious, the discontented. They came from technically-advanced countries like Britain and from primitive agrarian societies like that of Sicily. There were starving peasants and comfortable farmers, artisans and businessmen, unskilled labourers and people whose gifts had won them fame. Some immigrants were fugitives from persecution, others from justice. People crossed the Atlantic to escape from unsatisfactory marriages as well as from governmental tyranny. Immigrants included conformists and misfits, visionaries and remittance-men. They were not, however, a complete cross-section. They were mostly young, usually between fifteen and thirty-five, and were thus drawn disproportionately from the more active and productive elements in the European population. The one thing they all had in common was the conviction that in America things would be better.

But in leaving Europe emigrants were not necessarily repudiating the countries of their birth. Many crossed the Atlantic in the same spirit as the seventeenth-century founders of Virginia and New England: they emigrated not so much to create a new world as to preserve in more promising surroundings those things they had cherished in the old. That is why immigrants always sought at first to recreate in America the communities they had belonged to in Europe. Most retained feelings of warm affection for the old country, and displayed a deep interest in its affairs.

One of the factors encouraging them to do so was the coldness of their reception in the United States. America did not always extend a welcoming hand. Immigrants were at best tolerated and at worst treated with savage contempt. Sometimes they were victims of discrimination and even mob violence; they became the scapegoats for many of the evils that afflicted American society – crime, urban slums, political corruption. Moreover their adherence to foreign ways was increasingly held to be a threat to national unity.

Much in the immigrant experience applied to all who were exposed to it. Yet every part of Europe had its own emigration history, each exodus its own character and rhythm. To understand these realities we need to know what was distinctive about each group as well as what was common to all, and to look at the background to emigration in each of the major countries which contributed to it. We shall discover later that the ways in which immigrants responded to the 'land of the free' were very largely preordained by the characteristics and traditions which they brought with them from the old world.

OPPOSITE A bewildered Russian newcomer prepares to step ashore from Ellis Island, 1900.

2 THE JOURNEY

ON 25 JULY 1807 the *Kitty's Amelia*, a vessel of 300 tons commanded by Captain Hugh Crow, left Liverpool for the Guinea coast. She was the last slave ship to sail from a British harbour, Parliament having at last decreed abolition. Liverpool, whose prosperity had been built largely on this infamous traffic, would now need another source of revenue. It was not long in coming. Within twenty years the city became the greatest emigrant port in Europe.

By 1830 the transatlantic emigrant traffic had become both lucrative and highly organized. Ports throughout Europe were thronged each spring with those seeking passage to the new world. The scenes of departure – the bustle, confusion and tearful farewells – were already a favourite subject for newspaper comment and would supply the theme for countless engravings, ballads and poems. A typical verse reflected the belief of those left behind that emigration was tantamount to death:

> *Friends stood upon the shore in grief,*
> *And watched the bark dissolve and fade;*
> *And who it bore, in their belief,*
> *Were lost to sight in endless shade.*

In 1855 an American reporter described the scene as one of Train's White Diamond line packets, bound for Boston, sailed from Liverpool, her decks crowded with emigrants.

Unlettered and inexperienced, everything seemed dreamlike to their senses – the hauling of blocks and ropes, the cries of busy seamen as they heave around the capstan, the hoarse cries of the officers, the strange bustle below and aloft, the rise and expansion of the huge masses of canvas that wing their floating home, and will soon cover it with piled up clouds. Here are women with swollen eyes, who have just parted with near and dear ones, perhaps never to meet again, and mothers seeking to hush their wailing babes. In one place sits an aged woman ... listless and sad, scarcely conscious of the bustle and confusion around her.... The voyage across the Atlantic is another dreary chapter in an existence made up of periods of strife with hard adversities....

Some, however, left rather more cheerfully. In 1850 the London *Morning Chronicle* described the departure of the *Star of the West* on her maiden voyage to New York, with 385 passengers, 360 of them Irish. Even as the ship was being towed through the dock gates, latecomers were still arriving, carrying chests and bundles:

Many had to toss their luggage on board from the quay, and to clamber on board by the rigging. The men contrived to jump on board with comparative ease; but by the belated women, of whom there were nearly a score, the feat was not accomplished without much screaming and hesitation.... Here and there a woman becoming entangled, her drapery sadly discomposed, and her legs still more sadly exposed to the loiterers on shore, might be heard imploring aid from the sailors or passengers above. . . . Many a package missed its mark and fell into the dock, where it was rescued and handed up by a man in a small boat who followed in the wake of the mighty ship. When at last the ship cleared the gate and floated right out into the Mersey . . . the spectators on shore took off their hats and cheered lustily, and the cheer was repeated by the whole body of emigrants on deck, who raised a shout that . . . must have been heard at the distance of a mile even in the noisy and busy thoroughfares of Liverpool.

In the 1830s such scenes could be witnessed in any one of a hundred ports, but by mid-century the fiercely competitive emigrant trade had become concentrated in a handful of the larger ports such as Bremen and Le Havre. But though these captured a substantial slice of the traffic, Liverpool had no serious challengers during the age of sail. The number of emigrants who sailed from the Mersey for North America rose from 15,000 in 1830, to more than 50,000 in 1842. During the great mid-century rush annual departures were running at around 200,000 – more than half Europe's total. As well as the British, all the America-bound Irish now took passage from Liverpool, not to mention substantial numbers from Germany and Scandinavia.

Anyone who walked along the Liverpool waterfront in the 1840s would have noticed that a switch had taken place from one kind of human cargo to another. In the docks smart, well-kept American cotton freighters and packet ships lay at berths where ill-kempt English slavers had formerly been fitted out and armed. In the surrounding alleys, shops and warehouses which had once supplied handcuffs, leg-irons and chains were now selling provisions, cooking utensils and bedding. Regent Road, close to the docks and to the Irish steamer berths, had become a maze of lodging-houses and brokers' offices. The most significant change had taken place at Goree Piazzas, which owed its name to Fort Goree off the Senegal coast, where slavers had once taken on their cargoes. Formerly the slavers' headquarters, Goree Piazzas was now occupied by American passenger-agencies, such as the pioneer firm of Fitzhugh and Grimshaw.

Many contemporary writers likened the conditions under which emigrants travelled to those which had prevailed on the Middle Passage during the days of African slave trading. This was of course an exaggeration since little similarity could be found to the systematic brutalities that had so long disgraced the iniquitous transportation of Negroes – the shackling, the whipping and the callous ceremony of 'dancing the slaves' against scurvy and melancholy. Nor were emigrants ever packed as tightly as Negroes had been in the hold of a slave ship. Yet the 'horrors of the steerage' were real enough. Until sailing ships gave way to steam, the voyage took about six weeks, and adverse winds or bad weather could extend it considerably, some journeys having taken as long as a hundred days. And when hundreds of people were crowded together for weeks on end in cramped, dimly-lit and poorly-ventilated compartments, even a quick passage was one of squalor and misery. Sea-sickness, lack of proper food, tainted water and a total lack of hygiene contributed to the general wretchedness – as did the ruffianly crews. Worst of all, as will be seen, were the dangers of fire, shipwreck and plague.

The crossing itself was not the only hazard, for each stage of the journey presented its own problems. In May 1823, Johann Jacob Rütlinger set off for America from his native village in Switzerland. Travelling by barge, raft, waggon, coach and on foot, it took him a month to reach the Zuider Zee. On his journey up the Rhine he met rascally innkeepers and boatmen, and at each river toll station he was faced with extortionate demands. At the Dutch frontier he found he had to pay yet another set of freight, customs and passport charges, and when he finally reached Amsterdam he still had to run the gauntlet of prostitutes who lay in wait for departing emigrants. He reported: 'Everywhere the whores stood at the door, gaily dressed, and called out to us, "Come on in, farmer". Or sometimes they even pulled us by the sleeve. When you come upon parts of the city like this, you begin to think that there is not one decent house to be found.'

For the Irish, the journey across the Irish Sea was almost worse than the Atlantic crossing itself. Passages were extremely cheap on ships exporting cattle and pigs – but at the sacrifice of all human decency. The animals were under cover in the hold; the passengers, on the other hand, travelled on deck with no protection of any kind and suffered severely from exposure to the notoriously bad weather en route. Some were so debilitated when they reached Liverpool that they were in no condition to face the further rigours of an ocean voyage.

At Liverpool, emigrants were then exposed to what was almost an organized system of plunder. The moment an emigrant set foot on the quay he was pounced on by an army of petty criminals, all out to fleece him. Many passenger brokers, provision dealers and lodging-house keepers had the same objective. There were frequent stories of tickets being sold for non-existent ships, money-changers cheating and the over-charging of provisions. Officials appointed by the government did what they could to protect emigrants, but the task was beyond them. A sensible and humanitarian proposal, made in the early 1850s, to build an emigrants' home was defeated by local pressures and government *laissez-faire*. Quayside crime continued to flourish: an enquiry into Liverpool's prostitution in 1852 revealed that many of the city's street-walkers had come to Liverpool 'with unspotted characters and innocent hearts', intending to join their husbands in America. But, robbed of their passage money, they had been 'driven to a life of infamy by the demands of hunger'.

Yet despite its growing notoriety, emigrants continued to flock to Liverpool. Sailings from there were more frequent, the ships were larger and more seaworthy. Elsewhere in the British Isles the only vessels available were those engaged in the Canadian timber trade. These had the advantage of cheap passages. In the 1830s and 1840s emigrants could reach Quebec from Ireland for as little as thirty shillings – half the fare to New York. Thousands intending

OPPOSITE ABOVE The Emigration Agent's Office in Cork at the height of the mid-century exodus from Ireland.
BELOW A steerage passage ticket from Liverpool to New York dated 1851. Passengers were expected to cook their own food, but the master was required by law to provide weekly provisions which were stipulated on the ticket: $2\frac{1}{2}$ lb bread or biscuit; 1 lb wheaten flour; 5 lb oatmeal, 2 lb rice or 5 lb potatoes; $\frac{1}{2}$ lb sugar; $\frac{1}{2}$ lb molasses and 2 oz tea. In addition he was required to supply three quarts of water daily.

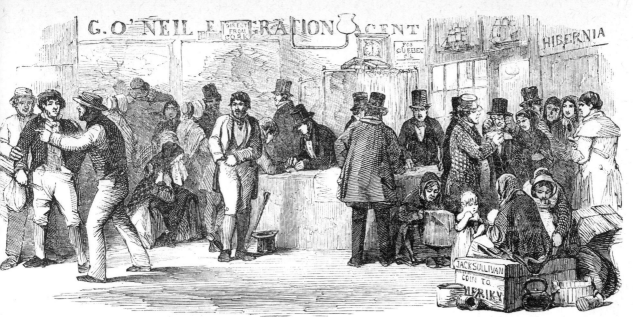

G. O'NEIL EMIGRATION AGENT
DIRECT FROM CORK · FOR QUEBEC · HIBERNIA

JACK SULLIVAN GOIN TO MERIKY

55-504

PASSENGERS' CONTRACT TICKET.

465

Ship *Princeton* of *1000* tons register burthen, to sail from Liverpool,
for *New York* on the *Twenty Eighth* day of *May* 185*1*

I engage that the Parties herein named shall be provided with a Steerage Passage to the Port of *New York* in the United States of America, in the Ship *Princeton* with not less than Ten Cubic Feet for Luggage for each Statute Adult, for the Sum of £ *3 - 5 - 0* including Government Dues before Embarkation, and Head Money, if any, at the place of landing, and every other charge ; and I hereby acknowledge to have received the sum of £ *3 . 5 . 0* in *full* payment.

In addition to any Provisions which the Passengers may themselves bring, the following quantities, at least, of Water and Provisions will be supplied to each Passenger by the Master of the Ship, as required by Law, and also Fires and suitable places for cooking:—
3 Quarts of Water daily.
2½ lbs. of Bread or Biscuit, not inferior in quality to Navy Biscuit; 1 lb. of Wheaten Flour; 5 lbs. of Oatmeal; 2 lbs. of Rice; ½ lb. of Sugar; ½ lb. of Molasses; 2 oz. of Tea— per week.

* 5 lbs. of good Potatoes may, at the option of the Master of the Ship, be substituted for 1 lb. of Oatmeal or Rice, and in Ships sailing from Liverpool, or from Irish or Scotch Ports, Oatmeal may be substituted in equal quantities for the whole or any part of the issues of Rice.

Signature, *Pat Connor*

On behalf of JOHN TAYLOR CROOK,

Date *May 23* 185*1*

Deposit £ *3 . 5 . 0*
Balance £ *None*
Total £ *3 . 5 . 0*

To be paid at the Office, 115, Waterloo Road, Liverpool, one day before the above date for sailing, or deposit forfeited.

NAMES.	AGES.	NO. OF STATUTE ADULTS.
James Farrell	26	

NOTICES TO PASSENGERS.

Scenes of farewell as Irish emigrants prepare to go on board at Queenstown, 1874.

to settle in the United States annually used the Quebec route in consequence. But the timber ships had an appalling reputation. Many were leaky old tubs, the cast-offs of other trades. An official enquiry into shipwrecks in 1839 was told that the timber trade was carried on by 'some of the worst kind of ships afloat'. The American vessels sailing between Liverpool and the United States, on the other hand, included some of the best. This was the heyday of the American merchant marine and vessels flying the Stars and Stripes were better built, sailed faster and were more competently manned than any others. The famous packet ships, like those of the Black Ball and Red Swallowtail lines, which eventually dominated the emigrant traffic, were extremely handsome vessels, carrying a huge spread of sail. Universally hailed as marvels of the shipbuilder's art, their most striking characteristic was their great size: some like the 2,050-ton White Diamond liner, *Chariot of Fame*, were among the largest sailing vessels ever built.

28

Nevertheless the packets were no more suited than their predecessors to carry emigrants in comfort and decency. Like sailing ships generally they were designed primarily for carrying cargo rather than passengers. They had room for emigrants because the outgoing freights, such as textiles and iron, took up far less space than the cotton or tobacco they carried on the eastward voyage. Shipowners came to regard emigrants as valuable return freight – and one that required little capital outlay. Apart from laying in provisions and water, all that was needed was a temporary deck, laid over the cargo in the lower hold, and rough pine berths which could be dismantled at the end of the voyage. Thus it can be imagined that steerage accommodation left much to be desired.

In 1851 a British Parliamentary committee was told that on American emigrant ships from Liverpool it was the practice 'to leave the whole deck on which emigrants were berthed undivided in any way.' Thus hundreds of passengers of all ages and both sexes were berthed together indiscriminately. Though this was forbidden by law, the proscription was widely ignored. But in any case, since berths were only separated from one another by a nine-inch plank, there was no division at all when the berths were filled with bedding. The result, as a witness commented, was that 'men, women and children [lay] in one promiscuous heap', stretching the whole length of the ship. Suggestions were frequently made that, in the interests of decency and morality, the steerage should be divided into three compartments, with single men forward, single women aft and married couples amidships, as on vessels carrying government-selected emigrants to Australia. But the travellers themselves were opposed to such a plan; they preferred to be berthed with the people they knew. Parents were violently hostile to the separation of the single women, fearing 'the contamination of their daughters, if removed from under their own eye, by improper characters among the [other] single women who might be on board'. Shipowners also opposed the plan arguing pragmatically that to partition the steerage would add to the problems of ventilation by impeding the flow of air.

In the end, when the British Passenger Act was revised in 1852, the separation of single men from other passengers was the only new requirement made. Even this, however, appears to have been ignored once vessels were at sea. A few years later a cabin passenger, William Hancock, noted that the principal activity in the steerage appeared to be lovemaking. 'Of this there is plenty – of its kind – at all times; most of the arrangements, or lack of such, being such as to permit of the most unrestricted intercourse and placing modesty and decency at a discount.'

Ventilation had long been a serious problem on emigrant ships. Up to the late 1840s the only way of admitting air into the steerage was by the hatches, but in bad weather these had to be closed to keep out the rough seas. That – coupled with the inadequacy of the lavatories and, indeed, the filthy habits of many of the passengers – accounted for the characteristic stench of the steerage. Speaking of the period around 1830, Dr Joseph Morin, a quarantine station inspector on the St Lawrence, declared that 'the harbour master's boatmen had no difficulty at the distance of gunshot, either when the wind was favourable or in a dead calm, in distinguishing by the odour alone a crowded emigrant ship.'

However, after 1848, all emigrant vessels going to the United States had to comply with a new American requirement. Every steerage compartment had to have at least two ventilators and, in addition, hatchways so protected that they could be left open permanently. Many of the new packet ships were fitted with iron ventilating tubes which functioned in all weathers – though it was impossible to stop emigrants blocking them up to keep out the cold. In an attempt to put a stop to the common practice of storing cargo in places intended for accommodation the 1848 American Passenger Act prescribed a legal minimum of space for each passenger; this, however, had the unintended effect of encouraging the construction of a new type of ship – the three-decker – a vessel with two steerage compartments, one above the other. Nearly all the new American packet ships built around 1850 were of this type. That they had three decks instead of two and consequently towered forty feet above the water line was one reason why they were so admired. But in fact these three-deckers were a deplorable innovation from the emigrant's point of view. Even with the new ventilating equipment, it proved extremely difficult to maintain a pure atmosphere in the lower of the two compartments. The result was that everyone suffered: those who were berthed in the lower steerage found it darker and more airless than on the deck above, while those in the upper steerage had to contend with the effluvium and stench rising constantly from below.

Nevertheless, most emigrant complaints were about the food and the behaviour of the crew. What they commonly endured in these respects was revealed by Vere Foster, a British philanthropist who sailed from Liverpool for New York in October 1850, as one of the 900 steerage passengers on the newly built Black Star liner *Washington*. He described the *Washington* as 'a magnificent vessel of 1600 tons register burthen ... very strong and dry, and probably as well furnished as the best of the emigrant ships between Liverpool and New York.... She had two lofty and well-ventilated passenger decks ... high bulwarks, over six feet, to protect the deck from the spray of the sea.'

But he severely criticized the brutal conduct of the ship's officers generally and also for their failure to supply the passengers with the food to which they were entitled. During the first few days of the voyage nothing but water was issued to passengers. Thereafter food was regularly distributed but correct amounts were never given and whenever provisions were issued passengers were 'cursed and abused ... cuffed and kicked by the mates' while a sailor stood by with a rope's end, capriciously laying about him. Vere Foster also complained of the favouritism shown by the cook to those who bribed him with money or whisky. They got as many as five or six meals cooked daily, while those who did not pay for the service were left waiting all day to have

Departure from Liverpool, 1850; an emigrant sailing packet is about to be towed out into the Mersey.

one cooked meal, and in some cases got a cooked meal only on alternate days. In the course of the voyage twelve children died from dysentery 'brought on by want of nourishing food' and on arrival at New York 128 other passengers signed a memorial drawn up by Vere Foster complaining of their treatment and warning future emigrants not to travel by the *Washington*.

The unsatisfactory state of the water aboard ship arose from the practice of storing it in wooden casks that had formerly contained oil, vinegar, molasses, turpentine, wine or indeed any commodity. Since little attempt was made to clean them out the result was frequently similar to that described by the Reverend William Bell, a passenger on the *Rothiemurchus* from Leith to Quebec in 1817. He wrote:

The Journey

Our water has for some time past been very bad. When it was drawn out of the casks it was no cleaner than that of a dirty kennel after a shower of rain, so that its appearance alone was sufficient to sicken one. But its dirty appearance was not its worst quality. It had such a rancid smell that to be in the same neighbourhood was enough to turn one's stomach.

Such complaints, however, did finally die away by the middle of the century, when water was stored in iron tanks, in which it rarely became unpalatable.

Food, however, was a thornier problem. After 1815 emigrant ships were required by law to carry provisions, though emigrants from Great Britain and Ireland were in practice allowed to bring their own. Irish emigrants usually took with them a bag of potatoes, some oatmeal, and a few dried herrings. But many arrived at sea ports with insufficient food to last the voyage. Sometimes, in order to deceive the inspecting officers, 'the same bag of meal or other provisions was shown as belonging to several persons in succession.' Frequently, when provisions ran low, the passengers plundered one another, while unscrupulous captains practised a particularly heartless form of extortion. Having encouraged the belief that the voyage would take only about three weeks, they waited until the emigrants' stores were exhausted and then sold them provisions at exorbitant prices.

The British Government was slow to remedy this state of affairs though the evils of the system were so glaring that in 1842 they finally adopted what was already accepted practice elsewhere, the issuance of provisions by the ship. However, to keep passage costs down only a bare level of subsistence was laid down: seven pounds of provisions a week, half of it in bread or biscuit, the remainder in potatoes, a much less generous dietary scale than that demanded by other countries. After the Irish famine, the British scale was gradually augmented to include such items as flour, rice, tea, sugar, molasses, beef and pork. But inspecting officers found it impossible to examine every barrel of provisions and much of the food taken on board was of inferior quality. The British consul at New Orleans, William Mure, attributed the fever that had raged on board the *Blanche* from Liverpool in 1850 to the atrocious quality of the pork. Moreover on Liverpool ships generally 'the bread is mostly condemned bread,' he reported, 'ground over with a little fresh flour, sugar and saleratus and rebaked. It would kill a horse.'

Mure also complained of the conduct of captains. The master of the *Blanche* had practised 'a most disgraceful system of extortion', charging grossly inflated prices for necessities, while the captain of the *Bache McEver*, which had arrived from Cork a year earlier, had been guilty of even darker deeds. According to Mure he had 'conducted himself harshly and in a most improper manner to some of the female passengers ... having held out the inducement of better rations to two who were almost starving in the hope that they would accede to his infamous designs.' That this was no isolated occurrence is clear from the petition sent to the United States Congress in 1860 by the New York Commissioners of Emigration.

The frequent complaints made by female emigrants arriving at [New York] of ill-treatment and abuse from the captains and other officers . . . caused us to investigate the subject; and from investigation we regret to be obliged to say that . . . after reaching the high seas . . . the captain frequently selects some unprotected female from among the passengers, induces her to visit his cabin, and when there, abusing his authority as commander, partly by threats, and partly by promises of marriage, accomplishes her ruin, and retains her in his quarters for the rest of the voyage, for the indulgence of his vicious passions and the purposes of prostitution; other officers of the ship . . . often imitate the example of their superior, and when the poor friendless women, thus seduced, arrive at this port, they are thrust upon shore and abandoned to their fate, without any remedy for the past wrong which has been done upon them; that such occurrences have become so frequent that [we] feel it our duty to ask for legislative interposition. . . .

Congress replied with a law providing that those found guilty of offences such as those complained of should be punished by one year's imprisonment or a fine not exceeding $1000. But there is no record of any officer being prosecuted under this law.

After Vere Foster's revelations no one questioned that the main cause of privation was the lack of cooked food. Even when provisions were issued regularly and in proper quantities passengers could be half-starved if, as often happened they were so prostrated by sea-sickness that they could not cook. Therefore, in 1852, it became obligatory for emigrant vessels leaving the United Kingdom to carry cooked instead of raw food and, with the adoption of the American Passenger Act of 1855, that became the rule on all emigrant vessels bound for the United States.

Thus during the sailing-ship era nearly all emigrants had to endure overcrowding, disorder, a foul atmosphere and poor food. But some had even greater trials to bear. They crossed the Atlantic in the knowledge that disaster might at any moment strike in any one of three forms: fire, shipwreck or plague. Those grim possibilities materialized often enough to ensure that a proportion of those who set out hopefully for the promised land never lived to see it.

In wooden vessels there was constant risk of fire. When it broke out the consequences were fearful. One of the most terrible disasters of the period was the burning of Train's White Diamond liner *Ocean Monarch*, in August 1848. This attracted unusual attention because it occurred within sight of land, the vessel having left Liverpool for Boston only a few hours before. No one knew for certain how the blaze began. One theory was that a steerage passenger had lit a fire in a ventilator, another that a seaman searching for stowaways had left a burning candle beneath one of the after-cabins. Whatever the cause, the fire was soon beyond control and although other vessels rescued the majority of those on board, including all the cabin passengers, 176 lives were lost. An eye-witness, Thomas Littledale, who was on board one of the rescue ships, described the scene as 'most harrowing and appalling'. He went on:

The flames were bursting with immense fury from the stern and centre of the vessel. So great was the heat in these parts that the passengers, men, women and children, crowded to the fore part of the vessel. In their maddened despair women jumped overboard; a few minutes more and the mainmast shared the same fate. There yet remained the foremast. As the fire was making its way to the fore part of the vessel, the passengers and crew, of course, crowded still further forward. To the jib-boom they clung in clusters as thick as they could pack – even one lying over another. At length the foremast went overboard, snapping the fastenings of the jib-boom, which, with its load of human beings, dropped into the water amidst the most heartrending screams both of those on board and those who were falling into the water. Some of the poor creatures were enabled again to reach the vessel, others floated away on spars, but many met with a watery grave.... We must not omit to mention an act of heroism exhibited towards the close of this melancholy scene. When only a dozen helpless women and children remained on the burning wreck, paralysed with fear and totally incapable of helping themselves ... an Englishman, Frederick Jerome ... a seaman of the American ship *New World*, stripping himself naked, made his way through the sea and wreck, and with a line in his hand succeeded in lowering the last helpless victims safely into the boats, being the last man to leave the wreck.

The following year 101 emigrants were burned or drowned when the Black Star liner *Caleb Grimshaw* caught fire 300 miles north-west of the Azores, and on Christmas Eve 1852, a further fifty-one emigrants died in the fire that destroyed the Red Star liner *St George* in mid-Atlantic. Sailing ships were not the only vulnerable ones: in September 1858 the Hamburg-Amerika iron steamship *Austria* caught fire when the hot tar being used to fumigate the steerage spilled on to the deck and ignited. Out of the 567 emigrants on board only sixty-seven survived. This was the worst fire disaster in Atlantic history though a similar incident in July 1865 on the sailing packet *William Nelson* came close to it, when more than 400 emigrants were lost.

Shipwreck too resulted in appalling losses. Not surprisingly, it was the timber ships that had the worst record: in one year alone – 1834 – seventeen were lost in the Gulf of St Lawrence and 731 emigrants were drowned. One of the worst winters on record was that of 1853–4, when gales and snowstorms raged almost without interruption on the Atlantic. Passages that winter were exceptionally long and several emigrant ships were severely damaged. Some, like the *Jacob A. Westervelt*, bound for New York with 700 passengers, arrived off the banks of Newfoundland in December 1853, stripped of sails and partly dismasted after weeks of battling against tremendous seas and head gales. Her exhausted crew mutinied and, supported by the passengers, compelled the captain to return to Liverpool. Other captains may have wished they had done the same for those same gales produced an unprecedented crop of disasters.

In several cases passengers were saved when their ship foundered, but 200 German emigrants were drowned when a fierce north-east wind drove the *Powhatan* on to the New Jersey shore. A final tragedy, proof of that winter's severity, occurred after the iron-hulled screw steamship *City of Glasgow* cleared the Mersey on 1 March 1854 with 480 emigrants and was never heard of again.

Few shipwrecks were attended with such horror as the one on which the Hollywood film, *Souls at Sea*, was based. The emigrant ship *William Brown* sank after striking an iceberg on 19 May 1841, five weeks out from Liverpool on her voyage to Philadelphia. Of her sixty-five steerage passengers, thirty went down with the ship. The captain, seven of the crew and a female passenger took to the jolly-boat and steered for Newfoundland, about 200 miles distant. They were not heard of again. The mate, Alexander Holmes, with eight of the crew and thirty-three passengers, crammed themselves into the long boat and steered south. That same night it came on to blow and, with the boat making water fast and in a sinking state, the mate decided that some of the emigrants must be thrown overboard in order to lighten it. On his orders the crew first tossed out six benumbed creatures who were too feeble to resist or even to know what was happening to them. Then they turned to a passenger named Frank Carr who was in better shape and was prepared to help bale out. But despite his pleadings and his offer of five sovereigns for his life till morning, he was manhandled over the side. In an attempt to save him Carr's youngest sister, Mary, called out: 'Oh! don't put out my brother – if you put him out, put me out too!' The sailors took her at her word and having thrown her into the icy water, seized hold of another sister, Ellen Carr, and dropped her overboard too, disregarding her pleas for a mantle to cover her nakedness. Next day the long boat fell in with the ship *Crescent*, eastward bound from New York, and the survivors were taken to Le Havre. Several of them made sworn depositions about what had happened and some months later Holmes was sentenced to a long term of imprisonment for manslaughter.

Shipwrecks and fires involving emigrant ships were reported in such detail in the contemporary press that today it seems that these were almost everyday occurrences. Yet a return presented to Parliament in 1852 showed that, during the previous five years, only forty-three emigrant ships had been lost out of the 6877 which had left United Kingdom ports, while out of 1,421,704 passengers only 1043 had died as a result of shipwreck or fire.

More common than disasters of this kind were the epidemics to which emigrant ships were prone. The disease which appeared most frequently was 'ship fever', or typhus. It was among the most loathsome of diseases, highly contagious and often fatal. Associated with poverty, filth and overcrowding, it became rampant whenever conditions favoured the spread of the lice that conveyed it. When it broke out in the steerage of an emigrant ship it ran through the passengers like wildfire. In the 1820s and 1830s scarcely a year passed without the appearance of typhus on at least some vessels. Sometimes there were scores of fever cases on a single ship. There were, for example, ninety sick passengers on the bark *Ranger* when she arrived at Quebec from Liverpool in 1836, and eighty (not counting the nine who had died during the passage) on board the ship *Phoebe* from Liverpool to Perth Amboy the following year.

In 1847, the blackest year of the Irish famine, typhus produced a frightful mortality rate. In that year no fewer than 7000 people, mostly Irish, succumbed to fever during the crossing, and 10,000 more died in hospitals and quarantine establishments in North America. The great majority of deaths occurred on vessels bound for Canada and New Brunswick. This was because the cheapness of the Canadian route had always attracted the poorest emigrants, and because the measures adopted by American states in 1847 to discourage pauper immigration had the effect of diverting to Canada an even larger number of people near to starvation and thus most susceptible to disease. Of the 89,738 emigrants who left United Kingdom ports for Quebec in 1847, 5293 died on passage and

another 10,037 in hospital in Canada; in all, 15,330 or 17.08 per cent of those who embarked. On some ships the mortality was much higher. The *Sir Henry Pottinger* which left Cork for Quebec with 339 steerage passengers, lost ninety-eight on the voyage with over a hundred others sick on arrival. The worst case was that of the *Virginius*, from Liverpool, of whose 476 passengers 158 died on passage and a further 106 were landed at Grosse Isle suffering from fever. Of the survivors the superintending physician at Grosse Isle, Dr Douglas, wrote: 'The few that were able to come on deck were ghastly, yellow-looking spectres, unshaven and hollow-cheeked and, without exception, the worst-looking passengers I have ever seen, not more than six or eight were really healthy and able to exert themselves.'

Conditions on the stricken vessels were graphically described in a book entitled *An Emigrant's Narrative; Or A Voice from the Steerage*. Its author was William Smith, a powerloom weaver from Manchester, who crossed from Liverpool to New York in the ship *India* in the winter of 1847–8 in company with emigrants from southern Ireland. Within a week of leaving Liverpool ship fever appeared, killing the captain and twenty-six passengers. Smith himself caught it and when, after a voyage of eight weeks, the *India* arrived at Staten Island, he and 122 others had to be taken to hospital. Of the voyage he wrote:

... the scenes I witnessed daily were awful; to hear the heart-rending cries of wives at the loss of their husbands, the agonies of husbands at the sight of the corpses of their wives, and the lamentations of fatherless and motherless children; brothers and sisters dying, leaving their aged parents without means of support in their declining years. These were sights to melt a heart of stone. I saw the tear of sympathy run down the cheek of many a hardened sailor.

Many contemporaries blamed the awful mortality of 1847 on overcrowding and poor food. But the death rate was highest, not on the most crowded or worst-found ships, but on those carrying emigrants from places where pestilence had been most rampant. Thus 'ship fever' was not generated in the steerage, but carried there by those who had been previously infected.

The way in which conditions on shore determined the incidence of epidemics at sea was also shown by the other great scourge of the steerage – Asiatic cholera. This was an even more malignant disease than typhus. It was characterized by violent diarrhoea, vomiting, cramps, collapse and usually death within hours. No one knew what caused it or how to treat it, for the science of epidemics was still in its infancy and doctors could only speculate about the source of this mysterious and terrible malady. Most of them thought it was caused by a poison in the air – a miasma arising from decaying matter, carried by the wind. The chances of catching it were thought to be increased by a weak constitution and such indiscretions as eating cucumbers or exposure to the night air.

In fact cholera was caused by an intestinal microbe, transmitted by contaminated water. Thus, inevitably, whenever cholera raged at the ports of departure

Life below deck, 1872. Even at this date steerage accommodation remained cramped. Emigrants line up for food from the ship's galley. Separate dining-rooms for steerage passengers were not generally introduced until later.

it would be carried on board by infected emigrants and, after a period of incubation, would break out during the passage. The first time this happened was in 1832, when cholera appeared on several vessels bound for Quebec. Perhaps the worst affected was the ship *Brutus* from Liverpool, which sailed on 18 May with 330 emigrants, all of them apparently healthy. On 27 May cholera broke out and by 3 June deaths were so numerous that the captain decided to return to Liverpool. By the time he reached there on 13 June, 117 cases had occurred, of whom eighty-one had died. Soon afterwards it became known that there had been several outbreaks on vessels bound for Canada from Irish ports. The first was the brig *Constantia*, which arrived at Grosse Isle on 28 April with 170 emigrants, having had twenty-nine cholera deaths during the voyage. Then in May two other Irish vessels, the *Robert* from Cork and the *Elizabeth* from Dublin, also reported cholera deaths. But it was not until the brig *Carricks* arrived on 3 June, having lost forty-two out of her 187 emigrants that the disease began to be recognized for what it was. Within a few days of the *Carricks'* arrival a cholera epidemic broke out in Quebec and Montreal. Before it was over there had been more than 4000 deaths in the two cities and a great many more in those parts of the United States to which it had been carried.

In 1848 cholera was again carried across the Atlantic by emigrants, and it reappeared yet again in the autumn of 1853. This particular epidemic exacted a far heavier toll of emigrants than either of the previous two. Indeed, more emigrants died at sea in 1853 than in any year of the nineteenth century except 1847. Vessels on the Liverpool-New York run suffered most. Of the seventy-seven vessels which left the port between 1 August and 31 October, forty-six were attacked by cholera, and 1328 emigrants were lost. The highest number of deaths occurred on the *Washington* – the ship Vere Foster had criticized three years earlier – which lost 100 passengers out of 898 (10.84 per cent). But on three vessels the mortality rate was even higher, the *Winchester* being the worst case with seventy-nine deaths out of 490 (16.21 per cent).

These calamities brought forth a chorus of complaint from both sides of the Atlantic. In England *The Times* blamed the cholera outbreaks upon the inadequacy of the law and the unseaworthiness of the ships. They were denounced for their rotten rigging and unsound hulls. The New York press took a similar line. But a British inquiry showed that such criticism was ill-informed. The ships in question were the best afloat and on previous voyages had carried just as large numbers of emigrants with minimal loss of life. What was significant about the 1853 outbreak was that it occurred only on ships which carried German emigrants who had come from regions where cholera was already raging when they left.

The state of the affected ships served to focus official attention on the need for a reform of steerage conditions. Responding to the public outcry, governments sought to extend their control of the emigrant traffic. By the mid-nineteenth century every maritime country in Europe as well as America and

Canada had built up an elaborate code of regulations. The various provisions of the Passenger Acts limited the numbers emigrant ships might carry, prescribed the quantities of food and water each emigrant was to receive, and laid down minimum standards of ventilation and sanitation. Standards required were still woefully low, however. Governments were reluctant to insist on anything higher lest the consequent increase in fares, which in the 1850s averaged about £3. 10s. od., might impede emigration. Nor did they wish to overburden shipowners with restrictions, fearing that these might be a handicap in the competition for emigrants. But the only real remedy was an international agreement, and though a proposal was several times discussed by the international maritime powers, no government cared sufficiently about the well-being of emigrants to make the necessary surrender of jurisdiction. Until the coming of steam the Atlantic crossing remained what it had always been: an exhausting, terrifying and hazardous affair.

An 1863 poster announces the opening of the Cunard emigrant service.

In the early days of steam, which began in earnest around 1840, government-subsidized ships of the Cunard Line only carried mail, a few cabin passengers and some valuable freight. As the aristocrats of the Atlantic, the line could afford to forget about the emigrant trade. In any case, said Sir Samuel Cunard, somewhat heartlessly, in the event of fire the ships' boats would have to be used to save the passengers – and then what would become of the mail? Cunard's American rivals, the Collins Line, which was also subsidized, likewise carried only cabin passengers. Others could not afford to be so choosy. It was a Liverpool steamship company, the Inman Line, that took the plunge in the 1850s when one of the partners, William Inman, decided to tap the profitable emigrant trade. After making the Atlantic crossing with his wife to study steerage conditions, he realized that there was a class of emigrant prepared to pay more for a faster passage. His company began with the daring decision to employ iron-screw steamers. Until this time iron hulls had been scoffed at. It was believed they would not withstand shot and so could not be used as transports in wartime; governments, therefore, would not subsidize them. Screws were thought to be too weak to propel a steamship – and there was the risk of their falling off. Loss of the screw was indeed a major hazard. It explained why even the biggest ocean steamships carried auxiliary sail until the 1880s when the problem was solved. Nevertheless, in spite of these hazards, the Inman Line inaugurated a regular service for emigrants in 1852; the *City of Manchester* and the *City of Glasgow* set out from Liverpool, each carrying 400 passengers, those in the steerage paying six guineas a head – about double the fare by sailing ship.

Two years later the *City of Glasgow* was lost without trace in the Atlantic with 480 passengers on board, and the *City of Philadelphia* was wrecked on her maiden voyage on Cape Race, though her passengers were saved. But, undeterred, the Inman Line was by 1860 running a fortnightly service with eight steamships, carrying an average of 16,000 emigrants a year across the Atlantic.

The Journey

In fact, the carriage of steerage passengers was quickly to become the most lucrative branch of the transatlantic trade and thus, within a very short time the Cunard and National Lines had joined the race. So too had German steamship lines, as well as many other smaller shipowners. The transition from sail to steam was greatly accelerated by the fact that during the American Civil War the heavily-armed Confederate raider, *Alabama*, drove virtually all the American sailing ships off the seas, thus in effect transferring transatlantic commerce to British-owned steamships. War-risk premiums rose so high that it became extremely difficult for American shipowners to remain in business. Consequently many ships were laid up and more sold to foreign owners. Two emigrant ships, both flying the Stars and Stripes, had the misfortune to meet Confederate raiders. One was the Black Ball packet *Isaac Webb*, which was intercepted on passage to New York in 1863. Her 750 emigrants saved her because her captor could not accommodate them. But she had to give bonds for $100,000 (£20,000) before being freed. The *Adriatic* was not so lucky: captured in 1864 by the *Tallahassee*, her 170 emigrants were taken off and she was then burned.

By the 1870s the westbound crossing was taking less than fourteen days, while Blue Riband holders had clipped it to less than eight days. Iron and steam were a good deal safer than wood and sail, particularly with regard to fire hazards: the burning of the steamship *Austria* in 1858, in fact, was the last occasion that an emigrant-carrying vessel was destroyed by fire. Shipwrecks became less common too, though when they did occur the loss of life was fearful. When the *Atlantic* went aground near Halifax in the teeth of a gale in April 1873 she broke up at once: of the 862 people on board 546 lost their lives. There would have been an even heavier toll but for the heroism of a quartermaster who swam through the raging surf to get a line ashore. This enabled about 200 people to reach a rock some forty yards away, though about three-quarters of them were drowned when they tried to get from the rock to the shore. Many of those who clung to the wrecked liner's rigging died of cold or were washed away and drowned. The survivors were rescued at daylight by local fishermen. A young Irishman, Patrick Leahy, told later of the scene he had witnessed while hanging in the rigging.

It was just gleaming day; a large mass of something drifted past the ship on the top of the waves, and then was lost to view in the trough of the sea. As it passed by, a moan – it must have been a shriek, but the tempest dulled the sound – seemed to surge up from the mass, which extended over fifty yards of water; it was the women. The sea swept them out of the steerage, and with their children, to the number of 200 or 300, they drifted thus to eternity.

Collision was another serious hazard. Usually the passengers were saved but in the 1890s it caused heavy losses. In January 1895 the steamer *Elbe* collided in dense fog with a coaster in the North Sea and sank immediately. All but twenty of the 352 people on board were drowned. In July 1898 *La Bourgogne* was rammed amidships off Cape Sable by a British sailing ship. She sank within minutes, losing 549 passengers. Icebergs, too, were a constant danger. On the night of 14 April 1912, the most terrible disaster in the Atlantic's history occurred: the 'unsinkable' liner *Titanic* went down, carrying with her 825 passengers and 673 crew.

The transition from sail to steam did not, however, entirely mean the end of steerage epidemics. Even in the 1880s there were occasional small-scale outbreaks of typhus and smallpox. And in 1866 there was another major cholera outbreak, though that proved to be the last to cause serious loss of life during the Atlantic crossing. The heaviest losses that year were suffered by three newly-built steamers belonging to the National Line. The *England*, carrying over a thousand emigrants from Liverpool to New York had already lost forty passengers from cholera when she put into Halifax for assistance, where no fewer than 227 passengers died. On the *Virginia* there were thirty-six deaths during the crossing, while the *Helvetia* put back to Liverpool when she was attacked by cholera four days out, losing forty-four passengers before she made port.

The pathology of cholera was still not understood – Robert Koch would not isolate the cholera bacillus until 1885 – but, although there was still talk of miasmas, there was also a growing tendency to look on the patient himself as

The wreck of the White Star liner *Atlantic* on Meagher's Rock, Nova Scotia, April 1873. More than 500 emigrants lost their lives.

a possible carrier. At least medical researchers were starting to think in terms of contact and contamination. Guesswork, perhaps inspired by the new thinking, led the Liverpool steamship owners to halt the sailing of a ship carrying German and Dutch emigrants who had already been in contact with the disease. Significantly, there were no more cases. Thus people were becoming less inclined to blame cholera outbreaks on the ships.

By 1873 American and British investigators were agreed that the coming of steam had made an enormous improvement in steerage conditions. A group of British doctors, having inspected a number of the Liverpool steamers asserted: 'A very cursory glance at the occupants of an emigrant ship when she is fairly out on the Atlantic will convince the observer that for the vast majority the much quoted "middle passage" has very few horrors.' Dr John M. Woodworth, the supervising surgeon of the US Marine Hospital Service was equally certain that the scandals of the steerage were now a thing of the past. With the gradual supplanting of sail by steam, he declared, had come 'shorter voyages, increased space, improved accommodation, more light, better ventilation, more abundant supplies of more wholesome food and water.' Indeed Dr Woodworth doubted whether one per cent of the emigrants 'were ever so well treated – fed, lodged and cared for – in their lives before as during their steerage-voyage on any average steamship'. The best proof of improvement, he went on, was the dramatic decline in steerage deaths as the proportion of steamships to sailing ships rose. Thus in 1870, the 156 sailing ships which brought immigrants to New York suffered 110 deaths on passage out of 18,824 passengers carried (0.58 per cent); but the 484 steamships making the same voyage lost only 155 out of a total of 194,088 passengers (0·08 per cent).

All the same there was still room for improvement. Ventilation was still inadequate and food a never-ending subject of complaint. Until the 1890s emigrants had to go on providing their own straw mattresses, to be thrown overboard at the end of the voyage. They also had to bring their own cups, plates and cutlery. Even on the best-managed ships, moreover, the steerage was still very cramped. Passengers were now accommodated in compartments of about twenty berths each and, on British ships at least, single men, single women and married couples were berthed separately. But berths were only two feet wide and were closely arranged in tiers on either side of a narrow aisle. Since there were no dining-rooms, meals had to be eaten at tables placed between the berths.

A lack of order and decency was inevitable in such surroundings, as Joseph Chamberlain was forced to admit when, as President of the Board of Trade in 1881, he presented to Parliament the results of yet another enquiry into steerage conditions. He was not surprised that 'kind-hearted and delicate persons' should from time to time complain at conditions on emigrant steamships. A crowded steerage packed with sea-sick emigrants, most of them poorly clad, many with unclean habits, was bound to arouse 'feelings both of pity and

Emigrants stretch out on the deck of the Red Star liner ss *Pennland*, on passage from Antwerp to New York, 1893. Built in 1870 for the Cunard Line and known originally as the *Algeria*, by the 1890s the *Pennland* was one of the oldest and slowest transatlantic liners.

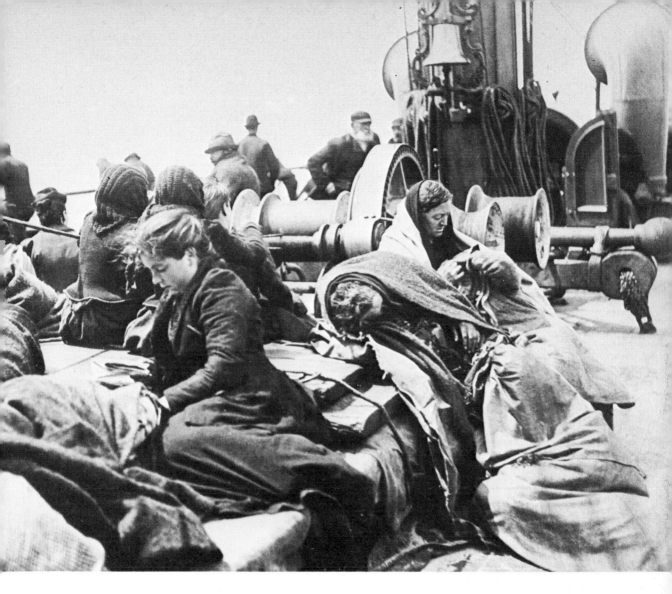

disgust'. But he felt that such conditions could not be improved without increasing fares beyond the capacity of emigrants to pay. He added, with some
insensitivity, that in any case steerage berths could only be judged in compari-
son with 'the crowded cottage of an English labourer, the close, narrow garret
of the workman, or the cabin of the Connemara peasant'.

The Board of Trade enquiry was prompted by a fresh spate of criticism in
the New York press of the steamship companies. Their avarice, it was said, led
them to cram in as many passengers as their vessels would take. Between
January and July in 1880 thirty-four steamships arrived at New York, all
carrying more passengers than was allowed, some with as many as 250 more
than their legal capacity. Enquiries elicited numerous now-familiar complaints
from steerage passengers. Typical was that of Owen McManus, a Scottish passenger on board the Anchor liner *Alsatia*. He declared that neither he nor his

fellow passengers had been able to eat what they had been given. The salt pork was hard, stringy and tasteless, the salt fish so bad that it was thrown overboard untasted; what little fresh meat was served proved to be tainted, and the oatmeal served each morning for breakfast was black and dirty, often with black beetles in it. Complaints of brutal treatment at the hands of the crew were also common: a German girl testified that a steerage steward on a Dutch steamer 'committed an assault upon her while she was in her bunk and nearly all the passengers were on deck.' Friedrich Eiseler, who was in an adjacent bunk, corroborated her statement and added that when he attempted to protect the girl, the steward hit him with a bottle.

In the eighties the huge profits to be made in the emigrant trade were reflected in the intense competition between steamship lines and in 'rate wars' which sometimes brought the cost of passage down for short periods to as little as £2 ($10). To ensure regular supplies of passengers the lines established a network of agencies all over Europe and in the United States too, where prepaid passage tickets could be bought for relatives and friends; by 1890 the Hamburg–Amerika line alone had 3200 American agencies. By 1890 nearly a third of all emigrants to the United States were travelling on prepaid tickets or tickets paid for with money remitted from America. A decade later nearly two-thirds were doing so.

The emigrant traffic continued to be dominated by the British and German lines, between whom there was fierce rivalry. Hamburg and Bremen were geographically better placed than Liverpool to tap the huge outflow from central and eastern Europe. This advantage was increased when they erected control stations along Germany's eastern frontiers, a system originating in the cholera epidemic of 1892 when Hamburg was badly infected and thousands died. The eleven control stations along the Russian and Austrian frontiers ensured that emigrants were medically examined before passing through Germany. The German shipping lines quickly took advantage of the control system to harass emigrants booked to travel on other lines, especially British ones. Sometimes the only way to avoid being sent back was to change to a German steamer.

In 1907 emigration to the United States reached a record level which has not been exceeded since: total arrivals in American ports came to 1,285,000, almost sixty per cent having sailed from one of four ports. Naples now led with 240,000, mostly Italians, but with large contingents of Greeks, Turks and Syrians. Bremen came next with 203,000, mainly Poles, Czechs, Croats, Slovenes and other Slavs. Liverpool, now pushed into third place, sent 177,000, the majority British and Irish, but with a large admixture of Swedes, Norwegians and Russian Jews. Hamburg's 142,000 were perhaps the most cosmopolitan of all; while east European Jews and Scandinavians predominated, virtually every ethnic group in central and eastern Europe was represented.

By this time the modern steamship had arrived. Now that nearly all had twin screws the risk of mechanical breakdown was minimal. Wireless telegraphy was also being introduced. But the greatest revolution had been the substitution of steel for iron. This meant that ships' lengths were increased almost as much as buildings on shore rose in height and each year saw the arrival of larger vessels on the Atlantic. The Inman Line's *City of Paris* (10,650 tons) was the world's largest ship when she was launched in 1889, but by 1907 the new Cunarder *Mauretania* had reached 31,950 tons. Such huge, magnificent floating palaces also carried emigrants and after the turn of the century a new third class was substituted for the steerage. On such vessels emigrants had little to complain about. But not all ships were up to their standard. Some of the worst were those under French or Italian ownership operating from Mediterranean ports. They were notorious for their lack of comfort, poor ventilation and bad food. Bad conditions were reported in 1906 on a White Star liner carrying emigrants from Naples. 'How can a steerage passenger', asked a journalist who travelled on the ship, 'remember that he is a human being when he must first pick the worms from his food ... and eat in his stuffy, stinking bunk, or in the hot and fetid atmosphere of a compartment where 150 men sleep, or in juxtaposition to a seasick man?'

Nevertheless, though conditions were still occasionally poor, by 1907 discomfort had been reduced to an endurable level – most evident from the fact that many thousands were now prepared to suffer the crossing not once, but several times. By now the 'bird of passage' was a familiar figure. It was becoming a common practice to go to America each spring when jobs were most plentiful and to return home for the winter.

Emigrants now found the European railway network so complete that the journey to the sea had become a less exhausting and uncertain business. Special trains conveyed passengers to the docks in hours or at most days, though they as yet provided only crude facilities. The steamship companies, fearful of the penalties they would incur if any of their passengers were refused entry on health grounds, now insisted upon a screening before embarkation which meant more supervision over passengers than in the past.

Arrangements did, however, vary between one port and another. At Liverpool the steamship companies provided emigrants with free accommodation while awaiting embarkation. Those arriving by train were met at the station by uniformed representatives of the steamship lines and taken to a company hotel. An American investigator who passed through the port in 1909 in the guise of an emigrant spoke highly of the Cunard hotel system. He described it as 'a village by itself in the centre of Liverpool', consisting of several buildings capable of accommodating 2000 people. He was kindly treated, well fed, supplied with towels and soap and given a clean bed in a room provided with steam heat and electric light. A company doctor visited the hotel daily to carry out medical examinations. In cases of infectious or contagious diseases emigrants were either rejected or held for further observation.

Among those at other European ports the emigrant hotel of the Holland–America Line at Rotterdam was a fine building, admirably managed, though before being admitted emigrants were first lodged in an observation shed, where they were medically examined and brought to a common standard of cleanliness. At least at the time of the cholera scare of 1893 the cleansing routine here was as degrading as it was thorough. While their clothes were being disinfected emigrants were required to take an antiseptic bath. Men and boys then had their hair cut close with clippers and their heads shampooed with a mixture of soft soap, carbolic acid, creolin and petroleum, the shampoo being applied with a stiff brush. Women and girls were spared the haircut but otherwise got the same treatment and were all required to comb their hair with a fine tooth-comb, one being attached to each bathroom by means of a small brass chain.

Similar indignities awaited emigrants at Hamburg. For those who had passed through a control station at the German frontier this was the second time in forty-eight hours that they had been compulsorily bathed and fumigated. Yet the Hamburg–Amerika Line's huge emigrant depot was a relatively humane institution. Laid out as a model village in the city suburbs, it was capable of accommodating 4000 emigrants at a time. Among its many facilities

LEFT The main hall at the Hamburg emigrant village, c. 1910–14.
RIGHT Emigrants embarking at Hamburg, c. 1910–14.
BELOW Hair inspection before embarkation, Danzig, c. 1910.

there were hotels, shops, restaurants and churches. There were even band concerts every afternoon. Emigrants were forbidden to go into Hamburg itself, but behind the depot's high brick walls they were at least secure from the fraudulent trickery of an earlier era.

By 1914 then, the hazards of the past had been largely eliminated. Emigrants were now spared the difficulties and uncertainties of travel to the sea port, and the Atlantic crossing itself had lost most of its terrors. But as one set of problems disappeared, another arose in its place. The era of free movement was drawing to a close. After three centuries of comparatively unrestricted immigration the United States was beginning to doubt the wisdom of opening its doors to all comers. From 1880 onwards, as we shall see later, American immigration laws grew steadily more complex and restrictive. Thus, as they travelled across the Atlantic the thoughts of those in the steerage were on the ordeal that they knew awaited them at New York. Before they could enter the Promised Land they would have to satisfy the guardians of the gate, stationed first at Castle Garden and then, from 1892 onwards, at much-maligned Ellis Island.

3
GUARDIANS OF THE GATE

N 1819, AS AMERICA was getting its first taste of wholesale immigration, the Society for the Prevention of Pauperism in the City of New York lamented: 'From various causes, the city ... is doomed to be the landing-place of a great portion of the European population, who are daily flocking to our country. . . .' That proved to be a remarkably accurate prediction, for New York, already handling the bulk of America's import trade, was destined to receive the same overwhelming share of human freight as it did of other commodities. Of the 5,400,000 immigrants who arrived in the United States between 1820 and 1860, about 3,700,000, or more than two-thirds, entered at New York. New Orleans was her nearest rival with about 550,000, followed by Boston with some 380,000, and Philadelphia and Baltimore, each with about 230,000. By the 1850s New York was receiving more than three-quarters of the national total, and by the 1890s more than four-fifths.

New York was, however, slow to regulate the immigrant traffic and slower still to provide adequate reception facilities. Until mid-century the city's chief concern, other than a desire to speed newcomers on their way, was to ensure that they did not bring contagion or add to the burden of poor-relief. Before being allowed to pass through the Narrows into the Upper Bay immigrant ships had to perform quarantine. The port health officers inspected the passengers, more or less perfunctorily, and those suffering from contagious or infectious diseases were sent to the Marine Hospital on Staten Island. This had been founded in 1797 and was financed by a fifty-cent tax, called hospital money, on each immigrant.

But as the forebodings of the Society for the Prevention of Pauperism imply, New Yorkers resented the arrival of needy immigrants who looked to the city for support. There was a widespread belief that Europe was deliberately casting its poor-house refuse on them. Statistics of the city almshouses and hospitals

OPPOSITE Immigrants file patiently past the registration clerk, Ellis Island, c. 1890.

48

seemed to bear out the contention. Hence in 1824 the State of New York – to whom, along with the other states, the federal government left control of immigration in this period – passed a measure requiring captains to report the names of their passengers to the mayor and to give bonds of $300 for each to guarantee that they would not become public charges in the next two years.

To dodge this requirement some passengers were landed at nearby Perth Amboy in New Jersey, where the regulations were more lenient. In 1837, more than 5000 immigrants arrived in the tiny port – more than the total for either Boston or Philadelphia. One ship, the *Phoebe* from Liverpool, put scores of sick passengers ashore at Perth Amboy, where they were forced to lie outdoors during a rainstorm. They were eventually taken by waggon to New York, where the almshouse commissioners successfully sued the passenger agents.

This verdict promptly put a stop to bond-dodging. But another evil now developed. Speculative bond-brokers, prepared for a small payment to relieve captains of liability, made their appearance. They knew that they would have to pay for the bonded passengers only in case of their sickness or destitution. In practice, however, bond-brokers avoided forfeiting bond-money by establishing their own hospitals and almshouses to lodge the poor wretches. These places became notorious for their ill-treatment of the immigrant poor. An investigation in 1846 revealed, for example, that Tapscott's Poor House and Hospital, across the East River at Williamsburg, was grossly overcrowded and insanitary and that the food consisted of mouldy bread and rotten fish.

The lack of proper reception arrangements meant a free-for-all at the docks. The weary immigrant, exhausted by weeks in the steerage, had once again to be on his guard against the kind of chicanery practised at the ports of departure. A brood of villainous runners, as plausible and as unscrupulous as those at Liverpool, infested the docks and battened on the unsuspecting. In 1846 an investigating committee found that most of the frauds committed on immigrants were the work of their own countrymen, 'the German preying upon the German, the Irish upon the Irish, the English upon the English'. The methods employed by these rogues were described in John F. Maguire's account of what befell a young Irish immigrant:

The moment he landed, his luggage was pounced upon by two runners, one seizing the box of tools, the other confiscating the clothes. The future American citizen assured his obliging friends that he was quite capable of carrying his own luggage; but no, they should relieve him – the stranger, and guest of the Republic – of that trouble. Each was in the interest of a different boarding-house, and each insisted that the young Irishman with the red head should go with him.... Not being able to oblige both gentlemen, he could oblige only one; and as the tools were more valuable than the clothes, he followed in the path of the gentleman who had secured that portion of the 'plunder'.... The two gentlemen wore very pronounced green neck-ties, and spoke with a richness of accent that denoted special if not conscientious cultivation; and on his [the Irishman's] arrival at the boarding-house, he was cheered

New York City, 1855. The bulk of the immigrants landed at New York. America's largest city and greatest port offered immigrants greater employment opportunities than elsewhere. It also had better communications

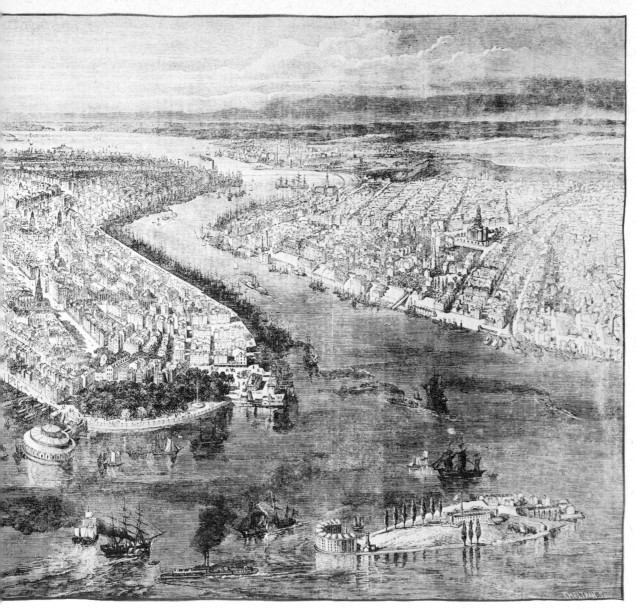

with the West than any other port on the eastern seaboard. The round building at the tip of Manhattan Island (left centre) is Castle Garden, which opened that same year as New York's first Emigrant Landing Depot.

with the announcement that its proprietor was from 'the ould counthry, and loved every sod of it, God bless it!'

Immigrant aid societies, like the German Society of New York and the Irish Emigrant Society, did what they could to check the abuses, but they lacked the necessary authority. It was clearly a task for the government and in 1847, when thousands of fever-stricken immigrants were arriving daily from Ireland, the State of New York established an Emigration Commission to care for and protect newcomers. The commissioners took over the management of the Marine Hospital and established an Emigrant Hospital and Refuge on Ward's

51

Immigrants landing at New York, 1858. Steamboats transferred them and their luggage to Castle Garden from the docks in the East River where the immigrant ships berthed.

Island in the East River. In the first eight years of the commission's existence, nearly 50,000 immigrants were treated in these hospitals. But the commissioners knew that they could not protect them against fraud without a landing depot from which runners could be excluded. In 1848 an attempt to lease a pier was frustrated when local residents obtained an injunction; they objected that the landing of immigrants 'would bring into a quiet part of the city a noisy population without cleanliness and sobriety ... endangering the health and good morals of the ward, and seriously affect the value of real-estate.' Similar objections were raised whenever other sites were proposed and in 1858 the Marine Hospital on Staten Island was actually burned down by residents fearful of epidemics of typhus and smallpox.

In 1855, however, the commissioners found what they sought at Castle Garden, near the Battery at the tip of Manhattan. Castle Garden had had a curious history. Originally a fort, built just before the War of 1812 to defend New York against a possible British attack, it later became a fashionable amusement centre, a place for concerts, firework displays and other entertainments as well as for the reception of visiting celebrities like the Marquis de La Fayette and President Andrew Jackson. Jenny Lind, 'the Swedish nightingale', made her American debut there in 1850, singing to packed audiences of the New York elite. On 1 August 1855 came another change: Castle Garden was officially opened as an Emigrant Landing Depot – the first anywhere.

Here it was easier for the authorities to keep a proper record of newly-arrived immigrants and to decide which were subject to special bonds under state law

– the blind, cripples, lunatics, paupers and others who seemed likely to become public charges. It also made possible a more orderly and systematic handling of passengers and their luggage, for only licensed runners and agents were allowed to enter. Inside the huge rotunda – an area of 50,000 square feet, capable of holding between 2000 and 4000 people – the immigrant could obtain food and information, collect letters, change money, book accommodation at a boarding-house, buy rail and steamboat tickets and arrange for his luggage to be forwarded. In 1867 a Labour Exchange was erected in an adjoining building; here immigrants could get information about jobs and some were engaged on the spot by employers. The whole enterprise was financed by a head tax on immigrants which ranged from one to two dollars and which captains usually added to the fare.

Castle Garden may not have succeeded in ending the deceptions practised upon immigrants: rogues still lay in wait outside. But the institution provided a range of welfare services remarkable in an age of *laissez-faire*. It thus offered immigrants a better introduction to their adopted land than they had formerly been given. Castle Garden's reputation added to New York's popularity with immigrants. In 1874 the *New York Times* asserted: 'Castle Garden is now so well known in Europe that few emigrants can be induced to sail for any other

The crowded interior of Castle Garden. In the main rotunda immigrants were registered after they had passed the medical inspection.

Guardians of the Gate

destination. Their friends in this country write to those who are intending to emigrate to come to Castle Garden where they will be safe, and, if out of money, they can remain until it is sent to them.'

In 1882, after the Supreme Court had declared state head taxes unconstitutional, the federal government took over from the states responsibility for immigration. State-appointed boards, however, were to continue inspecting immigrants and to exclude undesirables. Castle Garden thus continued to be used as a landing depot under the supervision of the New York Commissioners of Emigration. But throughout the 1880s there were repeated complaints about the way it was being run. It was alleged that employees were given to bullying and that railroad agents and money changers licensed to operate there were defrauding immigrants on an extensive scale. By the end of the decade Congress decided it was time for an enquiry. The Ford Committee's report, published in 1889, was fatal to Castle Garden. Immigration into the United States in 1888 totalled 546,889, of whom 418,423 (about 76 per cent) arrived at New York. The committee believed this was more than Castle Garden could cope with.

The committee visited Castle Garden on several occasions and witnessed the arrival and inspection of immigrants, and it was very obvious to them that it was almost impossible to inspect properly the large number of persons who arrived daily during the immigrant season ... and the testimony taken puts it beyond question that large numbers of persons not lawfully allowed to land in the United States are annually received at this port. In fact one of the commissioners of immigration himself testified that the local administration ... was a perfect farce.... Dr Hoyt testified [that] the State annually expends in taking care of paupers, insane persons, etc., $20,000,000 [£4 million] and that this condition of affairs is largely due to improper immigration.

The Ford Committee's report convinced the federal government of the need to assume direct control. In 1890 it set up a Bureau of Immigration and looked around for a site for a new immigrant depot. Its choice fell on Ellis Island, a low-lying islet in New York harbour close to the New Jersey shore. The naval powder magazine which had been there since the end of the Civil War was removed, the island's area was doubled by landfill and a group of buildings costing half a million dollars was erected. On 1 January 1892 Ellis Island was opened as a receiving station.

It soon acquired a sinister reputation – 'a cross between Devil's Island and Alcatraz' was one description. This was not because immigrants were pushed around by officials – though they often were – or even because cheating and exploitation were rampant. It was because in contrast to Castle Garden, whose main purpose had been to protect immigrants, Ellis Island was a gigantic sieve, whose sole function was to keep out undesirables. By the early 1890s the list of excluded classes was long and continually growing. As well as paupers, lunatics and idiots and those likely to become a public charge, it now included persons with criminal records for offences involving 'moral turpitude', those

Ellis Island, which succeeded Castle Garden as New York's immigrant depot in 1892. The red-brick building in this architect's drawing of 1898 replaced the wooden receiving station which had burnt down the previous year.

54

suffering from a 'loathsome or contagious disease', and contract labourers –
workmen induced to emigrate by the offer of a job and allegedly imported
for the purpose of lowering wages and breaking strikes. By 1914 new categories
had been added: polygamists, prostitutes, anarchists and persons advocating
the violent overthrow of the American government. In 1917 a literacy test was
introduced, together with an intelligence test to weed out the feeble-minded.

To be found inadmissible for any of these reasons meant being sent back
to Europe. Hence arrival day was as full of apprehension as of hope. Artists
liked to depict immigrant steamships nosing their way into New York harbour,
their passengers crowding the decks, their eager faces turned towards the Statue
of Liberty. In fact not all of them knew what the statue was: in 1913 one immigrant was overheard telling another that it was Columbus' tomb! But even those
who knew better were generally less concerned with the statue than with

'Heartbreak Island', as Ellis Island was popularly known, for there was great apprehension lest they fail to get through. The British author, Stephen Graham, who travelled with a shipload of Russian immigrants in 1913, described the ordeal of Ellis Island as 'the nearest earthly likeness to the final Day of Judgement, when we have to prove our fitness to enter Heaven.'

Arrival day began with the immigrants being ferried from the Hudson River pier, where their steamer had docked, to Ellis Island. Here they were shepherded into the main building, an imposing, red-brick structure built in 1898 to replace the original wooden building destroyed by fire the year before. Wearing identity tags corresponding to numbers on the ship's manifest, immigrants were ranged into single file and guided between iron railings that made the great Registry Hall a maze of open gangways. The sifting process began with the immigrants queuing up before two doctors of the US Public Health Service. The job of the first was to look for any kind of physical or mental abnormality. Suspected cases received a chalk-mark on the right shoulder: L for lameness,

OPPOSITE On the ferry to Ellis Island, *c.* 1900.

BELOW That immigrants were not uniformly drawn from the ranks of Europe's poor is evident from the appearance of this seemingly well-to-do Dutch family, pictured at Ellis Island, *c.* 1908.

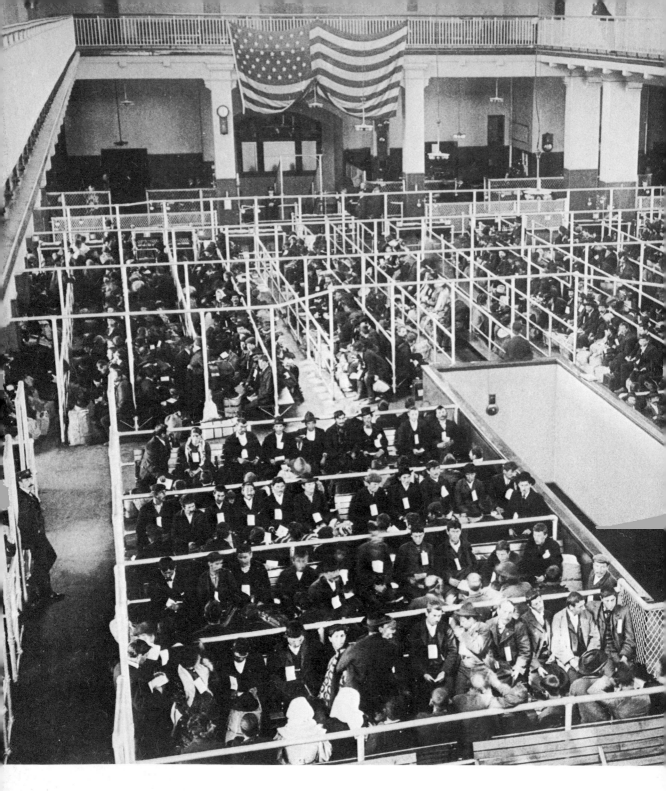

Part of the main inspection
hall at Ellis Island.

G for goitre, X for mental illness and so on. The second doctor was on the watch for contagious and infectious diseases. He looked especially at the eyelids for symptoms of *trachoma*, a blinding disease which, together with *favus*, a contagion of the scalp, accounted for a high proportion of the medical detentions. All who failed to pass both doctors had to undergo a more thorough examination. So had unaccompanied women who appeared to the matron's vigilant eye to be pregnant.

Medical inspection was the greatest trial of all. The writer, Angelo Pellegrini, son of Italian emigrants, recently recalled his stay at Ellis Island:

We lived there for three days – Mother and we five children, the youngest of whom was three years old. Because of the rigorous physical examination that we had to submit to, particularly of the eyes, there was this terrible anxiety that one of us might be rejected. And if one of us was, what would the rest of the family do? My sister was indeed momentarily rejected; she had been so ill and had cried so much that her eyes were absolutely bloodshot, and Mother was told, 'Well, we can't let her in.' But fortunately, Mother was an indomitable spirit and finally made them understand that if her child had a few hours' rest and a little bite to eat she would be all right. In the end we did get through.

Italian immigrants in the railroad waiting room at Ellis Island, 1905.

Ellis Island 1907
Immigrants had to
undergo various
examinations to determine
whether they were eligible
for admission.

ABOVE LEFT The medical
examination. Beside the
eye chart with Hebrew
lettering stands an
immigrant with the letter
'κ' chalked on his jacket,
indicating a suspected
hernia.
LEFT An immigrant
suspected of being feeble-
minded is given an
intelligence test. The
federal Immigration Law
of 1907 added a new
category of inadmissibles –
persons whose mental

Those who escaped tell-tale chalk marks moved on to the registration clerk. With the help of an interpreter he put a series of questions to each passenger. What is your name? What nationality? Where are you going? What occupation? Who paid your fare? Can you read and write? How much money do you have with you? Have you ever been in prison or an almshouse?

Names were a constant source of difficulty. Not all immigrants could spell their names, and baffled officials often simplified them. Sometimes this meant that immigrants left Ellis Island with a new name. The best known story relates

deficiencies might prevent them from earning a living.

ABOVE A Public Health Service doctor examines the lining of eyelids, with a buttonhook, for signs of *trachoma*, a blinding disease responsible for more than half of the medical detentions.

RIGHT Contract labourers awaiting deportation. In 1885 union pressure led Congress to ban the importation of immigrant labour on contract. On the eve of the First World War about 1000 immigrants a month were refused admission under the statute.

to a German Jew named Isaac who became so confused by the barrage of questions that, on being asked his name, he replied: 'Ich vergessen' ('I forget'), whereupon the official recorded his name as Ferguson. In Elia Kazan's film *America, America*, a Greek shoeshine boy, Stavros Topouzoglou, fearful that he will be excluded through the intervention of another passenger, answers to the name of his dead friend, Hohannes Gardashian. The immigration officer tells him that, if he wants to be an American, the first thing to do is change his name for something shorter. 'Hohannes. That's all you need here,' he says and writes the name 'Joe Arness'. Then he adds: 'Well, boy, you're reborn. You're baptised again. And without benefit of clergy. Next.'

It was not always easy for inspectors to obtain comprehensible answers to questions about immigrants' destinations. Frequently, immigrants would fish out a piece of paper bearing illegible or garbled addresses. It took imagination – and experience of immigrant speech – to work out that 'Pringvilliamas' was Springfield, Mass., and that 'Neihork, Nugers' was Newark, New Jersey.

Interrogation was usually brief, over in a few minutes. But where there was doubt about an alien's admissibility or his capacity to travel on, he was detained for more thorough questioning. Immigration inspectors did not enjoy a good press. They were frequently depicted as rigid bureaucrats who heartlessly turned back poor immigrants at America's very threshold. But theirs was an unenviable task for some of the immigration regulations were difficult, if not impossible, to enforce. Simple questioning was not likely, for example, to reveal whether prospective immigrants were, say, anarchists or prostitutes. Nor was it easy to detect contract labourers, especially when they had been coached to give evasive answers.

Dissimulation on the part of immigrants was in fact inevitable, given the contradictions embodied in the immigration laws. One set of statutes was designed to exclude paupers, those who would not or could not support themselves; another, the anti-contract labour laws, sought to exclude those who had provided themselves with a job beforehand. In 1901 the United States Industrial Commission commented:

The consequence is that the immigrant must summon all his ingenuity and subterfuge to dodge the two extremes. . . . If he cannot support himself he is sent back as liable to become a public charge. If he has provided beforehand for self-support he is sent back as liable to displace an American workman.

Apprehensions about Ellis Island were well-founded. It is true that about eighty per cent or more of the total were usually passed by both the medical officers and the immigration inspectors. That still meant that large numbers of people were held for longer or shorter periods. In 1907, for instance, there were no fewer than 195,000 detentions compared with 1,004,756 admissions at New York. Of the detainees, 121,737 were temporary, mostly women and children who were held briefly until relatives sent funds to enable them to reach

OPPOSITE Detainees at Ellis Island collaborate in writing letters. About eleven per cent of the immigrants were temporarily detained, mostly women and children coming to join relatives and friends but having no funds of their own. If no money was sent and no one called for them within five days they were turned over to benevolent societies or deported.

their destinations. Next, there were 9293 detainees who were sent to hospital. Lastly, 64,510 aliens were held for investigation by boards of enquiry. How many were excluded that year is not recorded, but in other years the proportion ranged between fifteen and twenty per cent of the cases heard. In 1914, for instance, about 70,000 were held for special enquiry and of these 16,588 were eventually excluded – about two per cent of the total immigration.

Those not detained made their way downstairs, stopping to claim their baggage and, if they so wished, to buy railroad tickets and food. Service tenders stood ready to take them to the Battery, a mile away. For many immigrants fresh ordeals still lay ahead: many still faced long journeys overland before they reached their goal. But as they stepped on board the tender, tired, harassed, clad in a variety of old country costumes and clutching their pathetic bundles, few can have failed to be uplifted. For the new life they had come so far to find had now begun.

The heyday of Ellis Island was comparatively brief. The outbreak of the First World War in 1914 stemmed the tide of immigration and no sooner had it revived in the early 1920s than it was again checked by drastic new restrictions. After the National Origins Act went into operation in 1929, Ellis Island had only a trickle of immigrants to deal with. During the Second World War it was used as a detention centre for enemy aliens and suspected spies. After 1945 the task of examining prospective immigrants was carried out by American consulates abroad and those whose entry papers were in order – the vast majority – by-passed Ellis Island. By 1954 only a handful of aliens awaiting deportation were held there and the federal government closed it down as an immigration station. After it was vacated there were protracted arguments about the island's future. Suggestions included turning it into a recreation centre, a women's prison, a university, a gambling casino, a clinic for alcoholics, a home for the aged, a school for international affairs. None of these proposals has come to anything, largely because the government felt that they were unsuitable for such a historic site. In 1965 Ellis Island was officially proclaimed a national monument, but plans for an immigration museum were dropped. Meanwhile the deserted buildings rapidly deteriorated, pilferers stripped them of everything that could be moved, smashed windows and broke down doors. Leaky roofs went unrepaired, pigeons invaded the upper storeys and the grounds became choked with weeds and refuse. Today its future still unresolved, Ellis Island, gateway to America for sixteen million immigrants, is a crumbling ruin.

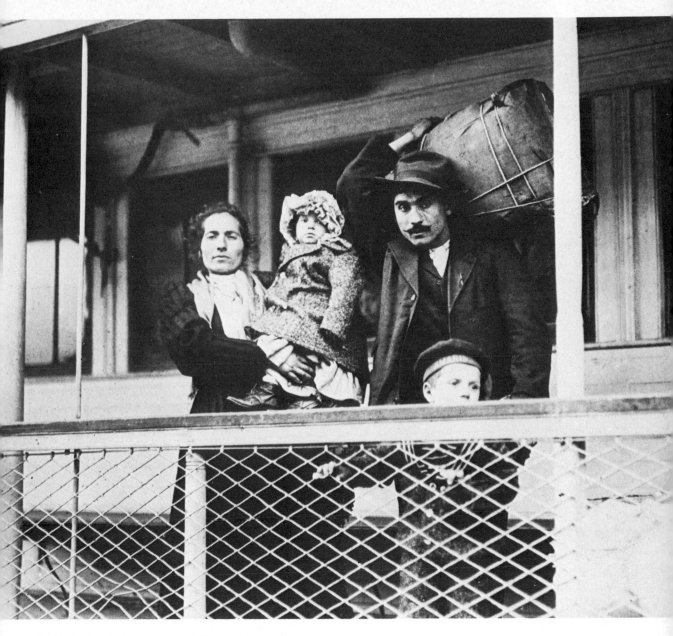

An Italian family, having successfully run the gauntlet
of Ellis Island, takes the ferry to the mainland, 1905.

4 FLIGHT

In the 1880s, despite Gladstone's land reforms, the bulk of the Irish peasantry lived close to subsistence level. For those, such as this Connemara family living on three shillings a week, emigration offered the only escape. The Monarch Line offered a direct transatlantic service from Galway but it was unable to compete with the more frequent sailings of the Liverpool lines.

FROM HUNGER

DISASTER, ON AN UNPRECEDENTED SCALE, struck Ireland in the middle of the 1840s. In the late autumn of 1845 the potato blight – ironically, it originated in America – made its first appearance, causing a partial failure of the crops. The following year it reappeared, bringing universal ruin. Throughout Ireland potato fields in full bloom changed overnight into a waste of blackened, putrefying vegetation. The potato being the Irish peasant's staple diet, famine began to stalk the countryside. Furthermore, the winter of 1846–7 was abnormally severe. The death toll from hunger and privation was frightful. By the spring of 1847 typhus and relapsing fever raged with terrible virulence, finding easy victims among a distressed and weakened population. The pestilence did not die out for more than a year.

Ireland was a land of horrors in 1847. Starving men roamed the countryside, workhouses and hospitals were swamped with fever victims, emaciated peasants lay dead and dying on the earth floor of their hovels, their bodies half-eaten by rats, while thousands of corpses were buried unrecorded in pits. Nobody knows how many died from fever, perhaps a million, and certainly more than those who died of starvation. Even when the epidemics subsided the death rate remained appallingly high. By 1847 it was thought the blight was dying out. But in 1848 it returned so malignantly that again the potato crop failed.

What actually happened in the black year of 1847 is all too tragically clear. But the British Government's part in it was – and still is – the centre of controversy. It has been widely believed that the successive policies of two prime ministers, Sir Robert Peel and Lord John Russell, were of deliberate extermination, and that they remained callously indifferent to Irish starvation because of their belief that the 'Irish problem' could only be solved by depopulation. After all, Peel did nothing to stop the export of Irish grain and those in most need of it had to watch it sail away to England. Deliberate starvation, it has been said, was what occurred, not merely famine. When the English girl in Shaw's *Man and Superman* refers to the Irish famine, the Irish-American, Malone retorts: 'No, the starvation. When a country is full of food, and exporting it, there can be no famine. Me father was starved dead; and I was starved out to America in me mother's arms. English rule drove me and mine out of Ireland.'

A famine funeral at
Skibbereen, Co. Cork,
during the winter of
1846–7. Dead bodies piled
up in the streets in such
numbers as to outstrip the
supply of coffins.

But however cold and indifferent Peel and Russell may have been towards
Ireland, they cannot be accused of deliberately starving her people – indeed,
by their standards, they thought they were doing everything possible. Like their
contemporaries generally, they firmly believed in a policy of *laissez-faire*, convinced that government interference in trade would impede the working of
natural economic laws, and further would hamper private charity – the only
tool that could tackle relief work. Such views today would be considered deplorable, but in the past they were sincerely and honourably held – not only in the
1840s, but by the British Government during the Lancashire cotton 'famine'
of 1862–3, and indeed by Herbert Hoover after the Wall Street Crash.

It is easy to see why the Irish should have been furiously resentful of Britain's
Irish policy. How, after all, could a starving country go on exporting food?
They were not to know that far greater amounts of grain were imported into
Ireland during the famine than were exported from it. Many also did not know
that large quantities of Indian corn and meal were also being imported to be
retailed at cost price. However, they thoroughly disliked what they dubbed
'Peel's brimstone', that is, Indian corn. It was probably so named because
it was yellow and hard and needed to be ground twice to be digestible. The
British Government had overlooked the fact that there were not enough of the
right sort of mills in Ireland to grind it properly – and no doubt this was why
they subsequently imported Indian meal. Nor were the Irish impressed by a
relief programme that assumed that road and canal-making were suitable work
for starving men. Finally, a cause of still greater grievance was the government's
decision to give no relief to those who held more than a quarter of an acre.

68

Russell's stated purpose was to encourage the resumption of agricultural work, halted by the famine. But the Irish naturally assumed it was done to make them choose between abandoning their holdings or starving.

Thus it was against a bitter background of catastrophe, resentment and misunderstanding that the Irish began to leave their homeland in vast numbers. In 1846 more than 100,000 left. The following year more than 200,000 did so; indeed for several years more, departures rarely dropped below that level. In 1851 there were 250,000 emigrants – an all-time record. By the end of 1854 nearly two million people – about a quarter of the population – had emigrated in ten years. Proportionately, it was a larger exodus than from any other country.

It was also, initially at least, the most headlong. In 1846 and 1847 the Irish did not plan their going: they simply fled from hunger and pestilence, from an accursed and dying land. So panic-stricken were they that they were undeterred by the prospect of a winter voyage and, indeed, paid little heed to where they were going. 'All we want,' said one group of emigrants, 'is to get out of Ireland. . . . We must be better anywhere than here.' Great numbers – not included in the emigration statistics quoted above – went to Britain, especially to Liverpool and Glasgow, which already had large Irish populations. Some of those who landed in Britain were sent back to Ireland, others emigrated later to the United States and Canada, but a sizable proportion, especially of the really poor, stayed on. By 1851, the number of Irish-born in Britain had increased in ten years by 300,000. Nevertheless it was across the Atlantic that the great majority of the Irish went. Despite the appalling ravages of ship fever in 1847, the United States remained henceforth their mecca.

The tremendous exodus that followed the Irish famine was, however, not wholly a consequence of that dreadful catastrophe. Long before the famine, particularly since 1815, the volume of Irish emigration had been steadily growing. It would probably have gone on doing so, though less spectacularly, had the famine never occurred. Even in the eighteenth century there had been a steady trickle of Irishmen across the Atlantic, especially from Ulster; the total that went in the half century before 1776 has been estimated at a quarter of a million. Then, after Waterloo, the pace quickened. By the early 1830s, the annual departures were exceeding 50,000. Many still came from Ulster but by now the majority of Irish emigrants were from the south and west of Ireland. During the period 1850–1900, nearly half of all Irish emigrants came from only six of the thirty-two counties – Galway, Mayo, Cork, Kerry, Tipperary and Limerick. These were the most infertile counties, as well as those most dependent on agriculture and the potato.

After 1815 the condition of the Irish population was deteriorating. A large and growing proportion lived permanently in a state of near starvation. Moreover, for Irishmen generally, the range of opportunities was steadily narrowing. This was the consequence not of over-population as such – although Ireland was undoubtedly the most densely populated country in Europe by 1840 – but of an evil land system and of accelerating economic change. Irish landlords, most of them Protestants, many of them absentees, regarded their estates simply as a source of revenue. They and their agents took advantage of the intense competition for land to charge rack rents which left tenants with almost nothing. If a tenant made improvements his only reward was a higher rent. These practices, together with insecurity of tenure, ruled out efficient farming and left tenants with a sense of hopelessness. It was the land system, moreover, which, along with the fact that the potato made it possible to survive on tiny plots, encouraged the frantic sub-division of land that became such a feature of Irish agriculture.

For a time the landlords acquiesced because it meant high rent receipts. But the collapse of grain prices and the growth of the British market for Irish provisions meant that it was now more profitable to convert land to pasture and to replace small farms with large. Thus estates were consolidated and tenants evicted. Some Irish proprietors, like Lord Palmerston and Lord Fitz-william, provided their evicted tenants with the money to emigrate. Most simply cleared their estates, sometimes with great ruthlessness, burning down cabins and leaving the evicted to become squatters in nearby bogs.

In view of the chronic state of wretchedness and misery the wonder is not that so many people left the country after 1815 but that so many stayed on, there being little reason to do so. As the population soared the number of those with no secure stake in the land increased rapidly. And as domestic industry declined, no alternative employment was to be had. But the Irish peasant was passionately attached to the soil; he was unwilling to abandon it as long as it was possible to hope for better times. The Great Famine finally showed him the futility of that hope. 'Poor Ireland's done' was now the verdict. So in the early 1850s, vast numbers of emigrants continued to leave, though the famine was over and relative prosperity had arrived.

The famine continued to be a cause of Irish emigration for the rest of the century in the sense that once emigration had become a national habit no special stimulus was needed to keep it going. It was heavy during the grim decade of the 1880s which began with a new famine in the west of Ireland and unrest throughout the country; it was heavier still during the 1890s, though by then the land question had at last been settled and some grievances removed. The fact was that in good times and bad the Irish had come to regard emigration as being part of the normal order of things, something to be fitted in, like marriage, between birth and death. They did so because the famine had convinced them of the truth of the Irish bull which ran: 'The only place in Ireland that a man can make his fortune is in America.'

Who were the Irish emigrants of the famine era? The evidence conflicts. In Ireland it was lamented that those who went belonged to 'the best and most substantial part of the agricultural population'; Irish papers commonly described them as 'the pith and marrow of the land', 'the lifeblood of the country'.

Eviction of Irish peasants, 1848. Backed by the military, the landlord's agents tear down a family's cabin to make way for large-scale farming.

Across the Atlantic, however, the complaint was that they were drawn from the most destitute of the population. Both classes were in fact represented. When the emigrant ship *Ocean Monarch* was destroyed by fire on her way to Boston in 1848, several thousand pounds in gold were found on the Irish victims' bodies. At the other extreme were the wretched, naked creatures shipped out to Canada and New Brunswick in 1847 by landlords such as Sir Robert Gore Booth and Lord Palmerston. But the mass fell somewhere in between. Sir Charles Trevelyan, who was responsible for Irish famine relief, believed that 'the emigrants generally belonged to that class of smallholders who, being somewhat above the general level of prevailing destitution, had sufficient left to make the effort required for their removal to a foreign land'.

Other Irish of the famine era got to America by assisted passages. Five thousand landlord-assisted emigrants, for instance, arrived in Quebec alone in 1847,

Flight from Hunger

while emigrants who had gone to America earlier sent a stream of remittances back to enable relatives to join them. To an extent unmatched by other groups Irish emigration was a family undertaking. 'The general routine of emigration established here,' reported a Londonderry official in 1834, 'is that in the first place the most enterprising of a family goes out; he then sends for one of his relations; and in this manner the whole of the family is brought out at successive intervals.' Even at that date one third of all Irish passages were said to have been paid for in this way. By the 1850s the proportion was believed to be as high as three-quarters. In aggregate the sums sent back were enormous: £34 million in the fifty years 1850–1900, most of it in small sums. It was a remarkable testimony to the strength of family ties.

Mary McBride left Ireland only in May 1847, but by the following October, having obtained 'an ecellant situation' as a domestic servant at Newburyport, Massachusetts, she was saving a pound a week to enable her brother and sister to emigrate. She promised that 'on St Paterick day I will send you money enough to bring them out.' A letter written by Edward Quinn from New York in March 1848 demonstrates that not all the money remitted was intended to finance emigration. To his parents he wrote: 'I am sending ye two pounds at Present but I had no oppirtinity of sending ye no more but yet I will not forget to send ye some more assitance as soon as I can.' The spirit in which the poor, famine Irish honoured the call of blood is, however, most movingly illustrated

Irish immigrant mothers and children, 1902. Irishmen usually emigrated alone, sending for their families as soon as they could afford to.

by the devotion of Thomas Garry, writing from Peekskill, New York, to his family in County Sligo:

Beekskeel march 8th '48
My dear and loveing wife and children I Received yours of January 20th 1848 which gave me to understand that yous were attacked by a Severe Fever but thanks be God that yous are Recovered and well as I am at Preaset thanks be to his kind merceys to us all be on the watch at the Post Office day after day I wont delay in Relieveing yous as it is a duty encumbered on me by the laws of Church and I hope God will Relieve me. I work on a Railway at 8 shillings per day and pays 18 Shillings per week for my Boarding this is a good Country for them that is able to work and nother person. So I will be able to pay yours passage withe the help of God on the First of August next the sending of this sum of money to yous Compells me to let it be Back tel then and i long to see that long wished for hour that I will Embrace yous in my arms there is nothing in this world gives me trouble but yow and my dear Children whoom I loved as my life. Be Pleased to let me know how my two sons is Patrick and Franciss and not Fergetting my dear Father and mother Friend and neighbours not Forgetting your sister Bridget thank God she was to mind yous in your sickness and sorrows which i will never forget to her i expect to go to newyork on the 17th of march to send you this Bill of Six Pounds which you will Get Cash for in the Provensil Bank of Ireland I will send it in the Revd Patrick ogara is care For you I feel very sorry for my Brother Francis that lived at St John I Fear he is dead.

dont answer this letter tull you Receive the next in which the money will Be for you.

Keep your heart as God spareed you, so long you will be shortly in the lands of Promise and live happy with me and our children.

No more at Pressent
From your Faithful husband till death
Thos Garry

I was ready to go to york to pay Passge for you and the children but I consider yous would not stand the wracking of the sea till yous be nourished for a time.

Inevitably, family ties sometimes snapped as a result of emigration. Advertisements seeking information about relatives appeared frequently in the immigrant press – there were sometimes scores in a single issue. One in the *Boston Pilot* of 16 November 1844 ran as follows:

INFORMATION WANTED
Of PATRICK BOYD, native of co. Roscommon, parish of Elphin, who left home in 1839. He resided at Pennysack, near Philadelphia, in 1842, where his brother Thomas Boyd, did then, and does still reside – since that period there has been no tidings of him by either his brother or any of his friends. Any information regarding him will be most gratefully acknowledged by his wife, Catherine Boyd, or Murphy, who has arrived lately in this country in search of him. Address to the care of Darby Whelan, 94 Quay St., Albany, N.Y.

"Micky M'Carty is Rising in the World, slowly, but surely—

Sister Norah is staying at one of the **Big Hotels**—

Ould Mr. Fogarty has been called to the Bar—

As for us, we are living on Fifth Avenue, near the Cinthral Park—

The role of the Irish in American life is unflatteringly depicted in this 1873 series of cartoons entitled *Letters to the Ould Country*.

Life in the young, restless, fast-growing American republic was bewilderingly different from anything the Irish had known at home. They exchanged a rural for an urban existence; they left a largely Catholic country for one which, at least until the 1840s was overwhelmingly Protestant, and they came in poverty, without skills or education. As President John F. Kennedy was to say of his own immigrant great-grandfather, they left Ireland carrying nothing with them 'except a strong religious faith and strong desire for liberty'.

In the eighteenth century newcomers from Ireland had usually settled in the rural frontier regions. This was a reflection of the land-hunger which accounted for much of the emigration from Ireland in that period. Most of the eighteenth-century emigrants had been Ulster Presbyterians, or Scotch-Irish, as they became known in America. Driven out by high rents and short leases, by famine and by depressions in the linen trade, the Scotch-Irish had enough capital to begin farming afresh. They clustered especially thickly in Pennsylvania which offered generous terms to those who were prepared to settle in frontier regions menaced by the Indians. By 1750 immigrants from Ulster had made the Cumberland Valley their own and had pushed south into the valley of Virginia and on into the foothills of the Carolinas.

In the nineteenth century, however, the pattern of settlement was completely different. The Irish now flocked to the cities, especially those on the eastern seaboard. 'The great bulk of the Irish,' remarked an English writer, 'have blocked up the channels of immigration at the entrance, and remain like the sand which lies at the bar of a river mouth.' By 1850 New York, Boston, Philadelphia and Baltimore had each become a quarter Irish. Even when they went west or south it was only to congregate in cities such as Albany, Cincinnati, Chicago, New Orleans and San Francisco. This was despite frequent warnings of the perils of city life and despite too, the attempts of some Catholic prelates to promote Irish agricultural settlements in the West.

Contemporaries found it difficult to understand why the Irish turned away from farming. Thomas D'Arcy McGee, the editor of the *Boston Pilot*, found it strange 'that a people who in Ireland hungered and thirsted for land, who struggled for conacre and cabin even to the shedding of blood, when they reached the New World, in which a day's wages would have purchased an acre of wild land in fee, wilfully concurred ... to sink into the condition of a miserable town tenantry, to whose squalor even European ports would hardly present a parallel.' But the fact is that the Irish were not suited either by training or temperament to American agriculture. Most of them knew nothing of turning a sod with a plough, their main experience consisting of planting, trenching and digging potatoes – no preparation for running a 160-acre farm in the American West. Having been used to the close neighbourliness of Irish life, they were repelled by the loneliness of Western farm life. An Ulster farmer in Missouri who had worked for sixpence a day in Ireland could, in 1821, rejoice that he now tilled his own acres, yet he missed the gregariousness of peasant life:

Flight from Hunger

I could then go to a fair, or a wake, or a dance, or I could spend the winter nights in a neighbour's house cracking jokes by the turf fire. If I had there but a sore head I would have a neighbour within every hundred yards of me that would run to see me. But here everyone can get so much land, and generally has so much, that they calls them neighbours that lives two or three miles off – och! the sorra take such neighbour, I would say. And then I would sit down and cry and curse him that made me leave home.

The Irish also disliked isolated rural regions because they were afraid they might lose the consolations of their religion. Such fears were encouraged by Bishop John Hughes of New York, the first prominent Irish-born member of the hierarchy, who strongly opposed rural colonization schemes, arguing that dispersal would lead to loss of faith. However, the Irish were seldom in a position, even when they wished it, to settle in the West. Many of the famine emigrants were incapable of moving beyond the ports. 'They fell', said one commentator, 'like tired migratory birds on the eastern shores of the shelter continent . . . the impulse of migration exhausted, their money gone, with no definite purposes or plans.' Very few possessed the money to buy land, tools, seed and stock and to support themselves until their first crops were harvested. The majority were so poor that they were forced to look for work which paid wages right away. That, above all, was why they congregated in the cities. In doing so they became the first American slum-dwellers. True, the tiny cabins of rural Ireland, with their stone, clay or turf walls, mud floors and thatched roofs, were dank and cheerless places, but in America they crowded together in courts and alleys, garrets and cellars, in the unhealthiest and most congested neighbourhoods – New York's Five Points area, Philadelphia's Moyamensing and Kensington, New Orleans's Irish Channel. Perhaps the worst Irish slums were in the North End of Boston. Because the city was waterlocked it was impossible to travel in any direction without the payment of tolls which the Irish could not afford. Therefore, they crowded into Boston's old commercial centre, where mansions and warehouses were roughly converted into tenements, and also into the innumerable hovels that enterprising landlords erected in yards, gardens and courts. They also lived in dark, underground cellars which lacked drains and privies. In 1849 a Boston health committee, investigating a recent outbreak of cholera described such places as 'the permanent abode of fever'. It also found that the spread of the disease coincided remarkably with the areas of Irish concentration. The committee reported that 'the average age of Irish life in Boston does not exceed fourteen years.' It went on:

In Broad street and all the surrounding neighbourhood, including Fort Hill and the adjacent streets, the situation of the Irish . . . is particularly wretched. During their visits last summer, your Committee were witnesses of scenes too painful to be forgotten, and yet too disgusting to be related here. It is sufficient to say, that the whole district is a perfect hive of human beings, without comforts and mostly without

Irish shantytown on Fifth Avenue
at 116th Street, New York, 1893.

common necessaries; in many cases, huddled together like brutes, without regard to sex, or age, or sense of decency: grown men and women sleeping together in the same apartment, and sometimes wife and husband, brothers and sisters all in the same bed.

The Irish-American community also included a leavening of men of education and skill – lawyers, teachers, journalists. Those with professional qualifications kept their status, some achieving distinction after emigrating. This was especially true of the political refugees who fled to America after the unsuccessful Irish rebellions of 1798 and 1848. Of the Ninety-Eighters, Thomas Addis Emmet and William Sampson became leaders of the New York bar and Dr William James MacNeven a luminary of American medicine. Among the hundreds of refugees in 1848 three had outstanding American careers, Thomas D'Arcy McGee and John Mitchel in journalism, Thomas Francis Meagher as a Civil War general and later as territorial secretary of Montana.

Nevertheless, the great mass of their fellow-countrymen of the famine era possessed neither money, education nor skills. They were thus able to find places only at the bottom of the occupational ladder. In 1855 half of the Irish working population of New York City was made up of unskilled labourers, carters, porters, stevedores, waiters and domestic servants. In Boston the proportion was two-thirds. Because of a strong American prejudice against the Irish even unskilled jobs were hard to find. In 1886 Patrick Ford, the editor of New York's influential *Irish World*, described his early struggles as an immigrant boy from Galway: 'I travelled footsore day after day through Boston for a place at a dollar a week, or at any price. I would see a notice, "Boy Wanted, No Irish Need Apply".' During the Civil War, the phrase, 'No Irish Need Apply', became the title of an ironical popular song. It contrasted the welcome accorded Irish recruits for the Northern Army with the cold reception they had received on arrival in America.

Rejection was apparently most common in domestic service. Many advertisements for domestic help debarred the Irish and not a few turned the knife in the wound by expressing preference for Negroes. 'Wanted. A Cook or a Chambermaid', ran a typical advertisement in the New York *Evening Post* of 4 September 1830. 'They must be American, Scotch, Swiss or Africans – no Irish.' This kind of proscription was sometimes due to religious bigotry, sometimes the result of other servants refusing to work with the Irish. But there was also a widespread conviction among the American middle class that the standard of the domestic arts in Ireland was so low that Irish girls were not sufficiently experienced as cooks and laundresses to make good servants. Nevertheless, by the middle of the nineteenth century the Irish domestic servant had become a familiar part of the American scene.

In America as in Britain, a common Irish occupation was heavy construction work. As early as 1818 there were 3000 Irishmen building the Erie Canal, while in the later railroad era, Irish gangs were to be prominent in such enterprises

Posters like this, issued by railroad contractors, were aimed especially at the Irish city-dwellers. On arrival in the West the Irish frequently found that only a few labourers were wanted, and that wages were well below the rate advertised.

as the Erie Railroad and the Union Pacific. Without them the United States could not have acquired its thousands of miles of roads, canals and railways so rapidly. An American newspaper remarked: 'There are several kinds of power working at the fabric of the republic – water-power, steam-power and Irish-power. The last works hardest of all.' Conditions in the construction camps were uniformly bad and exploitation common. Irish navvies were often forced to pay exorbitant prices at company stores, and sometimes were cheated of their wages. Construction work was as hazardous as it was exhausting, and safety precautions were non-existent. Accidents were common and many an Irish labourer found his last resting place alongside the railroad he had helped to build. A Boston Irish priest, the Reverend John O'Hanlon, believed that these harsh conditions largely explained the rioting and heavy drinking for which Irish construction gangs were notorious. He also felt that 'the disorderly conduct ... the half civilized and intemperate mode of life of too many of our countrymen' had been 'the occasion for fomenting dislike towards our country and her people amongst many Americans'. Yet the truth was that this was only one of several reasons for anti-Irish feeling. Another was the sharp rise in crime and pauperism as a result of the Irish influx. Serious crime was rare among the Irish; the vast majority of arrests were for minor offences – petty theft, drunkenness, disorderly conduct. All the same, most of the occupants of city jails, especially along the Atlantic seaboard, were Irish. So were the inmates of almshouses and those on poor relief. In the winter of 1837–8 the commissioners of the New York City almshouses reported that seventy per cent of the applicants for poor relief were Irish women whose husbands were out of the city working on railroads and canals.

Undoubtedly, however, it was their religion that accounted most for the hostility that set in against the Irish in the 1830s. They were the first large group of Catholic immigrants to enter the United States, and the building of American Catholicism was peculiarly an Irish achievement. The Irish cherished their Catholicism because of the solace it had afforded them during centuries of oppression. It was, in the words of one of their present-day descendants, John Doherty, 'the only thing they had when they were over in Ireland. It was the thing that held them together when everything else went wrong.' The Irish had made enormous sacrifices to preserve their religion at home and they were determined to do the same in America. Without money, and with few priests, such was the attachment to their faith that they made the building of a church their first priority. The consequence was that the American Catholic Church acquired a Hibernian tinge which it still retains. Today, about half of the Roman Catholic hierarchy in the States have Irish names.

The coming of the Irish rekindled in America the religious intolerance of the colonial period, and a new wave of hysterical no-popery agitation began. Feeling against Catholics sometimes led to violence. In 1834 a mob of Boston labourers marched out to nearby Charlestown and burnt the Ursuline convent.

Flight from Hunger

In 1844 several Catholic churches in Philadelphia were burned and a number of Irish Catholics was killed and injured. Moreover, the 1830s saw a flood of scurrilous anti-Catholic literature, much of it directed against Catholic religious houses. The best-known example was Maria Monk's *Awful Disclosures of the Hôtel Dieu Nunnery at Montreal*, which depicted convents and monasteries as hotbeds of sexual immorality. This kind of religious sensationalism enjoyed wide circulation, especially when it was presented in the form of pornography.

What lay at the heart of the agitation was the conviction that Catholicism was incompatible with American ideals. American Protestants regarded it as the inveterate foe of civil liberties: some overwrought individuals, like Samuel F. B. Morse, the celebrated painter and the inventor of the telegraph and morse code, were ready to uncover popish plots aimed at subverting free government in the United States. Though few shared Morse's fantasies, a great many Americans were concerned about the efforts of the Catholic hierarchy to win control of church property from boards of lay trustees. These fears of foreign influence were further stimulated when in 1853 a papal nuncio, Monsignor Gaetano Bedini, arrived in the United States to settle a number of such conflicts. Bedini, who had taken part in suppressing the 1848 Italian revolution, was pursued by demonstrations throughout his visit.

Strong feelings were also aroused by the prolonged schools controversy of the 1840s. Catholics had long complained of the sectarian instruction in New York's public schools. The school day began with Protestant hymns and prayers, and with readings from the King James version of the Scriptures, which the Catholic Church condemned. The Bible was sacred to Protestants as a patriotic symbol and as Holy Writ: to reject it was blasphemy. So in 1840 when Bishop Hughes demanded a share of the public school funds for parochial schools, he met violent opposition. And when the following year Bishop Hughes organized a separate Catholic ticket in the city elections his action was loudly condemned as a violation of the American principle of the separation of church and state. The New York *Observer*, convinced that the Catholic Church was plotting to gain political control of the country, was indignant that an 'ecclesiastic at the head of his flock actually nominated a ticket ... declared his official approbation of it, and enjoined upon his trembling followers to go to the polls and put that ticket into the ballot boxes....'

Fears that the Irish represented a threat to political freedom owed much to the conviction that they were debasing American politics. Complaints that immigrants were being naturalized without the five-year residential qualification came to a head after the 1844 presidential election, which the Democratic candidate narrowly won and in which the Irish vote may have provided the margin of victory. One of the Whig leaders, Daniel Webster, alleged that 'masters of vessels, having brought over immigrants from Europe have, within 30 days of their landing, seen those very persons carried up to the polls and give their votes for the highest offices in the national and state governments.'

St Patrick's Cathedral, New York, begun in 1858 and completed in 1879. Largely owing to Irish immigration, there were over 100,000 Catholics in New York City by the 1850s – far outnumbering any Protestant denomination.

A Congressional enquiry in 1845 found that hired witnesses and false testimony were common in naturalization proceedings and that on the eve of elections newly-arrived immigrants were naturalized in droves at the instigation of the political machines. Equally well-founded was the widespread belief that the Irish had turned American elections into the riotous occasions they had been in Ireland. One of the worst examples occurred on election day 1834 in the Sixth Ward of New York City, where organized mobs of Irish labourers used clubs to prevent their opponents from voting. For three days street battles raged and it took a detachment of infantry and two squadrons of cavalry to restore order.

Though few had emigrated for political reasons the Irish threw themselves vigorously into American politics at all levels. As their numbers grew, they came to be an important factor. From the start they identified themselves with the Democratic Party. As early as the 1790s some of the exiled United Irishmen, like Thomas Addis Emmet, were hardly off the boat before they were lending their support to the Jeffersonians. Their vigorous partizanship was to lead one of Jefferson's opponents to call the Irish 'the most God-provoking Democrats this side of Hell'. A generation later the Irish were among the staunchest supporters of Andrew Jackson, who appealed to them as the champion of the common man and who was consistently friendly to immigrant aspirations.

Even when the Democratic Party fell under the sway of Southern slave owners, the Irish gave it their votes. They had little sympathy with abolitionism or with the anti-slavery policy of the Republicans who were to elect Abraham Lincoln in 1860. The Irish feared that the slaves if freed would move north and threaten the jobs Irish immigrants had so painfully won. The Catholic hierarchy, too, were bitterly opposed to abolitionism, not because they favoured slavery, but because they felt abolitionists to be dangerous radicals. Newspapers like the New York *Irish American* denounced abolitionists as enemies of religion, as hypocrites indifferent to the fate of immigrant labour and as fanatics who threatened to plunge the country into civil war. John Mitchel, the revolutionary who escaped to America from Van Diemen's Land (Tasmania), was openly anti-Negro. In 1856 he wrote in his paper, *The Citizen*:

He would be a bad Irishman who voted for principles ... which jeopardized the present freedom of a nation of white men, for the vague forlorn hope of elevating blacks to a level for which it is at least problematical whether God and nature ever intended them.

Not even Daniel O'Connell, who was an uncompromising abolitionist, could persuade Irish-Americans to share his views. In 1842 O'Connell denounced George Washington and Andrew Jackson as slave owners, reproached his fellow-countrymen in America for their hostility to abolitionism and called upon them to speak out against slavery. 'How can you have become so depraved?' he asked. 'How can your souls have become stained with a darkness blacker

Flight from Hunger

than the Negro's skin?' But the only result of O'Connell's call was to destroy his influence and Irish-American support for his repeal movement fell away sharply.

Fear of Irish turbulence, of Catholicism, and of Irish political dominance contributed to the formation in the 1850s of a new, though short-lived, political party, the 'Know-Nothing' or American Party. It grew out of a secret society, the Order of the Star-Spangled Banner, founded in New York in 1849. The Order aimed to exclude pauper and criminal immigrants, to debar immigrants – especially Catholics – from public office, and to reduce the immigrant vote by extending the residential qualification for naturalization from five to twenty-one years. Like American secret societies generally, the Order had an elaborate apparatus of secret grips, signs and passwords which members swore never to divulge to outsiders. Secrecy was retained even after the Order grew into a political party. When questioned about its activities, members replied, 'I know nothing'. During the heavy mid-century immigration from Ireland and Germany, the Know-Nothings enjoyed a phenomenal growth and between 1854 and 1856 they controlled several states. Among them was Massachusetts, founded two centuries before by a group of Puritans led by John Winthrop and still recognizably a child of the Reformation. Antipathy towards Irish Catholics came naturally to those living in Boston, America's cultural capital. Bostonians prided themselves on their English ancestry and their social and cultural contacts with England. They also numbered in their ranks some of the most fanatical abolitionists.

In Boston and other towns Irish voters became so numerous that they threatened to block the aims of native politicians. There was bitter controversy between Puritan and Celt over the return of fugitive slaves and over a new state constitution. The existence of the Irish militia, composed exclusively of immigrants, was seen at best as a proof of clannishness and at worst as a threat to American unity. In 1854 high feelings were aroused when two Boston Irish militia companies escorted an escaped slave to the warship which was to take him back to Virginia. Hence when the Know-Nothings gained power in Massachusetts in 1855 they banned all foreign military companies. They also sought to crush Irish political power by introducing a literacy test for voting and by disfranchising foreigners until two years had elapsed since their naturalization.

On the eve of the Civil War the Irish were thus an exploited and unpopular minority. Abused as they were for their poverty, censured for their violence, suspect because of their religion, they must have felt that they had not escaped the evils that had prompted them to emigrate. Hardship, disease and discrimination had accompanied them to their new homes.

Were they, in fact, better off in America? Certainly there was no more anguished dependence on the potato crop, no more hunger. Instead they received high wages – always the main attraction of America for the poor. At $1.00 (4 shillings) or $1.50 a day, rates in the United States were five times higher

OPPOSITE Friends of the Negro bitterly denounced the Irish for their racial prejudices. In this cartoon, by the famous *Harper's Weekly* cartoonist, Thomas Nast, the Irish voter is shown combining with former Southern slaveholders and New York capitalists to deny the freed Negro the equality the Republicans sought to grant him.

82

The Columbian Artillery was one of several Irish militia companies formed in Boston in the early 1850s. Although they were social rather than military organizations, such companies were held to be inconsistent with loyalty to America and were compulsorily disbanded during the Know-Nothing agitation just before the Civil War.

than in Ireland, though the American cost of living was higher and they had to buy food and clothes, which they had once grown or made for themselves. Even so it was beyond question that the Irish were materially better off. The evidence of emigrant letters is suggestive of this. Margaret McCarthy's first letter home after landing in New York in 1850 contained a typically glowing account:

My dear Father I must only say that this is a good place and a good country, for if one place does not suit a man he can go to another and can very easy please himself. ... Any man or woman without a family are fools that would not venture and come to this plentyful Country where no man or woman ever hungered or ever will and where you will not be seen naked.

How quickly some of the Irish rose may be seen from the fact that as early as 1851 a substantial number of those in Philadelphia, for instance, owned their own homes. Above all, that many were able to send money back to their relatives, though they stinted themselves to do it, is proof that the promise of American plenty had been fulfilled. Some of the more striking success stories found their way into the newspapers. In 1850 *The Times* of London printed a letter from an Irishman who had emigrated to Wisconsin twelve months before. It read:

I am exceedingly well pleased at coming to this land of plenty. On arrival I purchased 120 acres of land at $5 [£1] an acre. . . . You must bear in mind that I have purchased the land out, and it is to me and mine an 'estate for ever', without a landlord, an agent or tax-gatherer to trouble me. I would advise all my friends to quit Ireland – the country most dear to me; as long as they remain in it they will be in bondage and misery. . . . What you labour for is sweetened by contentment and happiness; there is no failure in the potato crop, and you can grow . . . every crop you wish, without manuring the land during life. You need not mind feeding pigs, but let them into the woods and they will feed themselves, until you want to make bacon of them. I shudder when I think that starvation prevails to such an extent in poor Ireland. After supplying the entire population of America, there would still be as much corn and provisions left as would supply the world, for there is no limit to cultivation or end to land. Here the meanest labourer has beef and mutton, with bread, bacon, tea, coffee, sugar and even pies, the whole year round – every day here is as good as Christmas-day in Ireland.

If the immigrants themselves could count emigration a gain, their children were to be immeasurably better off. Hence, in spite of the painful nature of many of his experiences, the Irish immigrant came to look upon the United States with gratitude and affection. Even in the 1840s some regarded it, in the words of Thomas Colley Grattan, as 'the refuge of his race, the home of his kindred, the heritage of his children and their children . . . a sort of half-way stage to Heaven.'

For despite the hostility they faced, a fierce American patriotism was growing among the Irish. To quote Thomas D'Arcy McGee: 'Not even the natives of New England have a greater interest in the preservation of the Union than the Celts of America.' Their enthusiastic response to Lincoln's call for volunteers in April 1861 showed that McGee had been right. Some may have volunteered because the military experience they gained might come in useful in a future war of Irish independence, but their motive was mainly to defend a country which had, with all its limitations, treated them more fairly than Britain had done and which they now felt to be their own. The alacrity with which they sprang to arms brought a relaxation of discrimination. They were now encouraged to organize units under their own green flag and their own commanding officers – a practice some states had frowned upon only a few years earlier. Among the earliest Irish regiments was the New York 69th, commanded by Colonel Michael Corcoran, which departed for Virginia in 1861 and served with distinction at Bull Run. During the battle Corcoran was taken prisoner and spent over a year in a Confederate prison camp. On his release he at once recruited another Irish unit, the Corcoran Legion. It was designed to replace the Irish Brigade which, under the command of General Thomas Francis Meagher, had fought so gallantly at Fredericksburg that it had been virtually wiped out.

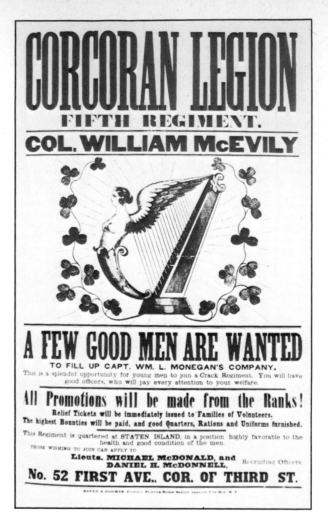

A Civil War recruiting poster of 1862. Separate Irish military units were encouraged once the Union needed soldiers to fight the Confederacy. The Corcoran Legion was named after Colonel Michael Corcoran, an immigrant from Sligo, whose popularity among the Irish was greatly enhanced when he refused to parade his militia unit in honour of the Prince of Wales's visit to New York in 1860.

A war for Negro freedom did not, however, engender the same enthusiasm among the Irish as one for the Union. Lincoln's Emancipation Proclamation of 1 January 1863 brought a sour response from Irish-Americans, and the Conscription Act passed two months later brought a violent one. The Irish protested that the wealthy could escape military service by paying a $300 fine and complained that the draft law was unfair to Democratic voters like themselves. They also objected to being compelled to fight for the freedom of their potential economic competitors. Their resentment boiled over in the New York draft riots of July 1863, when an Irish mob terrorized the city for three days, attacking and killing Negroes, destroying property and burning down a coloured orphans' asylum. Troops who had recently halted Lee at Gettysburg had to be brought back to restore order. Yet these outrages did not result in a resurgence of intolerance. By now the Irish were widely accepted as patriotic Americans.

But after the war, so long as the Irish persisted in demanding public funds for parochial schools and so long as there were fresh examples of Irish violence, so long would American antipathy continue. A series of 'Orange riots' in New York culminated in a bloodbath on 12 July 1871 when Irish Catholics broke up an Orangemen's march on the anniversary of the Battle of the Boyne. This tragic clash was closely followed by the violence of the Molly Maguires. The Mollies, a secret Irish labour organization, were responsible for a series of dynamite explosions and murders in the Pennsylvania anthracite fields in the early 1870s. Such episodes brought down upon Irishmen generally a chorus of denunciation and served as an excuse for Thomas Nast's vicious cartoons in *Harper's Weekly*, which depicted the Irish as drunken brutes with simian features.

In the 1880s Protestants became alarmed at the growing strength of the Catholic Church. This development, allied to the growing prominence of Irish Catholic politicians, revived talk of a popish plot and gave rise to organizations like the American Protective Association, pledged to defend the public school system and to oppose Catholic political influence. The APA soon vanished but prejudice against Catholics in politics lasted well into the twentieth century. No Catholic was to be elected president until John F. Kennedy in 1960.

So it was hardly surprising that the climb to prosperity and middle-class respectability continued to be a slow and often painful business for the Irish. Even in 1880 the Boston Irish were still doing most of the unskilled work and living in the poorest areas. New arrivals from Ireland still found it a hard struggle to escape from poverty. Dan Doherty emigrated to Boston in 1909 and got his first job working for the gas company, laying pipes: 'We worked nine hours a day, six days a week. And when we paid the landlady five dollars we had exactly three dollars left. We had nothing to spend. Most of us made out for nearly a year with the clothes we brought with us, including our underwear.' But with the growth of Irish political power, jobs in the police and fire departments became increasingly available. By the 1880s the Irish 'cop' and the Irish fireman had become familiar figures in American cities. Though even the second generation did not find it easy to get clerical and professional jobs, many managed to climb into the ranks of the semi-skilled and even the skilled.

Those Irishmen who reached the top did so by a variety of routes. There was, for instance, William O'Connell. Born in 1859, the son of Irish immigrant millworkers, he rose from being curate of a Boston slum parish to be successively bishop and archbishop of Boston and in 1911 the first American cardinal. Patrick A. Collins, a potato famine immigrant from Cork, was brought to Boston in 1848 at the age of four by his widowed mother. An errand boy in a Boston law office at twelve, a coal miner in Ohio at fourteen, he returned to Boston at eighteen and worked his way through college, then through Harvard Law School. After practising law for some years he entered politics and was rewarded with the Consul-Generalship in London. There was another O'Connell, James, who left his father's farm in Cork at the age of sixteen. The family had cousins in Dorchester, a farming town on the outskirts of Boston.

ST. PATRICK'S DAY 1867

RUM.   BRUTAL ATTACK ON THE POLICE. "THE DAY WE CELEBRATE."   IRIS

He got a job as a farmhand, and then after the Civil War he married and took up plastering. At a time when the city of Boston was rapidly expanding – so much so that it ultimately annexed the town of Dorchester – there was plenty of work. James O'Connell made enough money to start his own business and his five sons all had to work for him as soon as they were old enough. The profits of the family were used to educate the five boys. All of them went to Harvard. Three became lawyers. Joseph O'Connell went to Congress for two terms as a Democrat. Daniel T. O'Connell worked on the Boston journal *Republic* and became a leading light in the movement for Irish freedom. He was ultimately one of the American judges at the Nuremberg trials.

The Irish propensities
for violence and for drink
were mercilessly satirized
by Thomas Nast.

America's tremendous industrial expansion after the Civil War offered dazzling opportunities to businessmen who had the necessary ability, energy and ruthlessness. Some Irishmen made great business fortunes despite their humble beginnings. One was Thomas F. Ryan, son of a famine immigrant, who rose from being a Baltimore errand boy to become a millionaire financier. Another was Michael Cudahy, who arrived in America in 1849 at the age of eight, and later revolutionized the meat-packing industry by introducing summer curing under refrigeration. A third was William R. Grace, a native of Queenstown, who made a fortune in Peruvian mining, founded the Grace shipping line and in 1880 was elected mayor of New York.

Some of the most spectacular examples of rags to riches were those men who took Horace Greeley's advice to 'Go West, young man and grow up with the country!' Like many others in the California gold rush of 1849, the Irish did not make fortunes prospecting. Among those who rose to prominence in the West was Peter Donahue, born in Glasgow in 1822 of Irish parents. Arriving in California in 1849 he set up an iron foundry, started a steamboat line and constructed San Francisco's first streetlights. At his death in 1885 he was worth $4,000,000 (£800,000). Another remarkable business career was that of James Phelan, the founder of a Californian political dynasty. As a young immigrant from Ireland he worked first as a grocery clerk in New York before moving to San Francisco during the gold rush. There he opened a saloon, branched out into real estate and ultimately established his own bank. By 1870 he was one of San Francisco's ten richest men.

In California too, wealth brought the Irish social recognition. In the 1870s the tone of San Francisco society was set by the wealthy Irish whose mansions lined Nob Hill. The city's leading hostess was Mrs Edward Martin, wife of the founder of the Hibernian Bank and sister of John G. Downey, who had become governor of California in 1862, only thirteen years after he had arrived in Los Angeles with $10 (£2) in his pocket.

The Irish possessed peculiar talents for political organization. They brought with them from Ireland a well-developed taste for politics and a familiarity with the forms if not with the realities of representative government. They also had eloquent tongues and of course had no language barrier to surmount. Their political ascent was therefore remarkably rapid. In little more than a generation after the famine, men with Irish names had made their mark. Boston got its first Irish mayor, Hugh O'Brien, in 1886 and few but Irishmen have held the post since. By 1901 the Irish had a majority on the Boston City Council and a second Irish mayor in Patrick A. Collins. Twelve years later Massachusetts had its first Irish senator, David Ignatius Walsh. John F. Fitzgerald ('Honey Fitz') was narrowly beaten in the 1916 Senatorial election but was destined to be remembered in another way. When his grandson, John F. Kennedy, was elected president of the United States, *Honey Fitz* was the name chosen for the presidential yacht.

Flight from Hunger

Neither the political machine nor the boss was invented by the Irish. But in Irish hands these institutions became the instruments of a characteristic political style. Irish bosses had a shrewd appreciation of the needs and aspirations of the immigrant masses. They knew that the machine could win the votes of immigrants by finding them jobs, protecting them from the law, organizing picnics for the children, and sending round gifts of coal and turkeys at Christmas. Consequently most of the major cities in the North and the Midwest fell under Irish boss rule. Chicago, Boston and above all, Tammany Hall in New York, best exemplified Irish municipal control. The succession of autocratic Irishmen who ruled Tammany conformed to no single pattern. The first, John Kelly, reigned between 1873 and 1886, cherished the nickname 'Honest John' and was indeed honest by the standards of American municipal politics. His successor, Richard Croker, was not; 'Crokerism' became a synonym for graft. A Tammany boss once described the difference between honest and dishonest graft. The first he summed up in the saying: 'I seen my opportunities and I took 'em.' The second involved accepting protection money from gamblers, houses of prostitution and saloon-keepers who had broken the law. Most bosses preferred the first kind of graft; Croker enjoyed both. Though born in Ireland, he was of English descent and only became a Catholic when he entered politics. He began as a street brawler and on one occasion narrowly escaped conviction for murder. Politics made him a millionaire and when he retired he returned to Ireland to breed racehorses and pigs. Croker then became a familiar figure on the English turf and his horse Orby won the Derby in 1907. He also ran a farm, naming each of his pigs after a New York politician.

One of the last of the old-time bosses – and perhaps the most colourful – was James Michael Curley. Born in a Boston tenement in 1874, the son of immigrants from County Galway, Curley was exceptional among Irish bosses in seeking high political office rather than staying behind the scenes. During his fifty-year career he was a Congressman three times, mayor of Boston four times and governor of Massachusetts once. He was also in gaol twice. Denounced by his enemies as 'a political Barnum' and as 'the Irish Mussolini', Curley's power rested on the support of the Boston Irish. He appealed to their aspirations, played upon their emotions and won their affection by his efforts to improve their condition – the first of his two gaol sentences was for sitting a Civil Service examination in place of a constituent who would have been unable to pass it. That kind of gesture justified Curley's claim to be 'the mayor with a heart'.

No immigrant people displayed such an affectionate concern for the old country as the Irish, their moral and financial support sustaining a long succession of Irish causes: Catholic Emancipation, the Repeal movement, Fenianism, the Land League, Home Rule, Irish independence. Nationalist leaders like Parnell, Davitt and De Valera who made fund-raising visits to the United States could be sure of a rapturous reception. Sometimes Irish-Americans made more

Boston's most celebrated Irish-American mayor makes a characteristic appeal for support.

direct attempts to strike a blow for Ireland. There were Fenian invasions of Canada from the United States at the close of the Civil War, and in 1883 a Clan-na-Gael plot to torpedo British warships visiting New York. Moreover the Irish repeatedly used their political weight to oppose any State Department move that seemed to favour Britain. Their well-known Anglophobia led politicians, anxious for Irish votes, to make a practice at election times of twisting the lion's tail.

Such agitations attracted much criticism. Other Americans complained of divided loyalties and of the impropriety of attempts to influence American foreign policy in the interests of foreign lands. But this was to misunderstand the nature of Irish-American nationalism. Those who sought to explain it, and especially its vindictive hostility to England, assumed that it derived from bitter memories of the famine. Yet a British journalist visiting the States in the 1880s met 'men of the second generation, who had never set foot on Irish soil', but who were as fiercely devoted to Ireland as any inhabitant of Cork. William Mackay Lomasney, who was born in Cincinnati in 1841 of Irish immigrant parents, gave his life to the Irish cause. In 1884 he blew himself up while attempting to dynamite London Bridge. This seems to suggest that Irish-American nationalism originated not in what the immigrant brought from Ireland but in what he met in America. Though prejudice and discrimination diminished with time many second and third generation immigrants, even those who had prospered, felt excluded and inferior. Their spokesmen constantly told them that what prevented the Irish from being treated as equals in the United States was their origin: they were despised and rejected because they came from a despised and rejected land. The only remedy was to end Ireland's dependency on Britain and thus, in supporting Irish causes they would be seeking their own emancipation as much as that of Ireland itself.

Irish nationalist leaders did not always understand the basic reasons that lay behind their support in the United States. Michael Davitt was one who did. He was careful in his appeals to Irish-Americans to link the status of Ireland with that of his audience. 'Aid us in Ireland', he urged a New York gathering in 1880, 'to remove the stain of degradation from your birth and the Irish race here will get the respect you deserve.' De Valera, on the other hand, did not display that kind of perception. During an American visit in 1920 his claim to be the spokesman for the Irish in America brought him a monumental rebuff from a leading Irish-American. Judge Daniel F. Cohalan's words serve to illustrate both the paradoxical quality of Irish-American nationalism and the extent to which the Irish in America had become Americanized. 'What I have done for the cause of Irish independence,' he wrote, 'I have done as an American whose only allegiance is to America, and as one to whom the interest and security of my country are ever to be preferred to any and all lands.'

5 COUSINS AND STRANGERS

NATIVE-BORN AMERICANS, anxiously scanning the variegated army of newcomers arriving from Europe during the nineteenth century, tended to focus their gaze upon unfamiliar types. What caught their attention were the masses of Irishmen, Germans, Italians, Slavs and Jews; they paid much less heed to British immigrants. Sometimes, indeed, these were ignored so completely in contemporary journals and literature that one might have thought that, after independence, the tide of emigration from what had once been the mother country had turned elsewhere.

In fact nothing could be further from the truth. Statistics reveal that between 1820 and 1930 four and a quarter million Britons arrived in America, almost as many as those who came in the same period from Ireland or Italy. For the British, as for other Europeans, the United States was an incomparable magnet.

One reason why the British influx attracted so little notice was that it had no sudden, dramatic cause, such as the Irish famine or the waves of anti-Jewish persecution in Russia. Another reason was that, alone among the motley throngs who tramped down the gangplank at Castle Garden or Ellis Island, the British were not alien in appearance, language, religion or customs, while their standards of living and modes of thought were, more than any other group, close to those of America. Consequently they were more readily assimilated. To use the description of one historian, they were 'invisible immigrants'.

Yet the condition of the British immigrants was not essentially different from that of other newcomers. Though they stood high in the estimation of Americans and did not have to struggle so hard for acceptance, they nevertheless felt themselves to be arriving, as an English immigrant put it, 'in a foreign land among strangers'. For many this was an unexpected – and sometimes painful – discovery. Crossing the Atlantic in the belief that what they would find would be very like home, they were often surprised at the extent to which it was not.

The same underlying forces that were dislodging people from Europe were moving the British out in great numbers – these being the pressures of a rising population and the dislocating effects of the agricultural and industrial revolutions. In just over a century the population of Great Britain quadrupled – from ten and a half million in 1801 to forty-one million in 1911. During the same

An English family arrives in New York, 17 April 1908.

period, a series of economic changes caused the collapse of the old agricultural order, and the transformation of Britain into the world's leading industrial nation.

Agricultural change was chiefly responsible for emigration in the decades just after 1815. The trend towards large-scale scientific farming greatly increased output but made many agricultural workers redundant. To make matters worse, the collapse of wheat prices at the end of the Napoleonic Wars ushered in a long period of agricultural depression, which lasted for a generation.

Poor conditions led even wealthy farmers to emigrate during that period. One, Morris Birkbeck, sold his farm in Surrey in 1817 and emigrated to the prairies of Illinois, taking with him a large quantity of prize livestock and £18,000 ($90,000). Together with another rich landowner, George Flower, he established an English colony west of the Wabash River. Alas, Albion, as it was known, brought financial ruin to both its founders and even before Birkbeck's death in 1825 it no longer attracted other farmers.

William Cobbett remarked that all the farmers he saw leaving Lincolnshire for America in 1830 had money, some as much as £2000 ($10,000). Labourers, however, could go only when they were assisted. At that time parishes in southeast England made a practice of shipping off their paupers to America, believing that this would be cheaper in the long run than supporting them at home. But the numbers were never large and the practice ceased in 1834, when the new Poor Law stipulated that assisted paupers could only emigrate to a British colony.

Many English farmers adjusted successfully to their new conditions and wrote enthusiastically of the abundance they had found. In 1818, Edward Connor, who farmed 134 acres in Indiana, wrote back to his family in England:

We have plenty of game such as bears, wolves, deer, wild turkeys, pheasants, partridges, rabbits, wild pigeons in thousands.... The land is upon a limestone-bed; and will grow anything. It *has* grown 200 bushels of potatoes per acre and here they use no manure. No land in England is to be compared with it.... There is the sugar maple, which yields a great quantity of sugar.... We can make our own candles and soap; and grow our own tobacco; in short, we can do anything.

By about 1830 the emigration of farmers and labourers had become extensive, especially from the south-coast counties from Kent to Cornwall, and from Yorkshire, Derbyshire, Cheshire and Cumberland, the counties hardest hit by the agricultural depression. The majority of emigrants seem to have been small farmers and what Cobbett called 'the flower of the labourers'. A witness before a parliamentary committee in 1833 described emigrants to America from Yorkshire's North Riding:

They were small freeholders that were in debt and compelled to sell the land, and they went away, saying that if they stopped here there was nothing but poverty for them; and they got away with the remainder of their property under the fear of losing the whole.... The labourers that have emigrated have been in general the best of the labourers that we had, saying that they were going to be ruined if they remained here; a labourer that had got his wife and child and saved his £20 or £30 [between $100 and $150] in service, got off before his money was gone.

It seems from this and other evidence that it was not the pressure of absolute want that induced the agricultural population to emigrate, but uncertainty about the future. Emigrants consisted of men who were not yet engulfed by poverty but feared they might be soon.

Farming in Britain improved during the middle decades of the nineteenth century. The long-drawn-out depression that began after Waterloo ended and the repeal of the Corn Laws in 1846 did not, as many had feared, ruin the British farmer. Overseas supplies of wheat did not, as yet, constitute a threat. Agriculture was enjoying a brief 'golden age'. But the last quarter of the nineteenth century again witnessed a severe agricultural depression. The main cause was the flood of American grain that began to arrive in the 1870s. Wheat prices fell catastrophically, went on falling for twenty years and did not recover before the First World War. All over Britain stark necessity compelled farmers to lay ploughland down to grass, adopt labour-saving machinery and dispense with a large proportion of their labourers. The result was that between 1871 and 1901 the number of agricultural labourers fell by a third.

Many of the dispossessed gravitated to the industrial districts of Britain. Others forsook Britain in large numbers to seek new farms overseas. In the 1880s many of them settled in Australia and New Zealand, having received assisted passages. In the decade immediately before 1914, Canada enjoyed a tremendous vogue, both with country folk and with town dwellers. Even so, the American census of 1890 showed that there were more than 90,000 British-born farmers in the United States and well over 100,000 British-born farm labourers. Not all had worked on the land in the old country – it was not un-known for British textile workers and miners to turn farmer in America – but it may be assumed that most of them had.

Welsh farming emigrants, as we shall see, tended to herd together in American rural communities. But most English and Scots farmers and agricultural labourers merged into the American landscape so quickly and successfully that it is difficult to discover where they settled. Certainly some took up land in the West in response to the recruiting efforts of American railroads. In the 1870s and 1880s the Northern Pacific Railroad, the Santa Fe and the Burlington and Missouri conducted vigorous colonization campaigns in Britain, employing hundreds of agents, publishing emigration newspapers and flooding the country with advertising posters extolling the advantages of their lands. Western states, like Minnesota, Kansas and Texas, did the same, vying with each other in the extravagance of their propaganda. Missouri was a place where 'forty million people can subsist in plenty and comfort'; Colorado was 'a mecca for

all classes and conditions', while Minnesota was a demi-paradise where the hardworking and ambitious could 'exchange the tyrannies and thankless toil of the old world for the freedom and independence of the new.' But the results were hardly proportionate to the effort. In 1870 the state of Kansas persuaded 300 Sussex emigrants to settle in Geary County, and in the following year a group of Scots was induced to establish a colony in western Minnesota to raise pure-bred cattle. In 1872 Burlington railroad company planted a colony of English farmers in Kansas while in 1873 the Northern Pacific brought over several hundred farmers and artisans to Clay County, Minnesota, where they founded a colony called Yeovil. But state and railroad schemes accounted in aggregate for only a few thousand British emigrants.

Bizarre experiments occurred. Colonies of English 'gentlemen' were at one time planted in different parts of the West. The best known was the one in Rugby, Tennessee, established in 1880 by Thomas Hughes, the author of *Tom Brown's Schooldays*. This was an attempt to turn young men from public schools and universities into hardy pioneers. Not surprisingly it failed within

96

a few years. So did a similar colony at Le Mars, Iowa, founded in 1879 by three Cambridge oarsmen. Here it was possible to 'see the heir-apparent to an old English earldom mowing, assisted by the two sons of a viscount' and to 'watch the brother of an earl feeding the threshing-machine'. But a visitor was struck by the fact that the young fellows at Le Mars treated their work as though it were a picnic and he could not have been surprised that they soon became bored and drifted away to the cities or back home.

Even Englishmen better acquainted with the soil were sometimes defeated by American farming, especially in the West. Their experiences had not prepared them for the extremes of climate, the larger scale of Western farming, the new techniques and the amount of capital required. Farmers failed to appreciate that there was a world of difference between British and American farming and their letters home were often disgruntled.

The greatest attraction of all was that America offered the chance to become independent and to own land. This was the theme of countless letters from immigrants throughout the century. James and Betty Rous, for instance, wrote from their 165-acre farm in 1817:

You can ask if we like it here as much as in our native land, to which I answer, that were I sure of a good life in England and a good prospect for my children, I should prefer the company of my old friends and native place. But ... here with common industry and frugality a man may soon get a good farm of his own, and may be as independent as your country squires, but not quite so lazy.

Scotland lost a much higher percentage of her people than either England or Wales. In 1841, for example, when Scotland's population was one-sixth of England's, Scottish emigrants were almost as numerous as the English. However, relatively few Scottish farmers went to America, most of those who did being Lowlanders. To understand why it is necessary to appreciate that Scotland was not one country but two, each having its own emigration tradition. Nature had divided Scotland into Highlands and Lowlands and the differences between them were greatly accentuated after the defeat of the Jacobite rebellion of 1745. While Lowland Scotland prospered under the stimulus of the current economic changes, the Highland half of the country stagnated and became a chronically impoverished backwater. In 1841, nearly seventy per cent of the emigrants from Scotland came from the Highlands, almost half of these from the five counties of Perth, Argyll, Inverness, Ross and Sutherland, including the Western Isles from Islay to Lewis.

Large-scale Highland emigration had begun in the eighteenth century. The fundamental cause was the destruction of the clan system after Culloden. For the tacksmen (superior tenants), this meant a loss of prestige and a sharp rise in rents. Rather than accept the new dispensation many tacksmen led their tenants across the Atlantic to upper New York, Nova Scotia, Cape Breton, Prince Edward Island and above all to the Cape Fear region of North Carolina.

Cousins and Strangers

Dr Samuel Johnson, during his Highland journey of 1773, was struck by the feverish urge to emigrate both on the mainland and in the islands. He reported that great numbers were leaving from the glens of Inverness-shire and that something approaching a mass exodus was taking place from the Western Isles – Skye, Lewis, North and South Uist, Jura, Islay and Arran.

After 1800 the Highland problem became even more acute. The spread of large-scale sheep rearing resulted in the notorious Highland clearances, in the course of which thousands of crofters were cruelly evicted and whole glens denuded of their inhabitants. The expulsion of the Highland people to make way for sheep was as traumatic an event as the Irish famine and it left equally long and bitter memories. What made matters worse was the decline, one after another, of the industries which might have revived the Highland economy – fishing, kelping, and linen manufacturing.

Most nineteenth-century Highland emigrants went to Canada and the Maritime Provinces. Highlanders were clustered especially thickly in Upper Canada (Ontario) which by 1850 or so was dotted with tiny Scotch-Canadian settlements. But in spite of its Canadian orientation the Highland emigration movement must be seen to some extent as a chapter in the history of the United States, for many of the clansmen, who first settled in Canada, moved to the States after a time in search of wider opportunities.

Emigration from the Welsh countryside began during the French Revolutionary Wars when hill farming suffered acutely from the shortage and high price of corn. Scores of upland farmers from Llanbrynmair, Montgomeryshire, were the first to go in 1795 to take up farming in frontier regions of New York, Pennsylvania and Ohio. Around these pioneer settlements sizable Welsh agricultural communities grew up during the next half century, notably near Utica in Oneida County, New York, and in Jackson and Gallia Counties, Ohio. The depression which affected British agriculture generally after 1815 brought distress to Wales too and there was especially heavy emigration from the Welsh rural counties. In 1841 Cardigan and Carmarthen accounted for nearly half of all Welsh emigration and Montgomery for a further one-fifth.

Even when the long agricultural depression came to an end about 1850 there remained much in the state of Welsh agriculture to cause discontent. The Welsh land system in many respects resembled that of Ireland and Welsh peasants shared many of the grievances of the Irish. They especially resented the harsh treatment they received at the hands of Church of England landlords who, although neither alien nor absentee as in Ireland, were separated from themselves by religious and social distinctions. In the 1850s a popular agitation developed for land reform. It was led by the Reverend Samuel Roberts, a Montgomeryshire minister and tenant of an upland farm, who wrote a series of pamphlets denouncing the tyranny of landlords, tithes and church rates. In 1857, concluding that the only hope of emancipation lay in emigration, he attempted with William Bebb to found a Welsh colony in eastern Tennessee, to be known as Brynyffynnon. Only a handful of Welsh farmers could be persuaded to follow him, however, and the venture ended in fiasco. In March 1858, one disillusioned settler, John R. Jones, wrote bitterly to Samuel Roberts:

I wish I had never seen Mr Bebb ... and that I had never heard of Tennessee. Undoubtedly we have all been disappointed in our venture. . . . It was terrible indeed of Mr Bebb to persuade us to buy land in Tennessee without knowing more about it and with the titles being so uncertain. . . . When I heard Mr Bebb in Wales sighing and groaning that we were suffering such oppression, living on hopeless and sunless farms, boasting of the great fortune that he had made for us and the paradise that was to be had on this side of the Atlantic, who would not have expected something from him!! I have not seen him proving any of his claims and I judge that he had nothing in view except his own pocket.

Agricultural discontent persisted, however, fanned by a series of evictions in Merionethshire after the 1859 election and, more extensively, in Carmarthenshire and Cardiganshire after the fiercely fought election of 1868. Some tenants who abstained from voting or who voted for Liberal candidates were punished with eviction; others had their rents increased or were told to join the Anglican church if they wanted to renew their tenancies. This oppressive treatment created a storm of indignation in Wales and was popularly believed, then and since, to have caused large-scale emigration to America. Some of the evicted tenants did indeed emigrate but neither at this time, nor during the so-called 'tithes war' of 1886–91, was there the massive overseas exodus of popular tradition. In fact emigration from rural Wales declined shortly after 1870. This was because those uprooted from the countryside by landlordism and agrarian change were absorbed by the mines, mills and factories of South Wales and of nearby England.

The recurrent nationalist dream of an extensive Welsh settlement on American soil had inspired the Reverend Samuel Roberts' venture. But not all those attracted to the New Wales idea were agreed that the United States was the place to put it into practice. A young Congregational minister, Michael D. Jones, emigrated from Bala to Cincinnati. In 1849 he expressed alarm at the rapidity with which his countrymen were losing their identity. In his view Americanization carried with it the taint of moral deterioration. The Welsh there, he complained, were more worldly, more frivolous, less righteous than they had been at home. He felt that the only way to preserve their pristine virtue was to establish elsewhere in the new world an exclusive colony where the Welsh language, faith and culture could be kept alive. In 1865 Jones succeeded in founding such a colony in Patagonia, but his efforts to persuade the Welsh in America to go there met little response – only three shiploads of Welsh-Americans went to Patagonia, and their misfortunes discouraged others from following.

But despite failure to establish an exclusive Welsh colony in America some rural communities retained a Welsh flavour for decades. There was, for instance the group of settlements in Waukesha County, Wisconsin. Welsh emigrants bought government land and occupied farms to which they gave old country names like Maesmawr, Bronyberllan, Tanrallt and Glandyffryn. The entire community – it numbered 1800 by the time of the Civil War – was made up of farmers. Even those who followed other occupations or professions were farmers as well – preachers, blacksmiths, stonemasons, shoemakers – a duality characteristic of Wales itself. Here as elsewhere the Welsh gave a high priority to establishing familiar forms of worship. Welsh chapels bearing such names as Bethania, Moriah, Bethel and Tabernacle brought an Old Testament flavour to Wisconsin, and when the Jerusalem Church Society built an enlarged chapel in 1859, its deacons ensured that it was exactly the same distance from the Jericho chapel at nearby Mukwonago as Jerusalem was from Jericho in the Holy Land.

Fifteen hundred miles west of Wisconsin, in the arid wastes of Utah, another group of British immigrants helped a unique experiment to succeed. Mormon missionary activity in Britain set in motion a stream of emigration with its own special characteristics. The Church of Jesus Christ of Latter-Day Saints, usually called the Mormon Church, was founded in New York State in 1830 by Joseph Smith. Smith claimed to have had a series of visions in which the golden tablets containing the *Book of Mormon* were revealed to him by the angel Moroni. This work identified the American Indians as the lost tribes of Israel and prophesied the rebuilding of Zion and the reign of Christ on earth. Smith and his followers established themselves first in Ohio, then in Missouri and, in 1839, in the town of Nauvoo, Illinois. But Smith's announcement in 1843 of a divine revelation sanctioning polygamy, or plural marriage as he called it, was the last straw for his non-Mormon neighbours. In 1844 he was lynched by a mob. Soon afterwards the main body of Mormons trekked westward across the continent under the leadership of Brigham Young to the remote valley of the Great Salt Lake in Utah. There they established a cooperative society. They settled in a desert; within a decade they had fulfilled the Scriptural prophecy, making it 'blossom as a rose'.

One of Mormonism's earliest and most distinctive doctrines was the gathering together of the elect. This made emigration to Zion a religious duty for converts. Hence Mormon missionaries in Europe gave a stimulus to the peopling of the American West. A British mission was established in 1837, when two Apostles of the church, Heber C. Kimball and Orson Hyde, together with five Elders, arrived in Liverpool. Three years later the first group of British 'Saints' was on its way to Nauvoo. They formed the vanguard of a movement which, in the course of half a century, involved nearly 50,000 British converts and about an equal number from continental Europe, especially Scandinavia.

Mormon missionaries employed a skilful mixture of spiritual and secular arguments to promote emigration. They held out Zion (first Nauvoo, then

Council Bluffs Ferry and a Group of Cottonwood Trees. This engraving, of Mormon immigrants crossing the Missouri, was the work of Frederick H. Piercy, a British artist who accompanied a group of British Mormon converts on their journey to Utah in 1853.

Utah) as a sanctuary from the destruction which would sweep over the ungodly in the last days – but they also promised guaranteed jobs and all the land that could reasonably be farmed. Charles Dickens, who witnessed the embarkation of a shipload of Mormons at London docks and wrote about it in *The Uncommercial Traveller*, thought that mundane considerations were what really motivated them; their conversion seemed only skindeep to him. But he was greatly impressed by the efficiency and discipline of the embarkation arrangements, which contrasted pleasingly with the usual chaos. Indeed it was the organized and supervised character of the Mormon movement which, together with its Utopian purpose, distinguished it from the main stream of British emigration. Mormon emigrants were relieved of the anxieties of the journey because the church authorities shepherded them every inch of the way to the Great Salt Lake, arranging all the details of outfitting, feeding, lodging and transportation. Some even had their fares paid by the Perpetual Emigrating Fund, set up in 1849 to make loans which were repayable after the recipients had established themselves in Utah.

Mormons crossed the Atlantic in specially chartered vessels and, until the transcontinental railroad reached Utah in 1869, journeyed overland from Iowa by handcart or covered waggon, escorted by church leaders. Mormons found the journey across the plains and over the mountains slow, fatiguing and full of hardship. In August 1856, David Grant wrote from Laramie, Wyoming, to a friend in Wales:

We left Iowa City on the last day of June, three hundred of us. We travelled seven or eight miles the first day, and we thought that that was quite a task. After we had been travelling a week we did ten miles a day which we thought a great deal, but before we arrived in winter quarters we could travel fifteen or twenty miles as easily as we travelled seven miles at first. It was hard work in the beginning because of our previous idleness. . . . While we were settling in old Sister Brooks died, together with Brother David Davies of Newtown, and they were buried in the Saints' cemetery. We left winter quarters on 30 July all well and happy and 225 in number. Some Saints had permission to stay behind there. From Iowa City to winter quarters we had three waggons and from there on four waggons loaded with food. Besides this, each tentful of people, that is twenty, carried four hundredweight of flour in their carts. You can see that we have only been travelling a month and we have already covered nearly half our journey. We hope to reach Salt Lake City on 4 October if God wills.

In the ever-present heat, dust and flies, sickness and death took a regular toll; there were thirteen deaths out of a company of 450 in 1855, seventeen out of 400 in 1865. Cholera broke out in 1854 and two years later a number of handcart companies which started late from Iowa were fatally trapped in the winter snows and nearly a hundred died.

Critics often said that Mormon missionaries systematically recruited single young women to become the plural wives of the Elders. This did not in fact happen. The passenger lists of Mormon ships show that the sexes were very evenly balanced and that all ages were represented. The strikingly high proportion of children, nearly one-third of the total, and the number of middle-aged and elderly emigrants show that Mormon emigration was essentially one of families. They came from only a few places: London, the West Midlands, South Wales, Lancashire, the West Riding and central Scotland, all heavily industrialized, urban areas. All ranks of British urban society were represented, from unskilled labourers to shopkeepers and professional men, with a large proportion of artisans. In Utah some artisans continued to follow their old occupations. Nevertheless in a planned rural society, many who had worked in British mills and mines had to become frontier farmers. Not all of them welcomed the change; they would have preferred more familiar tasks while awaiting the millennium. Some of their women found adaptation to Mormon principles painful, as witness a letter written back home by a Welsh woman:

As to polygamy, *you* are without a dread of anyone claiming a share with you; this dread has made me so miserable in past times that I almost wished myself at the bottom of the sea instead of in Utah, but so far I have been spared that trial. Oh … you cannot conceive what women here have to suffer with a view to obtain some great glory hereafter, which I for one am willing to forgo, if I can escape the purgatory they think necessary.

Yet some Mormon wives were unperturbed at the prospect of a plural household. A Cardiff woman, Ann Ellis, reported from Utah in 1855: 'James has no other woman than myself yet; and when we have got more property – that is, when we are in a way to maintain her without injuring ourselves – then it will be my duty to look out for another woman for him – that is my duty, not his.'

The industrial growth which made Britain the 'workshop of the world' stimulated emigration in three ways. First it created a pool of technological skill which its possessors were prepared to transfer elsewhere, given sufficient inducement. Second, with industrialism came unemployment, due not so much to automation as to a recurrent cycle of boom and slump which regularly threw great numbers out of work. Thirdly the new industrial system increased mobility. By drawing countryfolk into the towns it weakened traditional attachments and predisposed people who had moved, say, from Kent to London or from Wales to Liverpool, to contemplate venturing even further afield. Interestingly a large proportion of those who finally left Britain for America were making not their first but their second, third or even fourth move.

Until 1825, when restrictions were swept away, it was illegal for British artisans to leave the country in order to practise their trades. But the law was easily evaded and artisans did in fact emigrate in considerable numbers. Thousands went to France to work in the factories of Rouen, Calais, Charenton, Chaillot and elsewhere. Thousands more managed to slip away to the United States. If challenged they presented false documents certifying that they were agricultural labourers or farmers. The migration of skill across the Atlantic set in soon after the United States had become independent and by the early 1800s visitors to the textile mills of New England, New York and Pennsylvania were commenting upon the number of Englishmen and Scots who were supervising and instructing Americans in the new manufacturing techniques.

LEFT Wherever granite was worked in the United States Scottish colonies sprang up. Scottish quarrymen and granite-cutters were especially numerous in New England, in such places as Quincy, Massachusetts and Barre, Vermont.

RIGHT A Welsh miner in Pennsylvania, *c.* 1908. Miners from the valleys of South Wales flocked to the anthracite regions of north-eastern Pennsylvania, especially around Scranton and Wilkes-Barre.

It was one of these illegal emigrants, Samuel Slater, who founded the American cotton-spinning industry. Born in Belper in 1768, Slater was apprenticed at the age of fifteen to Jedediah Strutt, a partner of the famous Richard Arkwright, inventor of the spinning frame, and himself the inventor of cotton manufacturing machinery. In 1789 Slater emigrated by stealth to the United States carrying with him in his head – for the export of textile machinery was forbidden – the plans of a spinning jenny. This knowledge enabled him in 1793 to construct at Pawtucket, Rhode Island, the first American cotton factory.

Samuel Slater's role as a carrier of the new industrial technology was one which British artisans increasingly assumed in the following decades. British skills came to be a key factor in the rise of American industry. Each of the basic American industries – textiles, mining, iron and steel – leaned heavily during their formative stage upon the technical know-how brought by British artisans, operatives and managers.

Some of the heaviest outflows of industrial workers occurred during periods of slump. During the acute depression of 1841–2, for example, the Lancashire and Yorkshire papers were full of accounts of the way unemployment and distress were emptying the industrial towns of the North. Emigration was said to be especially heavy among cotton spinners, power-loom weavers, calico printers and woollen operatives. Another period of heavy industrial emigration was in the 1860s when in quick succession there occurred the Lancashire cotton 'famine', the collapse of the Cornish mining industry and a slump in the coal and textile trades.

Many of those who had emigrated to escape social hardship were enthusiastic about American abundance. Typical of those who wrote glowingly home of the improvement in their condition was Edward Kershaw, a Rochdale weaver, who emigrated to Lynnfield, Massachusetts in 1831. A few months after his arrival he wrote to his wife: 'I am between 20 and 30 pounds heavier than I was when I came to Lynnfield. Our common living would astonish you. Our breakfast is something like the old rush-bearing dinners in Rochdale. I never set me down to a meal but I think of the starving weavers of Rochdale.'

However, emigration was not always the product of distress. Even in prosperous times the stream did not dry up. As early as 1829 a cabin passenger on an emigrant ship from Liverpool to New York remarked on the number of mechanics, 'who had nothing to complain of either on the score of work or pay, but who wished to visit this wonderful America, or El Dorado of the age'. Contemporaries, accustomed to think of emigration as the remedy for hard times, were sometimes puzzled when it did not fall off as trade revived. They talked of emigration as a 'mania', and of those who spurned high wages at home to look for higher wages elsewhere as being, in the words of *The Times* in 1865, 'the victims of false representations and deluded hopes'. The truth was, however, that even when conditions were good in Britain they were better in America – or at least were believed to be so.

American manufacturers frequently sent emissaries to Britain to recruit skilled labour. In 1811 a group of manufacturers at Ballston, near Albany, New York, decided to establish a factory for making superfine broadcloth. To find a qualified man to take charge of it they explored the west of England, the home of broadcloth. Such arrangements were of course illegal before 1825 when Parliament removed the ban on the departure of artisans, a step taken partly out of deference to free trade ideas but mainly because it had become clear that the laws against emigration could not be enforced.

But while skilled hands could thereafter be recruited openly up until 1885, when Congress prohibited the practice, American manufacturers often found contract labour too unreliable and used it only for particular jobs or new processes. Thus, in 1869 the Amoskeag Woollen company of Manchester, New Hampshire, imported about fifty Scottish girls skilled at weaving ginghams. But most American employers found it unnecessary to go to such lengths; they simply asked their British workmen to inform their friends at home that jobs were available.

The encouragement of emigration by trade unions gave a further stimulus to the departure of skilled men. For a large part of the nineteenth century, unions saw emigration as a panacea for distress. They believed that to thin out the ranks of labour would be to benefit those who went and to improve the condition of the workers who stayed behind. Hence many unions assisted unemployed members to emigrate. Some unions, like the Durham Miners' Association, gave emigration benefit only to 'members who have become marked men, or "victims", for taking an active part in the society's business, or who have been prominent in any trade dispute.' Lack of funds limited the amount of assistance. The Iron Founders' Union, one of the most active in promoting emigration, spent less than £5000 on emigration between 1858 and 1874 – barely enough to pay the fares of eight hundred men.

British skilled emigrants gravitated to the American centres of their crafts, their occupation determining their location. Thus Lancashire and Yorkshire textile operatives congregated in Massachusetts mill towns like Fall River, New Bedford and Lawrence. Fall River, on the coast about fifty miles south of Boston, possessed the natural advantages needed to become a cotton manufacturing centre: water power, a moist climate and good communications. Its textile mills were among the first in Massachusetts. Just after the Civil War they enjoyed a boom which made the 'spindle city' the cotton capital of the United States. New Bedford, a few miles away, had once been a famous whaling port and long retained a nautical flavour. Here too the cotton industry became pre-eminent after the Civil War, while Lawrence, a planned industrial city established in 1845 by a group of Boston capitalists, built and populated by New England farm boys and Irish immigrants, grew with astonishing speed. Only fifteen years later it had 18,000 inhabitants, one-third being employed in the woollen and cotton mills.

These towns to which British textile workers flocked by the shipload in the 1860s were not unlike those they had left. Roused from bed at six each morning by the familiar sound of the mill whistle, Lancashire and Yorkshire immigrants gazed out at forests of chimneys, acres of brick and granite factories and rows of houses. Among the spindles and the shuttles they were surrounded by old neighbours speaking familiar dialects. It must have been difficult to believe they were not still in England – indeed, a Yorkshireman visiting Lawrence in 1880 found the mills full of Bradford loom-fixers, wool-sorters, managers and machinery. Many shopkeepers and saloon-keepers were also from there, and he called Lawrence the 'Bradford of America'. Five years later the Lancashire

A Massachusetts textile worker, *c.* 1910.

dialect humorist, Ben Brierley, met so many weavers and spinners from Pres-
ton, Oldham and Mossley while on a visit to Fall River that he wrote: 'I soon
forget wheere I wur, an' fancied I're i' England.' Fall River was a bastion of
Lancashire culture. Folk there still indulged their passion for football and dialect recitations, their taste for black puddings, pork pies, tripe and cowheel.
To complete the illusion of being in Lancashire one could even see housewives
on their knees scrubbing and whitening the front doorstep.

What was true of the concentration of cotton and woollen operatives was
equally true of other occupations. Macclesfield silk-workers were to be found
in Paterson, New Jersey; Stoke-on-Trent potters in East Liverpool, Ohio;
Kilmarnock carpet-weavers in the Connecticut mill town of Thompsonville.
Miners too developed distinctive patterns of settlement, those from Wales
favouring Pennsylvania, Scots and Geordies, Illinois.

Nevertheless those who came from the mining districts of Cornwall ranged
more widely. 'If you want to see our Cornish miners,' an American visitor to
Cornwall was told in 1881, 'you must go to Pennsylvania, to Lake Superior,
to Nevada; you'll find very few of them in Cornwall.' With the exhaustion
of Cornish ore deposits and the competition of Bolivian and East-Indian tin,
some Cornishmen went to diggings in Australia, others to the gold and diamond
mines of Witwatersrand. But the great majority crossed the Atlantic. After 1830

or so Cornish colonies grew up wherever mining was carried on in the United
States: the lead-mining regions of Illinois and Wisconsin, the iron and copper
ranges of the Michigan upper peninsula, the copper-rich town of Butte, Montana. 'Cousin Jacks', as they were known, also clustered in scores of mining
camps in the Rockies, the High Sierras and the south-western deserts; they
drilled, blasted and dug in places with violent and gaudy reputations like Virginia City, Nevada, Deadwood, South Dakota and Tombstone, Arizona. So
ubiquitous were the Cornish on the mining frontier that a popular saying had
it that wherever there was a hole in the ground in America, a Cousin Jack could
be found at the bottom of it.

Sometimes the immigrant's education and skill were found in the new world,
not the old. Andrew Carnegie illustrates the point. He was the son of a Dun-
fermline handloom weaver who had been active in the Chartist and anti-Corn
Law movements. In 1848, at the age of thirteen, Andrew emigrated to America
with his family and went to work as a bobbin boy in a cotton factory in Pennsylvania. Educating himself in his spare time he got a job with the Pennsylvania
Railroad and then became an iron manufacturer. His energy, ambition and
organizing skill, coupled with his gift for choosing able associates, enabled him
to become the dominant figure in the development of the American steel industry. By the time he retired in 1901 to devote himself to philanthropy, the

immigrant boy from Scotland had become one of the richest men in the world. In his retirement he enjoyed the friendship of Gladstone, Theodore Roosevelt and Mark Twain. He was also the proud owner of a Scottish castle, where he spent much time, entertaining nobility and discoursing with intellectuals.

In 1892 Carnegie was in Scotland when a great and bloody strike began at his steelworks at Homestead, near Pittsburgh; although he attempted to pass the buck to his lieutenant, Henry Clay Frick, he was responsible for the harsh treatment meted out to the strikers. The Homestead strike fatally injured Carnegie's reputation, branding him permanently as an enemy of labour. In vain the great steelmaker gave away millions 'with no more noise than a waiter falling downstairs with a trayfull of dishes', as Mr Dooley, Finley Peter Dunne's fictional bar-tender, put it. It was as a hard-faced capitalist rather than as a philanthropist that Carnegie would be remembered by most of his contemporaries.

British immigrants played a leading part in the early development of American trade unionism. As experienced unionists in the old country they were uniquely qualified to strengthen the infant American labour movement. In every trade they supplied – along with Irishmen who had gained industrial experience in Britain – an extraordinarily high proportion of union officials and organizers. The first president of the United Mine Workers of America was a Scot, John Rae, and the first secretary, Robert Watchorn, a miner from Derbyshire.

Once the steamship had robbed the Atlantic of its terrors British workmen began to shuttle back and forth between their homeland and the United States in response to the fluctuations of the American economy. When American industry was booming they streamed westward; when trade was slack they tended to go home. There were even times during the long American depression of the 1870s when the eastbound movement exceeded that in the opposite direction. Many people now took passage each spring with the fixed intention of returning to Britain in the autumn. This practice was especially popular with building workers – bricklayers, plasterers, painters, carpenters, plumbers – whose trades shut down in the American winter. In the 1880s seven or eight hundred English and Scots bricklayers came to work in New York annually. 'In the winter', it was said, 'you can't see none of them; they work their way over here in the steamers. . . . What they earn in one week will carry them back again.' After a summer's work at wages more than double those in Britain they could take several hundred dollars home, enough to keep them through the winter even if they were out of work. American trade unionists looked resentfully at these 'swallows'. Their lack of commitment to America weakened union solidarity and attempts were made to discourage their coming.

Immigrants possessing industrial skills needed in America usually found it easy to gain an economic foothold. Not that they were always satisfied with their new jobs. Cornish miners frequently protested that, although wages were higher in America, hours of work were longer, accidents more frequent and, in the far west particularly, the heat and dust underground resulted in more cases of 'miners' con', or psthisis, than at home. British coal miners echoed their complaints. A South Wales miner who in the old country had worked a fifty-four-hour week found on arrival in Pennsylvania in 1872 that soft-coal miners worked between sixty and a hundred hours weekly. They got an extra dollar a day, but he 'could not see that their condition was any better than the British miner' because of the higher cost of living in America. Textile workers too complained of the hectic pace of American industry. Besides having to work longer hours they found the pressure of work more intense because machinery

A mining crew drifting for gold below Discovery Point, Deadwood, Dakota Territory, c. 1876. Deadwood Gulch, in the Black Hills region, was the scene of the last of the great Western gold rushes. Consisting mainly of saloons, gambling dens and dance halls, and frequented by such legendary figures as Wild Bill Hickok and Calamity Jane, it was for a time the most lawless spot on earth.

was operated at higher speeds and they had to tend more looms than was usual in England. 'My work requires constant application and rapidity of motion,' declared an English carpet-weaver in Massachusetts in 1872. 'There is no let-up.' Others complained of the tyranny of American employers. 'I always thought they were tyrants at home,' said one spinner, 'but found out differently when I came here. We could always make a complaint of any grievance there; but here ... we are told that if we don't like it we can get out.' Another textile worker, Samuel Moores, drew on his experience in both countries for an investigating committee in 1872. In England, he recalled, operatives had been worked on a loose rein. He continued:

We might sing and talk. As a proof that we were not overworked I would state this fact. On one occasion, in the course of half a day, I committed to memory the twenty-fourth chapter of *Matthew*, besides minding my work. [But in America] we are driven all we can possibly bear; and have to strain every nerve to give satisfaction. . . . Some employers refuse to let you out when really sick, unless they happen to have spare hands. They will not let the machinery stand, but will discharge you if you leave work.

Moores earned more in America but 'my earnings have not supplied my wants any better here than they did at home, though nominally higher.' British immigrants were discovering that the dehumanizing effects of industrialization were sometimes worse in America than they had been in England.

But a further, and important, discovery made emigration worthwhile for many people. This was that in America there was no industrial working class in the European sense of the term. Americans did not expect to remain wage-earners indefinitely, still less that their children should follow in their footsteps. Moreover the greater social equality prevailing in America meant that wage-earners enjoyed an enhanced status. The English radical, George Jacob Holyoake, touring America in 1880, was struck by the difference he saw in immigrant workmen: 'They were no longer the same men. . . . In Lancashire it never entered their heads to introduce me to their employers. But when I met them in America they instantly proposed to introduce me to the mayor as a "friend of theirs" . . . in an easy, confident manner, as one gentleman would speak to another.'

By the end of the nineteenth-century mechanization, improved production methods and a flood of cheap, unskilled labour from southern and eastern Europe brought an end to the importation of British skilled labour. In one industry after another the British were displaced. In the Massachusetts textile mills the English and the Irish had given way by the 1890s to French-Canadians, Syrians, Greeks, Italians and Portuguese. In 1910 it was said that while there were still enough Welshmen in the Pennsylvania anthracite mines to 'make up a big Eisteddfod', there were not enough in the bituminous mines of the state to 'organize a prayer meeting'. Displacement did not generally mean redundancy since many Englishmen, Scots and Welshmen moved upwards to supervisory and managerial positions. But it did mean that the range of opportunities for British immigrants was narrowing. From about 1890 therefore skilled emigration from Britain declined and by 1914 had virtually ceased.

However, as the number of skilled emigrants declined the proportions of unskilled labourers rose; between 1873 and 1918 they accounted for fully a quarter of the total. These people, the victims of urban destitution at home, sometimes had a struggle to establish themselves in the United States, finding that other nationalities were preferred. Clerks and bookkeepers, too, found little demand for their talents. But such was the scope for advancement in America, especially for those able to speak English, that most of these people seem to have risen. At all events they were rarely to be found in the lowest-paid occupations.

The high standing of the British in American society was further demonstrated by the paucity of newspapers, churches, societies and other organizations catering exclusively for them. Unlike other immigrants they had no need of distinctive institutions to maintain their identity and perpetuate their heritage. The Welsh were exceptions because of their language. They conformed to the usual immigrant practice of establishing an organized life of their own. Eisteddfodau and singing festivals were prominent features of Welsh-American life. Utica, New York, the cultural capital of Welsh-America, published several Welsh language magazines as well as a newspaper, *Y Drych*, which at its peak claimed 125,000 subscribers. But the English and the Scots made only half-hearted attempts to follow suit. No newspaper addressed exclusively to them circulated widely or lasted long. How could it with the American press so readily available? Equally there was little point in setting up separate churches when their own denominations were widely represented in the United States. British immigrants did sometimes establish their own societies and orders, but it was difficult to prevent Americans from joining them. Conversely, because of the frequency of intermarriage between the British and the Americans, it soon became possible for second generation British-Americans to claim membership in such exclusive and prestigious American orders as the Society of Mayflower Descendants.

There was, however, one step that many Britons hesitated to take, namely, that of becoming an American citizen. They did not share the eagerness of most European newcomers to acquire American citizenship. Rather did they glory, as George III had once done, in the name of Briton. That was not surprising. The British were conscious of coming from the heart of the most powerful empire in the world to a country which, for all its rapid rise, had once been a British colony and which, in their opinion, owed most of its virtues to that fact. Moreover as products of Victorian Britain they tended to be badly infected with the prevailing jingoism. Some of them saw no incongruity in treating America simply as a place to work and make money. They saw no necessity to become American citizens and when pressure was put on them to do so they were apt to expostulate as did one Englishman in 1915:

If circumstances lead me to Mexico, Turkey or Germany, am I to give up my birthright and become a subject of Mexico, Turkey or Germany? . . . Your suggestion that unless a Briton is prepared to give up his nationality he should stay at home seems to me utterly preposterous. . . . An American living in Britain is never pestered to become a British subject. . . . May I ask, therefore, why an Englishman over here should be heckled into becoming an American citizen?

Candidates for naturalization had to swear not only to support the Constitution but also to forswear their former rulers by name. This may have produced

few qualms among those not attached to their former monarchs. But it was objected to by the British whose affection for the land of their birth expressed itself in an unshakable royalism. Queen Victoria's two Jubilees, in 1887 and 1897, brought forth an extraordinary outpouring of loyalty from the British in America – even from the Welsh, who had sometimes been given to making sour remarks about the Queen of England. This residual loyalty to the Crown, coupled with a reluctance to pledge themselves to fight against any country with which the United States might find itself at war – and throughout the nineteenth century Britain seemed the most likely enemy – led British immigrants to hesitate longer than most before applying for citizenship papers. John Spargo, the Cornish-born writer who became for a time a pillar of the American Socialist Party, wrote an angry account of what he had to go through in 1908 in order to become naturalized. He was insolently treated by the clerk, a 'young man of a class closely related to the yahoo and the hoodlum', against whom Spargo knew an indictment to be pending for election frauds. At a later examination he was disgusted to find that he had to wait until all the applicants brought in by crooked vote-catching politicians had been dealt with. Affronted by questions on such matters as polygamy and anarchism, Spargo asked himself

The elaborately furnished home of an English immigrant family in New England (*c.* 1890) testifies to its middle-class status.

CERTIFICATE OF NATURALIZATION.

BE IT REMEMBERED, That at a District Court held at *Waukesha* for the County of *Waukesha* — in the Territory of Wisconsin, in the United States of America, on the *Twenty Second* day of *February* in the year of our Lord one thousand eight hundred and forty- *eight* *Hugh Elias* a native of *Wales* exhibited a petition praying to be admitted to become a citizen of the United States; and it appearing to the said Court that he had declared on oath, before the *District* Court for the *County* of *Milwaukee* on the 14 th day of *August* A. D. *1843* ; that it was bona-fide his intention to become a citizen of the United States, and to renounce forever all allegiance or fidelity to any foreign Prince. Potentate, State or Sovereignty whatsoever, and particularly to *Victoria Queen of Great Britain & Ireland* of whom he was at that time a *Subject* and the said *Hugh Elias* having on his solemn oath declared, and also made proof thereof by competent testimony of *David Roberts & James Lewis* citizens of the United States, that he had resided one year and upwards in the Territory of Wisconsin, and within the United States of America upwards of five years immediately preceding his application; and it appearing to the satisfaction of the Court, that during that time he had behaved as a man of good moral character, attached to the principles of the Constitution of the United States, and well disposed to the good order and happiness of the same; and having on his solemn oath declared before the said court, that he would support the Constitution of the United States, and that he did absolutely and entirely renounce and abjure all allegiance and fidelity to every foreign prince potentate, state and sovereignty whatever, and particularly to *Victoria Queen of Great Britain and Ireland* of whom he was before a *Subject* Thereupon the court admitted the said *Hugh Elias* to become a citizen of the United States, and ordered all proceedings aforesaid to be recorded by the clerk of the said court; and which was done accordingly.

In Witness Whereof, I have hereunto affixed my hand and the seal of the said District Court, at *Waukesha* this *Twenty Second* day of *February* in the year one thousand eight hundred and forty- *eight*

Geo, S. West **Clerk.**

whether the change was really worth making. 'Did I really want to give up English freedom for citizenship in a land where I would not be free to read what books I liked?' He went through with the ceremony but appreciated the feelings of an old Scot who, the week before, had scornfully returned his naturalization certificate with the words 'Take this paper. I do not want it, for I am sick of the corruption and favouritism shown everywhere. I don't want to be a citizen of a land where there is no justice.'

The heart of the matter was that the British were immigrants who did not always know it: 'we didn't think of ourselves as foreigners' was how one immigrant put it. Accordingly they were not sufficiently sensitive to the need to change. When all was said and done, the British found it no easier than other foreigners to throw off old ways and adopt new ones. Even in a country whose culture so closely resembled their own they could not repress the nostalgia and yearning for the old country common to all newcomers. 'I would have walked the ocean to go back', was how one homesick Englishwoman put it. Many, unable to settle in America, did go back. Yet not infrequently they found that the Britain they had yearned for no longer existed, perhaps never had. Some found it shabbier and more primitive than they had remembered. After years in America it was sometimes difficult to fit in back home. Emigration had turned them into what sociologists would call 'marginal men', people suspended between two ways of life, belonging wholly to neither.

As for those who remained in America, memories of the old country could be stirred by attendance at a St David's Day Eisteddfod, the visit of a Scottish pipe band, or the news of Britain's ordeal in two World Wars. But what happened in Britain was always less urgent, less relevant, than events in America. Theodore Roosevelt and Woodrow Wilson inevitably figured more prominently in the consciousness of British-Americans than Asquith or Lloyd George; whether Lancashire could win the county championship meant less than the efforts of the Boston Red Sox to win the pennant. Under the pressure of the American environment, the ways of speech peculiar to Lancastrians, Geordies, Cockneys and Scots became blurred and overlaid with American idioms and intonations. Those who still expressed pride in Britain tended to do so in an American accent. Finally, however, it was the children of the immigrants who completed the transition, rarely thinking of themselves as anything but American. The process was helped by what they learned at school. How loyalties changed with the generations was brought home to one Yorkshire immigrant in 1900 when his young son came home after a history lesson on the American Revolution and told him: '*You* had the king's army, and *we* were only a lot of farmers, but *we* thrashed you.'

OPPOSITE The naturalization certificate of an early Welsh settler in Wisconsin Territory, 1848.

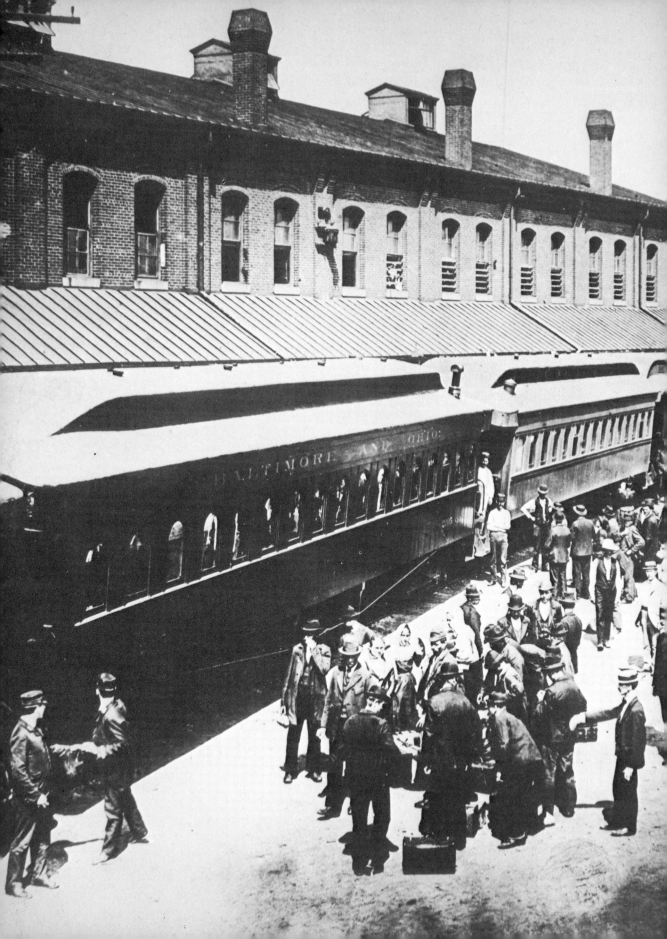

6
THE WAY WEST

An immigrant train at the Baltimore and Ohio
Railroad pier, Locust Point, Maryland, in the
1880s. After the Civil War, special trains carried
immigrants from the eastern seaboard to Chicago,
St Louis and other Mid-West cities.

ON THE EVE OF HIS RETURN to America in 1849, Friedrich Hecker, the German revolutionary, wrote to a friend: 'With true longing I gaze across the ocean to the Far West and to my forest solitude.' In fact Hecker had never known 'forest solitude' during his earlier stay in America. His well-established farm, to which he was now returning after the collapse of the 1849 uprising in Baden, was within walking distance of the town of Belleville, Illinois. But that he should still cling to his romantic illusions about the American West was proof of the region's extraordinary appeal for aspiring immigrants. Hecker's idyllic dream of an agrarian Eden may have been shared by only a few, but countless thousands of Europeans nevertheless fixed their hopes of a more abundant life upon America's vast, empty heartland – the region the nineteenth century called the Far West, and which we have come to know as the Middle West.

Immigrants were not the only people to respond to the pull of the West. Americans were themselves a restless people and after 1815 they surged westward in unprecedented numbers. Land-hungry settlers from the eastern states swept into the Ohio and Mississippi valleys, turning primeval forests and rolling prairies into a land of farms and, further south, of plantations. The subjugation and 'removal' of the Indians, the building of a railway network, the development of agricultural machinery – these paved the way for the westward advance that moved America's centre of gravity hundreds of miles nearer the great central valley. In 1810 one American in seven lived west of the Appalachians; forty years later the proportion was one in two. When the Civil War began in 1861 the tide of westward migration had carried the pioneer across the Mississippi. The frontier ran through Minnesota, Iowa, Missouri, jutted out into Kansas and Nebraska and out further still into Texas. The American people were now poised to conquer one last frontier, the vast, arid plateau known as the Great Plains, home of immense herds of buffalo and of nomadic and warlike Indian tribes – Sioux, Blackfeet, Crow, Pawnee, Apache and Commanche. By the end of the century that conquest was complete; the buffalo was virtually extinct and the civilization of the Plains Indian was destroyed.

The Europeans who joined the westward-moving army of pioneers came especially from Germany, Scandinavia, Switzerland and the Netherlands. Here as elsewhere, the great increase in popular knowledge of the United States was one of the most important causes of mass emigration. A flood of emigrant guidebooks and travel accounts poured from the presses to satisfy the common man's curiosity about America. Ole Rynning's *True Account of America for the Information and Help of the Peasant and Commoner*, written in 1838 by a Norwegian settler, had a tremendous impact on the Numedal district of southern Norway. No other Norwegian book was purchased and read with such avidity, people travelling long distances to hear it read publicly and some teaching themselves to read from it. In Germany, Gottfried Duden's *Report of a Journey to the Western States of North America* enjoyed a similar vogue. Published in 1829,

it contained a glowing account of Missouri farm life. It was an idealized and one-sided picture. Duden said nothing about the harshness of the climate, the crudity of frontier manners, the lack of cultural activities. But his lyrical descriptions of the West – its virgin soil, its majestic forests, its bountiful harvests – appealed strongly to a generation of Germans who harboured romantic notions about America and were anxious to confirm them. Neither could Duden's descriptions of bountiful America also fail to impress people for whom meat was a luxury:

As long as the settler does not have sufficient meat from domestic animals, the hunting grounds keep him in provisions. . . . There are so many deer, stags, turkeys, chickens, pheasants, snipe and other game that a good hunter without much exertion provides for the needs of a large family. Throughout the entire United States, hunting and fishing are completely free, and in the unenclosed spaces anyone can hunt how and when he pleases.

Duden also drew an appealing contrast between American intellectual freedom and the stifling atmosphere of Europe. He soon returned to Germany but his widely-read *Report* fired the imagination of thousands of his countrymen.

Duden's style was later copied by railroads and states anxious to people their empty acres. Railroads, as we have seen, spent more lavishly on advertising than the states and offered greater inducements – reduced fares, easy terms for land purchase and accommodation while prospective settlers chose their tracts. But the states, too, employed agents in Europe who were themselves usually immigrants. Thus Henry Hospers, one of the founders of the Dutch settlement

The scramble for newly-opened lands in the West: an immigrant family poses beside their covered waggon in Loup Valley, Nebraska, 1886.

121

at Pella, Iowa, in 1870 having become mayor of Pella, went back to his old home in Zuid-Holland, in order to stimulate immigration to Iowa. His efforts resulted in the establishment of a large Dutch settlement in the north-west part of the state.

The economic difficulties which caused European peasants to seek improvement in the American West were much the same in Scandinavia, Germany and the Netherlands. Nevertheless, to grasp the realities of the European exodus it is as well to remember that every country – indeed every province and region – had its own distinctive response to the forces shaping emigration.

Between 1825 and 1914, for example, emigration from Norway to the United States exceeded three-quarters of a million – more people than there had been in Norway at the beginning of the nineteenth century. In fact Norway lost a higher proportion of her people through emigration to America than any other European country except Ireland. This was because three-quarters of Norway's land consists of mountain or dense forest, most of the rest being either lake, bog or icefield, and only about four per cent of the land being tillable. Since Norway has no iron or coal for an industrial base she could not support her rapidly increasing population. John Haug's situation was typical. His son recalls:

My father came from a really poor family. His father and grandfather were both tenant farmers in a little valley in a remote spot in Norway – Fortun, near Luster, almost at the end of Sogne Fjord. It's a lovely place but the whole valley was owned by three people: the rest of the inhabitants of the valley were tenants and there was no chance whatever of getting ahead.

Conditions were much the same in Sweden, though the main cause of Swedish emigration was the huge increase in the landless agricultural classes. Whereas the number of peasant proprietors remained relatively stable, the number of crofters, cotters and farmhands increased rapidly. It needed only a succession of poor crops and famine, such as occurred in the late 1860s, to set in motion large scale emigration.

From Germany emigration slowly gathered momentum in the 1830s and in the decade after 1846 more than a million people left for the United States. It used to be thought that this mid-century German exodus was in some way connected with the failure of the revolutions of 1848. The emigrants, it was held, were drawn from the shattered ranks of those who had tried to unify Germany under a constitutional and popular government. But the Forty-Eighters, as the revolutionaries were called, accounted in fact for only a small fraction of the departures; most of the emigrants were drawn from those 'classes which had been little concerned with politics and with revolution not at all'. Although revolutionaries had gone to the barricades all over Germany in 1848, the bulk of the mid-century emigration came from the south-west, from the smallholdings of Württemberg, Bavaria and Baden. Some, however, certainly left in order to escape the revolutionary turmoil. John Kerler, for example, was a prosperous innkeeper and forester, who left Bavaria in the summer of 1849 because of his dissatisfaction after 'the year of Revolution, with its blessings of violence, anarchy and stirring up of the people'. A few months later he wrote from his Wisconsin farm:

I would prefer the civilized, cultured, Germany to America if it were still in its former orderly condition, but as it has turned out recently, and with the threatening prospect for the future of religion and politics, I prefer America. Here I can live a more quiet, and undisturbed life. One lives in such safety here in the country that you seldom lock your door at night, leaving cattle, waggons, plows, everything, out in the open without having to fear thievery.

The German emigration which reached its peak in the 1850s was a rural and village movement. It was the cumulative result of long-term social and economic changes – the growth of population and the subdivision of holdings to the point where they could no longer support those who depended upon them. In these circumstances periodic pressures were more likely to drive the peasant off the land. Then the only alternatives were to become a propertyless labourer or to emigrate. The emigrants consisted very largely of small farmers, many of whom, as in England, did not wait to be dispossessed but got out while they could. The fierce competition for land which prevented small farmers from acquiring sufficiently large holdings in Germany at least enabled many to dispose of their property at prices high enough to buy larger farms in the American West. Those unable to do so usually stayed behind. Declining standards also meant that shopkeepers and artisans faced a loss of independence if they stayed at home.

By the mid-1850s the rage for emigration had spread northward to Brunswick and Hanover, eastward beyond the Elbe to Saxony and Thuringia, north-eastward to the Prussian provinces of Pomerania and Mecklenburg along the Baltic. Subsequently these became the chief sources of German emigration. The next great wave of departures, occurring in the 1870s, was essentially a flight from the agricultural regions of the north and east, especially from areas where great estates predominated. Small farmers still contributed largely to the outflow along with a higher proportion than before of agricultural labourers.

Yet to stress the economic causes of emigration is not to say that they were the only ones. Successive revolutionary upheavals in Europe caused the departure of streams of exiles. Among those who fled were intellectuals who had taken part in the *Hambacher Fest*, the liberal demonstration held at Hambach in the Bavarian Palatinate in May 1832. Then there were the Forty-Eighters, a group whose influence was far beyond their numbers, since they included many intellectuals – journalists, doctors, musicians and teachers. How many Forty-Eighters there were is difficult to say – perhaps somewhere in the region of 5000 or so. The term Forty-Eighters is itself misleading for most of the refugees did not arrive in the United States until the early 1850s, some because they had been imprisoned in Germany, others because they spent several years in England before crossing the Atlantic. Then again, some of those who fled to America did not stay there. Gottfried Kinkel, for example, the Bonn professor imprisoned for his part in the revolution, spent only a year or so in the United States before going back, first to England, then to Zurich. Others returned to Germany, sometimes after a lengthy interval.

The avoidance of conscription was often said to have been an important cause of emigration. Whether it was so in reality is less clear, though military service was unpopular, and undoubtedly there were times when it induced young men to leave who might not otherwise have done so. A Norwegian writer commented in the 1860s that, whereas a young *bonde* used to maim himself to stay out of the army, he now chose to emigrate. Similarly, a prosperous young German rancher said that although he had to work harder in America, life was a thousand times better than in Germany 'because here I am free. In Germany I cannot say at all how I shall be governed. They govern the people with soldiers. They tried to make me a soldier, too, but I ran away.' He planned, he added, to go back to Germany in three years' time to bring out his sweetheart and marry her. He was not afraid of being arrested for evading military service for by then he would have become an American citizen. But the numbers emigrating for this reason do not seem to have been large, except perhaps in Hanover and Alsace-Lorraine, neither of which had conscription until they were annexed by Prussia in 1866 and 1871 respectively.

In some instances religion played a part in the decision to move to America, though precisely what part is not easy to say. The sloop-folk who left Norway in 1825 were Stavanger Quakers who had experienced persecution at the hands of the official clergy. But they nevertheless left in response to economic pressure. The Old Lutherans who began emigrating from Silesia in 1836 and later from other parts of eastern Germany stated specifically that religion was their reason for going. Like the English Puritans two centuries earlier they wanted to preserve their church from corrupting influences. Some genuinely felt they must leave Germany in order to escape damnation. Thus when one of the Old Lutheran leaders, Johann Friedrich Buenger, was asked: 'Must we really leave our beautiful country and emigrate to the wilds of America and live among the Indians?' Buenger replied: 'Well, if you want to go down with this country like Sodom and Gomorrah, then stay here.' But according to a recent historian 'the religious motive was mixed, not to say dubious' since many joined the Old Lutherans as a way out of their economic difficulties.

An equally confused relationship between piety and profit emerges from the history of Dutch emigration. When it began to increase in 1846 emigrants came from the province of Gelderland and consisted mainly of *Afgeschiedenen* – seceders from the established Dutch Reformed Church. The movement was indeed led and organized by two seceder dominies, Albertus van Raalte and Antonie Brummelkamp. In an appeal for help the two clergymen made it clear that the wretched condition of their flocks was as potent a cause of emigration as religious oppression; they had heard with great satisfaction that 'in the interior of America, together with all the privileges of religious ... liberty,' there is still a great abundance of fertile ground and profitable labour to be found.' In such cases it is often impossible to decide which motive was paramount. What can be said is that religious dissenters, often being the first to leave a region, helped implant the idea of emigration in the minds of their neighbours.

How far the motley peoples pouring into the West would carve out separate empires along the lines of nationality would depend upon where they settled and with whom. Congress, concerned for national unity, gave no encouragement to schemes for exclusive ethnic settlements. Foreign observers, on the other hand, were sometimes fired by the prospect that each of the newly-settled states and territories might develop a distinctive ethnic character. 'What a glorious new Scandinavia might not Minnesota become,' exclaimed the Swedish novelist Fredrika Bremer, when she toured the Middle West in the 1850s. Likewise the dream of a New Germany within the borders of the American Union was one which fascinated German nationalists for decades. German colonization societies made several attempts to concentrate immigrants in places where they could preserve their culture, the earliest being that of the Giessen Emigration Society whose leaders led a group that settled in Warren County, Missouri, in 1834. The plan failed, but about ten years later a more grandiose scheme was hatched by a group of German nobles led by the Duke of Nassau. They founded a society known as the *Adelsverein* for the purpose of planting a German colony in Texas, then an independent republic. The *Adelsverein* settled several thousand Germans in west Texas but, unable to fulfil its promises, the project was abandoned soon after Texas was annexed by the United States in 1845.

Colonization schemes were in any case exceptional, most immigrants moving not in groups but in families. They were free to settle where they liked and normally did so indiscriminately. Thus talk of a New Germany or a New Scandinavia was chimerical. Of course the immigrants' preference for being with their own kind produced a natural clustering. In 1860 more than half the Norwegians in the United States were in Wisconsin and virtually all the rest were in Minnesota, Iowa and Illinois. The Swedes favoured Minnesota and Illinois, the Dutch, Michigan and Iowa. But to discuss the pattern of settlement state by state is to tell only part of the story: the fact is that scattered throughout the Middle West there were many hundreds of tiny rural settlements inhabited by groups who, in Europe, had lived together in the same villages.

Some ethnic enclaves were the product of internal migration. Once they had crossed the Atlantic Europeans were quick to pick up the American habit of following the frontier west. The Norwegian sloop-folk of 1825, for instance, settled first near Kendall in upper New York State; nine years later the colony broke up when they moved to cheaper land in the Fox River valley in Illinois.

Harvest time in a
Norwegian settlement
near Madison, Wisconsin
in the 1870s. The rich soil
of south-eastern
Wisconsin was a powerful
attraction to Norwegians
from the 1840s onwards.

The same thing happened when Norwegians moved into Wisconsin in the late
1830s and early 1840s. The first Norwegian settlements, Koshkonong and Mus-
kego, later became parent colonies of those in Iowa, Minnesota and the Dakotas.
Thus in the 1870s newcomers might buy farms from earlier immigrants who
were about to exchange a log cabin in Wisconsin for a sodhouse in North
Dakota.

Immigrants arriving fresh from Europe had no experience of subduing a
wilderness. They lacked the American frontiersman's skill with the axe, his
knowledge of clearing a forest, building a log cabin, fencing his land. For that
reason most immigrants preferred to buy farms that had already been cleared.

A greenhorn who succeeded as a pioneer farmer was Friedrich Münch, the
German poet, philosopher and journalist. In his old age Münch reminisced
about his early amateurish efforts to farm in Missouri, his difficulty in learning
how to plough a straight furrow with a pair of oxen, his efforts to cut the corn
with a sword worn by his elder brother in the Prussian campaign against Napoleon in 1813. 'Our ignorance', he declared, 'led us to perform a great many
toilsome tasks which later proved to have been useless.' But he soon learned
to do things the American way. At the end of his life he could look back with
pride on the way he had with his own hands transformed a tract of primeval
forest into fertile fields, meadows and orchards. He not only became an authority on grape-growing but continued to follow his intellectual pursuits. He

was a frequent contributor to German-American periodicals and was an active politician, being elected to the Missouri state senate in 1862.

On the other hand, some intellectuals, or 'Latin' farmers, as they were called, were ludicrously out of place in the American West. In 1900 a historian wrote of them: 'They had wielded the pen, but had never handled the hoe; they had lectured from the cathedra and pleaded in court, but had never driven an ox-team. They were but little prepared for the hardships that were in store for them.' Their behaviour was a constant source of astonishment and amusement to their American neighbours. One made a chemical microscopic analysis of the soil before digging holes for fence posts. Another, a musician, wore a dress suit to milk his cows. Many of them were ruined; others, their idyllic vision faded, dragged out monotonous lives in uncongenial surroundings. Frederick Law Olmsted painted a revealing picture of some Latin farmers he came across: madonnas hung incongruously upon the log walls of their homes; 'they drank coffee out of tin cups upon Dresden saucers . . . and had bookcases filled, half with classics, half with sweet potatoes'.

But such farmers were the exception. Ever since the eighteenth century, when they first established themselves in force in America, Germans had had a reputation for hard work, frugality and thoroughness. These qualities, together with their shrewd choice of soils, made them outstandingly successful as farmers. Commenting in 1798 on German superiority in the agriculture of Pennsylvania, Dr Benjamin Rush, the celebrated Philadelphia physician wrote: 'A German farm may be distinguished from the farms of other citizens of the state by the superior size of their barns; the plain but compact form of their houses; the height of their enclosures; the extent of their orchards; the fertility of their fields; the luxuriance of their meadows, and a general appearance of plenty and neatness in everything that belongs to them.' Similar tributes could be paid half a century later to the Germans who farmed Illinois, Iowa, Missouri, Wisconsin and other parts of the upper Mississippi valley. Their spare, unpretentious houses contrasted with their huge, well-built barns and stables, their spartan style of living with the care they lavished upon their animals. These characteristics set them apart from their neighbours. So did their careful farming methods. Shunning the wasteful practices of the native American pioneer, the German farmer was prodigal of his labour, and of that of his wife and children.

Many other nationalities shared in the prosperity which these German farmers came to enjoy in the West. An account by a Swede, John Z. Sandahl, in a letter written from Iowa in 1860 was a good example of the 'America letter' which became so potent in stimulating emigration fever in those back home. He wrote: 'We are so exceedingly well satisfied with our emigration from the fatherland that the pen is powerless to capture it.' He was renting a large farm and had saved enough to buy a bigger one. Although he had harvested the hay the grass had since grown 'to the bellies of the grazing cattle'. Women

FRENZENY. TAVERNIER

never worked in the fields as they did in Sweden. Thus he had only learned to milk in America and at first got most of it up his coat-sleeves. But his circumstances, he declared, left nothing to be desired.

One must not, of course, accept at face value everything that immigrants wrote home. Anxiety to justify their decision to emigrate led many to exaggerate their success and play down the harsher side of their experiences. Only in later years, when frame-houses had been built and immigrant communities bore the marks of prosperity, were they willing to recall their early hardships – the primitive log cabins thrown up in a day which sometimes served both as barn and home, the crude sod-houses scooped out of the earth. Furniture was equally spare; log stumps served as chairs, bunks had mattresses of straw.

Sometimes there was more to endure than lack of comfort. Fever and ague, the common terms for malaria, took a heavy toll on settlers throughout the Middle West. The comment of President Garfield's mother – 'We was sick every spring regular' – was one which countless immigrant families could have echoed. Immigrant women had a particularly hard time of it. Worn out by constant drudgery and child-bearing, they were commonly said to be old at thirty-five.

The most horrifying experience to befall immigrants in the rural Middle West occurred during the Civil War, when the fierce Sioux went on the warpath in western Minnesota. Frontier settlers were scalped and killed; many abandoned their farms in panic. A Norwegian immigrant wrote to his friends in Stavanger:

The Indians have begun attacking the farmers. They have already killed a great many people, and many are mutilated in the cruelest manner. Tomahawks and knives have already claimed many victims. Children, less able to defend themselves, are usually burned alive or hanged in the trees, and destruction moves from house to house. The Indians burn everything on their way – houses, hay, grains, and so on ... even if I describe the horror in the strongest possible language, my description would fall short of the reality.... These troubles have now lasted for about two weeks, and every day larger numbers of settlers come into St Peter to protect their lives from the raging Indians. They crowd themselves together in large stone houses for protection, and the misery is so great that imagination could not depict it in darker colours. A few persons arrive almost naked, others wounded by bullets or other weapons, and some with their hands and feet burned off. May I never again have to see such terrible sights.

The heaviest immigrant casualties were at Norway Lake, where the Indians massacred Swedish and Norwegian settlers. The Sioux War of 1862 produced an immigrant heroine in Guri Endreson, a humble Norwegian woman who lived with her husband and five children in a small log cabin near the frontier village of Willmar. A party of Sioux braves burst in upon the family, killed the husband and one son, wounded another and carried off two of the daughters. Guri managed to elude the Sioux, getting her wounded son and another

OPPOSITE On arrival in the West the pioneer's first task was to build a log cabin that would provide shelter until a more substantial frame house could be constructed.

daughter to a neighbouring cabin, where she found two badly wounded men. She put the whole party into an ox-waggon and drove it to safety at Forest City, thirty miles away. Her two daughters escaped from the Sioux, but her wounded son died a few months later. Many years later the state of Minnesota erected a monument to Guri Endreson, 'in memory of her heroic deeds'.

Pioneer farming, always a risky and uncertain business, was plagued by periodic droughts, hail storms, prairie fires and, most of all, locusts. Prairie fires spread with terrifying rapidity and could destroy a year's labour in a few hours. In the autumn of 1871 they reduced scores of families to destitution in south-western Minnesota. Those who survived this disaster had then to withstand a series of locust plagues. In periods of drought the locusts drifted north like a mighty cloud, blotting out the sun, settling everywhere, devouring everything green. Gro Svendsen, the wife of a pioneer farmer in Iowa, complained repeatedly in her letters home of the losses they caused. In February 1877 she wrote: 'The locusts took all the corn, and all the potatoes and all the vegetables we had planted. We did get enough for our needs this year, but we were not able to pay off any of the debt.' Three months later she reported:

The locusts have returned; they are swarming everywhere. People have planted nothing but a little corn. On the twenty-fourth of this month all the prairie grass in this county was burned. It was agreed that we should all set fire to it everywhere, all at the same time, in order to kill the eggs. We were partly successful, but there are still many eggs left so that the future looks hopelessly dark.

Loneliness, as we have already seen in the Irish experience, was for some the greatest ordeal of all. Coming as most of the immigrants did from close-knit European villages, they found it difficult to adjust to life on the semi-arid Great Plains, with their isolated farms and huge expanses. The climate was itself a trial; blisteringly hot summers alternated with bitter winters. Worse still was the absence of neighbours. In whichever direction the pioneer gazed from his sod-house he could see nothing but flat and rolling plains, devoid of trees, stretching endlessly to the horizon. Melancholy and nostalgia, especially among immigrant women, is the theme of the classic novel *Giants in the Earth*, by the Norwegian immigrant Ole E. Rölvaag. Its main character, Beret, is a tragic figure, incapable of reconciling herself to a homesteader's life fifty miles from anywhere.

All night long Beret had been lying there with her eyes wide open, staring up at a picture that would not go away; a picture of a nameless, blue-green solitude, flat, endless, still, with nothing to hide behind....

The picture had been full of unearthly, awful suggestions. She had lain awake in terror, lost in her own imaginings, wrestling with fearful thoughts that only increased the dread in her soul....

It seemed plain to her now that human life could not endure in this country. She had lived here for six weeks and more without seeing another civilized face than those of their own company. Not a settled habitation of man lay nearer than several days'

A pioneer family's sod-house in the Dakotas, 1885. The loneliness of life on the Great Plains was for some the greatest ordeal.

journey; if any visitor came, it was a savage, a wild man, whom one must fear. . . .
To get what supplies they needed they must journey four whole days, and make pre-
parations as if for a voyage to Lofoten. . . . What would happen if something sudden
should befall them . . . attack, or sickness, or fire . . . yes, *what would they do?*

. . . Ah no, this wasn't a place for human beings to dwell in. . . . And then, what
of the children? Suppose they were to grow up here, would they not come to be
exactly like the red children of the wilderness – or perhaps something worse?

The tragic conclusion to this novel was Beret's final lapse into insanity.

Yet the majority prospered. One indication among many was the 1870 report
of the Swedish-Norwegian *chargé d'affaires* at Washington, Count Lewenhaupt. He found that many Scandinavians who had arrived with few resources
twenty years earlier had become well-to-do farmers. Such people lived in handsome white frame-houses, 'surrounded by luxuriant corn and wheat fields'.
After travelling extensively in the West, Lewenhaupt felt convinced that the
hope of bettering their condition, which had induced immigrants to leave home,
had become for most a reality.

Immigrants from the northern countries of Europe did not, of course, always settle in rural areas. Many Germans, for example, were to be found in the great ports of arrival. There were more than 100,000 of them in New York by 1860, while in the Middle West too cities like Chicago, St Louis, Cincinnati and Milwaukee harboured a sizable proportion of the newcomers.

Some of the German and Scandinavian city-dwellers, like their Irish counterparts, worked as labourers or domestic servants. But a much larger number were artisans who found it easy to get jobs. In some places Germans monopolized these crafts. They also strongly supported the American labour movement, sometimes forming their own trade unions.

German workers of the more literate and highly skilled kind brought with them a militant class consciousness. They gave to early American socialism a marked German flavour which persisted throughout the nineteenth century. In the 1880s German was the language employed in the conventions of the Socialist Labour Party and one of the first cities to elect a Socialist mayor was the German stronghold of Milwaukee. For similar reasons Chicago became the centre of American anarchism. German anarchist weeklies flourished there and five of the six anarchists sentenced to death for their alleged part in the Haymarket bomb outrage of 1886 were German.

A few German immigrants made huge fortunes. Frederick Weyerhaeuser, who arrived in 1852 as a penniless youth, acquired vast timber holdings in Minnesota and became known as the 'Lumber King'. Henry Villard, born Ferdinand Hilgard in Rhenish Bavaria, emigrated in 1853 at the age of eighteen. After a dazzling career as newspaper proprietor, financier and railway promoter – he was the main force behind the building of the Northern Pacific Railroad – he retired to devote himself to philanthropy. But a more characteristic German contribution was to found new industries. In doing so, several German immigrants made their names household words; among them the pencil maker Eberhard Faber from Nuremberg, who arrived in 1849, and the piano manufacturer Henry E. Steinway (originally Steinweg), who followed him two years later. Two other young arrivals of 1849, John J. Bausch of Württemberg and Henry Lomb of Hesse-Kassel, combined forces to establish the Bausch and Lomb Optical Company. Beer brewing was another German importation – indeed it became a German monopoly. Many of America's most popular beers today carry names of Germans who introduced brewing to Milwaukee in the 1850s and 1860s – Pabst, Schlitz, Blatz, Miller. An even more widely known name was that of H. J. Heinz, the inventor of the '57 Varieties', the son of German immigrants in Pittsburgh.

The professional men so heavily represented among the Forty-Eighters found an economic foothold more difficult to obtain. The reason was their inability to speak English: the physician, lawyer, journalist or teacher needed to be really fluent before he could apply his skills and training. Carl Schurz, however, the best-known of the political refugees, had a distinguished career in American public life; he was successively American minister to Spain, a Civil War general, senator from Missouri and Secretary of the Interior in Hayes' cabinet, as well as being on the editorial staff of the *Nation* and *Harper's Weekly*. But Schurz arrived in America at twenty-three and his wife's wealth spared him the customary early struggles.

The German-language press gave employment to some of the Forty-Eighters; German schools to others. But many highly qualified men, including some who later became well-known,-had to accept menial employment. Karl Heinzen, later the editor of a radical weekly, *Der Pionier*, at first lived with his family in a garret in Hoboken, supporting them by gilding frames at three dollars a week. Fritz Anneke eventually became Wisconsin state librarian, but his first job in America was swinging a pick and shovel on the railroad. But personal tragedy was more common than success. Some Forty-Eighters, finding the adjustment too difficult to make, died in despair; others took to drink; others again remained anchored in poverty, doing jobs below their capacity. Gifted musicians worked as piano tuners or played the fiddle at beer gardens; former teachers earned their living as bartenders or waiters. By going to America such men had gained freedom but had suffered a permanent loss of status.

In many Middle West cities certain neighbourhoods became unmistakably Germanic. Thus in Cincinnati's 'Over the Rhine' – as it was universally known – German signs and inscriptions were universal in shops, restaurants, churches, beer gardens and theatres. Pipe-smoking Germans, some in peasant costume, filled the streets; German bands played; for news people turned to dailies like the *Cincinnati Volksblatt* and the *Cincinnati Freie Presse*. Small wonder that Fredrika Bremer, visiting Cincinnati in 1850, commented: 'The Germans live here as in their old Germany. They are *gemütlich*, drink beer, practise music, and still ponder here "*über die Weltgeschichte*". . . .'

Milwaukee, known as the German Athens, vied with Cincinnati as the centre of German-American culture in America. But Germans also set the cultural tone in quite small towns like Watertown, Wisconsin, where Margarethe Schurz, Carl Schurz's wife, founded the first American kindergarten in 1856 and where orchestral concerts and grand opera were introduced soon after.

Here and elsewhere there were hundreds of *Männerchöre* (singing societies), *Turnvereine* (gymnastic clubs) and *Schützengesellschaften* (sharpshooting clubs). Parades and festivals, such as the annual picnics, the *Volksfeste*, were also regular features of German-American life. Most of these societies were organized along provincial rather than national lines, being associations of Bavarians, Badeners, Prussians, Saxons, for people from different parts of Germany varied greatly in outlook and custom and were frequently unable to understand each other's dialects. What is more, the centuries-old rivalries between various German states were carried on in America; until the German Empire was proclaimed in 1871, German communities in the United States

Germans in the Middle West

ABOVE Cincinnati, a mere village at the beginning of the nineteenth century, had grown by 1872 into a city of 300,000. German immigrants, constituting thirty per cent of its population, were an influential element.
RIGHT Germans carried their love of music with them to the new world; immigrant musicians practise in Winnequah Park, Madison, Wisconsin, 1897.

ABOVE A German hardware store in Watertown, Wisconsin, July 1888.
LEFT Members of a German social club in Cincinnati, c. 1890.

were deeply rent by factional struggles – probably a reason why the Germans did not enjoy the political influence to which their numbers entitled them.

Religion was another source of German disunity. Most immigrants were Protestants, chiefly Lutherans of varying degrees of orthodoxy. But something like a third were Catholics and there was a sizable proportion of Jews. Finally, there was a small but highly vocal band of free-thinkers and atheists – many Forty-Eighters being violently anti-clerical – attacking all forms of organized religion, especially the Catholic Church. They in turn were bitterly denounced by prominent German Catholic journals.

Religion was the chief concern of most immigrants. Not only were they deeply pious; in Europe the church had been the institutional centre of their lives. Their yearning for continuity thus led them to reconstruct familiar forms of worship. In Germany and the Scandinavian countries immigrants had been members of established churches, but in America church and state were separated, churches being purely voluntary institutions. That meant that the organizing and support of a church rested upon the immigrants themselves. In America immigrant churches tended to become more rigid and orthodox and even in the twentieth century insisted on strict standards of behaviour. Jack Holzheuter remembers his childhood in a German Lutheran community in Wisconsin in the 1940s:

We were an extraordinarily pious family. Church and prayers all the time and every-thing was thought of in terms of whether it was good or evil and the ultimate effect it would have. If you went to our church you didn't dance because that led to thoughts of immorality, which were shunned just as much as immorality itself.

Determination to preserve their religious heritage led many immigrant com-munities to accord a special position to their clergy. Some pastors exercised an influence that went far beyond religion. Dominie van Raalte, the Moses who led the Dutch to Michigan, remained their adviser on economic no less than on spiritual matters, while Pastor T. N. Hasselquist was a highly influential figure among the Swedes. A pioneer preacher, he became editor of *Hemlandet*, the first Swedish-language newspaper in the United States, acting in addition as land agent for the Illinois Central Railroad.

German Catholics brought with them a distinctive set of Catholic traditions and customs – processions, feast days, church music and church architecture. They found, however, that the Irish-Catholic hierarchy was unsympathetic to these traditions, seeking instead to Americanize them with all possible speed. German Catholics were ill at ease with the more puritanical Irish Catholicism and deeply resented the hierarchy's refusal to organize national parishes under their own priests. In 1886, a group of these priests decided to take their grie-vances to Rome. They asked the Holy See for independent German parishes and for separate German bishops. The Vatican declined to choose bishops on any but a territorial basis, but national parishes were tacitly conceded in time.

There were also bitter controversies over the language of worship, language being more than a means of communication. The Church became the chief rallying point for those determined to preserve the mother tongue. In areas of German strength in the Middle West, Catholics, Lutherans and Methodists alike established parochial schools where religious instruction – not allowed in state schools – was given in both German and English. In 1888 English-speaking parents in places like Rhineland and Fredericksburg, Missouri, were up in arms at the fact that their children were being taught only in German in the public schools. Nevertheless, schools such as these were too few to accomplish their purpose. Most immigrant children learnt English at school and grew up speaking a different language from their parents. The churches found they could only retain the traditional tongue as the language of worship at the risk of losing the younger generation. To avert that danger English services were

The dedication of the Norwegian Lutheran Church at East Blue Mounds, Wisconsin, *c.* 1873.

A Model School Among the Germans: this 1859 cartoon satirizes the boastfulness and drinking habits of the German immigrants. The speaker declares:
'The School which we have formed here, Gentlemen (*drinks!*), will show the enervated Americans what a miserable farce their System of Education is. Looking around this assembly of blooming enlightened Young Men, I feel that German Education is now, as ever, the cradle of pure action, ennobling sentiment, strong intellect and manly courage, which commands the respect of every civilized nation on the face of the earth.' (*Drinks – immense applause!*)

introduced, first once a month, then on alternate Sundays. These compromises were frequently arrived at only after violent quarrels between ministers and among congregations. But few found it possible to sail against the prevailing wind for very long.

Factionalism finally gave way, however, in the later decades of the nineteenth century to a growing sense of unity. This was mainly due to two new factors: the founding of the German Empire and the rise of the prohibition movement in the United States. The victory of German arms in the Franco-Prussian War and the proclamation of German unity in 1871 were greeted enthusiastically by most Germans in the United States. Many had serious reservations about the kind of Germany Bismarck had created. The Forty-Eighters, especially, were repelled by its autocracy and militarism. Others were angered by Bismarck's policies: the Catholics by the *Kulturkampf*, the socialists by the repressive legislation of 1878. But virtually all German-Americans took pride in the growing power and prestige of Imperial Germany, feeling this enhanced their own standing in America. They had been patronized and slighted by Americans, dismissed as a race of sentimental, good-natured but ineffectual beer-drinkers. The popular verse (1878) of Charles Follen Adams reflected the Yankee view of the fat, jolly German:

> *Mine cracious! mine cracious! shust look here and see*
> *A Deutscher so habby as habby can pe!*
> *Der beoples all dink dot no prains I haf got;*
> *Vas grazy mit trinking, or someding like dot.*

The stereotype persisted even after 1871 but now at least Germans could hope that they would soon stand higher in the estimation of their neighbours. Even Carl Schurz, whose ideal of German unity was very different from Bismarck's, could contrast in 1893 his new-found pride in the German name with the humiliation he had felt 'when the old Fatherland lay powerless and torn asunder'.

What is more, the boastful self-confidence and assertiveness that came to characterize Germany's rulers in the late nineteenth century communicated themselves to the Germans in America. Frequently and loudly proclaiming their German background, German-American spokesmen went out of their way to stress both the achievements of German culture and its superiority to that of the United States. To what lengths this attitude could be taken was revealed in an editorial in the influential *Illinois Staats-Zeitung* in February 1889. Commenting upon the columns of attention recently given in the English language press to gory descriptions of a prize fight, the editor asked whether a nation which found pleasure in such spectacles had any right to call itself civilized. He added: 'It arouses a suspicion, indeed, that the English-Irish-Americans are what Napoleon said of the Russians, namely, varnished over barbarians, and that when the varnish is scraped off the Sioux Indian stands revealed.'

Animus of this kind was more frequently displayed after 1900, when prohibition began to receive increasing attention – this being an issue upon which all Germans were united. They regarded prohibition as an abomination. It was not only an infringement of personal liberty but an attack upon one of their most cherished social customs. They denounced the crusade against drink as part of a deliberate campaign by intolerant Puritans to eradicate all traces of the German way of life. The demand for prohibition came when German-Americans were already alarmed at the erosion of their communities. With the virtual ending of German immigration after 1890, there were no reinforcements to keep alive old ways, and the second generation was becoming rapidly Americanized. In 1901 the Germans united to form the National German-American Alliance, its aim being to preserve the German language and literature and to fight prohibition. By 1914 it claimed a membership of over two million.

The Alliance had no links with Germany and had no sympathy with Pan-Germanism. But with the outbreak of the First World War it at once became violently and uncritically pro-German. So did the entire German-language press. It was not so much that German-Americans cared about Germany as such. It was rather that they felt that Germany was fighting the same battle for survival as themselves and against the same enemy. In their eyes Britain was trying to deny Germany her place in the sun, while in America the descendants of Britons were trying to erase German ways by such means as prohibition.

In any case German-Americans saw nothing improper, so long as America remained neutral, in expressing sympathy for Germany or even in demanding an embargo on war shipments to the belligerents. They claimed simply to be countering the pro-British bias of the American press and the allegedly un-neutral conduct of the Wilson Administration. But most other Americans interpreted their agitation as an attempt to influence American policy in the interest of – perhaps even at the dictation of – a foreign power. 'Germany', commented the *Houston Post* in 1915, 'seems to have lost all of her foreign possessions with the exception of Milwaukee, St Louis and Cincinnati.' Hence German-Americans found themselves denounced for acting as 'tools of the Kaiser' and accused of 'hyphenism', the popular phrase for divided loyalty.

When America entered the war in April 1917 German-Americans were placed in the cruel predicament of having to choose between their ancestral and their adopted lands. The vast majority did not hesitate. They loyally accepted the situation and played their full part in the American war effort. That did not prevent their becoming the chief victims of 'one hundred per cent Americanism', that coercive and intolerant nationalism which swept the United States in 1917-18. Hostility to all things German was carried to extreme, indeed grotesque, lengths. People with German names were bullied into Americanizing them. Towns, streets and buildings which commemorated famous Germans were renamed. Even sauerkraut appeared on menus as 'liberty cabbage'. The German-American Alliance had its charter withdrawn. German-language newspapers had to supply to the Justice Department translations of everything they published. The playing of German music was held to be un-patriotic; among other absurdities Beethoven was banned for a time in Boston.

Nor did hysterical anti-Germanism end with the war. As part of a drive for social unity several states passed laws providing that all instruction in primary schools, public or private, must be in English. Two states, Nebraska and Ohio, went further, prohibiting the teaching of foreign languages to students below the ninth and eighth grades respectively. There could be no mistaking which group these extraordinary measures were aimed at. In a message to the state legislature on 1 April 1919 – the date was ironically appropriate – the governor of Ohio described the teaching of German as 'a distinct menace to American-ism, and as part of a plot by the German government to make the school children loyal to it'. Four years later the Supreme Court was to declare such laws unconstitutional.

The First World War was a watershed in the fortunes of German-Americans. It undermined their self-confidence and dealt their organized life a blow from which it never recovered. German societies which suspended their meetings at the height of the storm found it difficult to resume. German-language newspapers, starved of advertising and boycotted by news-stands, collapsed by the score in 1917 and 1918. Then on 1 January 1920 came a further blow. The Eighteenth Amendment, enacting prohibition, went into force. The Anti-Saloon League and their allies owed their final triumph, at least in part, to their success in giving prohibition a specific anti-German character. In 1919 the German-American Alliance which had fought with equal fervour against prohibition and against American involvement in the war, was shown to have been financed – not indeed from Berlin, as many Americans had suspected – but by German-American brewers. In the light of that revelation prohibition could be presented as an assertion of American patriotism.

For German-Americans the Eighteenth Amendment was the final humiliation. It was not merely that they lamented the loss of their beer-gardens: they felt that their right to maintain their own culture had been denied. To be accepted in America immigrants had in future to conform wholly to a single set of values – those of the English-speaking majority. That was something that a group as self-assured and as well-established as the Germans found hard to accept. Their mood in the 1920s was one of bitterness and resentment. Some of them, reflecting on what the war had done to them wondered wryly what had become of the American freedom that had lured the Forty-Eighters.

Other immigrant groups also suffered from the general xenophobia and the new emphasis upon assimilation. The pro-Germanism of the Swedes and the Dutch created difficulties for them once America had entered the war. To many, forced Americanization was as bewildering as it was distasteful. A Swedish immigrant was heard to remark that he failed to see why, because of a shot fired at Sarajevo, it should be against the law to speak Swedish on the telephone in Minnesota.

On election night 1924 the results were for the first time announced by radio. In the Middle West there were so many Schultzes, Schneiders, Olsens and Swenssons among the candidates that the results were said to sound like 'a roll-call of the steerage'. The Progressive Party candidate for President, Robert M. LaFollette, who had opposed America's entry into the war, did well in areas of German and Scandinavian strength; he carried Wisconsin and polled heavily in Minnesota and the Dakotas. But the man who was re-elected to the Presidency was an archetypal Yankee, Calvin Coolidge, who a few months earlier had signed into law a bill which virtually brought mass immigration to an end. That meant that there would be no more reinforcements from the steerage. What little chance there still remained of a New Germany or a New Sweden in America's heartland was thus finally destroyed.

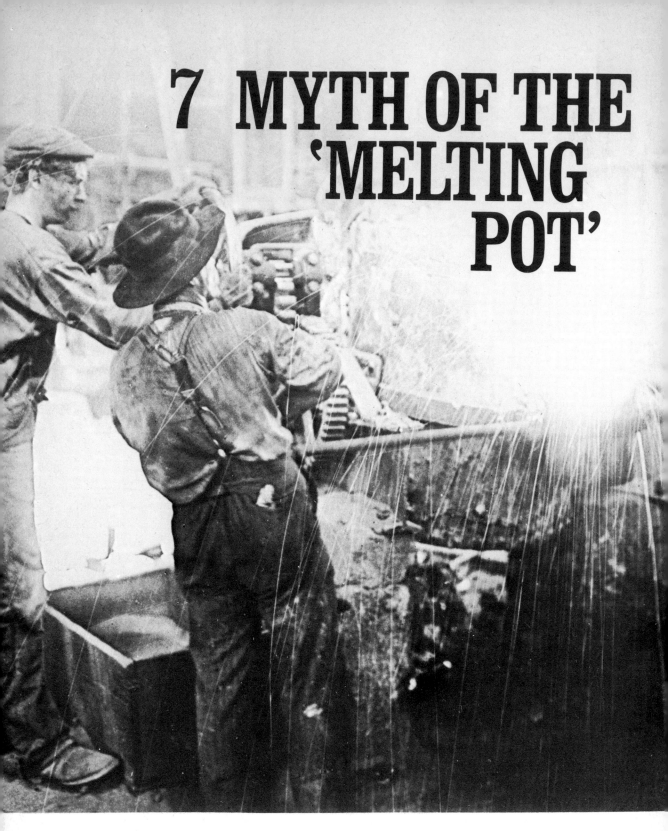

7 MYTH OF THE 'MELTING POT'

Pittsburgh steel workers, 1908. By the beginning of the twentieth century immigrants formed the bulk of the labour force in each of America's basic industries.

THE 'MELTING POT' IDEA is as old as the United States itself. It was first formulated by a Frenchman living in New York, Michel Guillaume Jean de Crèvecoeur, in his *Letters from an American Farmer*, published in 1782. Crèvecoeur insisted that Americans were not simply transplanted Europeans but a new stock, the blend of many different strains. 'I could point out to you,' he wrote, 'a family whose grandfather was an Englishman, whose wife was Dutch, whose son married a French woman, and whose present four sons have now four wives of different nations. . . . Here individuals of all nations are melted into a new race of men.' By the time of the Civil War Americans themselves had grown accustomed to the idea that they were a nation which had the capacity to absorb alien peoples and turn them into a unified, superior type. 'We are the Romans of the modern world,' claimed Oliver Wendell Holmes in 1858, 'the great assimilating people.' Much the same thing was said by Ralph Waldo Emerson, Herman Melville, Walt Whitman and other nineteenth-century writers and intellectuals.

But it was not until much later that the term 'melting pot' came into vogue. It owed its popularity to an English Jew, Israel Zangwill, who visited the United States only briefly and whose interest in America was merely a by-product of his concern for the future of the Jewish people. Zangwill's play, *The Melting Pot*, was a four-act melodrama written in 1908. The hero of the play is David Quixano, a Jewish refugee from Tsarist persecution. Escaping to 'waiting, beckoning, shining America', he rhapsodizes in the final scene about its mixture of peoples.

. . . America is God's Crucible, the great Melting Pot where all the races of Europe are melting and reforming! . . . Here you stand in your fifty groups with your fifty languages and histories, and your fifty blood hatreds and rivalries, but you won't be like that for long, brothers, for these are the fires of God you've come to – these are the fires of God. A fig for your feuds and vendettas. German and Frenchman, Irishman and Englishman, Jews and Russians – into the Crucible with you all! God is making the American. . . . He will be the fusion of all races, the coming superman.

The critics were not impressed with the play when it opened at the Capitol Theatre, Washington in October 1908. They complained of the thinness of the plot and the rhetorical excesses. One described it as being filled with an 'endless amount of hollow declamation'. But President Theodore Roosevelt, who was in the first night audience, was enthusiastic. 'That's a great play, Mr Zangwill!', he shouted across the theatre to the author. That turned out to be the popular verdict. Zangwill's play was a huge box-office success and ran for months on Broadway.

The play struck a responsive chord not because it was thought to be a realistic description but because it represented an ideal, a pious aspiration that the variegated army of newcomers from abroad would one day be fused into a single nation.

Myth of the 'Melting Pot'

Everyone knew that the reality was different. That things were not working out in practice in the way described by Crèvecoeur and Zangwill had been evident even during the period of the so-called 'old' immigration, that is, between 1820 and 1880. The 'old' immigrants, coming predominantly from northern and western Europe, were held to be sufficiently similar to Americans to encourage the belief that they would be assimilated quickly and would soon be indistinguishable from the rest of the population. But, as we have seen, that did not happen, or at least not with the Irish, or even the Germans.

It was, however, the radical change that took place in the sources of immigration in the late nineteenth century that demonstrated the gap between the ideal and the realities of American life. As we saw earlier, by 1896 southern and eastern Europeans were in a majority; by 1914 they constituted over eighty per cent of the total. These 'new' immigrants came from the most backward and reactionary regions of Europe. The cultural differences between them and the Americans were infinitely greater than had been the case with the 'old' immigration. Hence the 'new' immigrants would be correspondingly more difficult to assimilate. Their arrival raised new doubts. Could these heterogeneous masses really become one people? Americans were less sure of the answer than they had been fifty years earlier. They began to question whether intermingling was a desirable national goal; even those who continued to argue that it was, now doubted whether the melting pot functioned automatically and felt that positive steps were needed to Americanize immigrants. Moreover, as we shall see later, the arrival of the 'new' immigrants was the principal factor in the growing demand for immigration restriction.

In any case it was becoming apparent that the immediate effect of immigration was to fragment, rather than unite American society. Although the concept of class was alien to American thinking, a great gulf was developing between the native-born upper and middle classes and the predominantly foreign working class. Under the impact of immigration the United States became in effect two nations, differentiated by language and religion, by residence and occupation. The two nations had no more contact with one another than they had had when separated by 3000 miles of ocean. Each inhabited a separate world. A Serbian Orthodox priest, ministering to 'new' immigrants, remarked that his flock did not live in America but under it. What he meant is illustrated by a letter written by a Polish immigrant to the 1914 Massachusetts Commission on Immigration:

I am polish man. I want be American citizen.... But my friends are polish people – I must live with them – I work in the shoes-shop with polish people – I stay all the time with them – at home – in the shop – anywhere. I want live with american people, but I do not know anybody of american. I go four times to teacher and must pay $2 weekly.... The teacher teach me [English] – but when I come home I must speak polish and in the shop also. In this way I can live in your country many years ... and never speak – write well english – and never be good american citizen.

The native-born tended to close their minds to the immigrant presence. When an American businessman was asked: 'How many Poles do you have in town?', he replied, 'I'm not sure. The electric people have a couple of hundred, and a new company is putting some down.' When it was pointed out to him that the question related to Polish people, his answer was: 'Oh! I don't know; they're no good.' That kind of attitude, not at all uncommon, was of course a world away from the cosmopolitanism implicit in the melting pot idea.

However, cut off as they were from 'the real America', as some of them called it, immigrants did not in any way constitute an undifferentiated mass. On the contrary, they were divided by the varying backgrounds and cultures they brought from Europe. Suspicious of those who differed from themselves in speech, appearance and custom, each group tended to cluster together in separate neighbourhoods and to move elsewhere whenever newcomers appeared. Within these ethnic enclaves, immigrants followed their own distinctive ways, worshipping according to traditional modes and associating with their own kind. Yet this sort of exclusiveness, never absolute to begin with, soon broke down. However much their clannishness led them to attempt to organize their lives along the lines of nationality, that proved impossible in practice. Immigrants discovered that, like it or not, they had to mix with people of different backgrounds at work, at worship, and, above all, at school. To be sure such contacts stopped a long way short of the ideal. They seldom intermarried and it was soon clear that intermingling, far from producing social unity, generated ethnic discord which could erupt into open violence. Insofar as the melting pot functioned at all, it did so slowly and imperfectly. Even today, fifty years after the ending of mass immigration, the different ethnic elements in America are a long way from being fused into a single, uniform type.

Chicago, that most American of cities, serves to illustrate the size of the task facing the melting pot. The distinguished poet, Carl Sandburg, himself the son of Swedish immigrants, captured Chicago's essence in a celebrated poem:

> *Hog Butcher for the World,*
> *Tool Maker, Stacker of Wheat,*
> *Player with Railroads and the Nation's Freight Handler;*
> *Stormy, husky, brawling,*
> *City of the Big Shoulders.*

Chicago's rise coincided with the era of mass immigration. In 1830 it was a struggling frontier village, menaced by Indian attack. Thirty years later it was a city of more than 100,000 people; by 1870 the number had trebled. The 1871 fire only momentarily interrupted the city's progress. It was rapidly rebuilt and by 1890 its population exceeded a million. W. T. Stead, who visited the Columbian Exposition there in 1893, thought that 'the building of the city, and still more its rebuilding, is one of the romances which light up the somewhat monotonous materialism of modern America'. Others thought that Chicago

Polish women bring an old world flavour to Chicago, 1904. Large Polish populations congregated in such centres of heavy industry as Detroit, Milwaukee, Cleveland and Buffalo, but above all in Chicago, which had over 125,000 Polish-born residents by 1910.

personified materialism gone mad. Rudyard Kipling found the city particularly repellent, 'Having seen it,' he wrote, 'I anxiously desire never to see it again. It is inhabited by savages . . . [and] crammed with people talking about money and spitting about everywhere.'

The emphasis on money-making that Kipling found so distasteful was of course the secret of Chicago's appeal. From its earliest days it was an immigrant city. Even in 1850, more than half its population had been born abroad, mostly in Germany and Ireland, and by 1890 immigrants and their children made up seventy-eight per cent of the city's population. The Germans and the Irish were still the largest ethnic groups, but the city had now become a mecca for 'new' immigrants as well. In 1905, a visiting Hungarian aristocrat described Chicago as the most cosmopolitan of American cities:

It is a veritable Babel of languages. It would seem as if all the millions of human beings disembarking year upon year upon the shores of the United States were unconsciously drawn to make the place their headquarters. Chicago is the land of promise to all malcontents and aimless emigrants. . . . Nowhere else has immigration assumed such huge proportions.

In fact both New York and Boston had higher proportions of immigrants. Yet Chicago was undoubtedly more heterogeneous. By the time of the First World War it had more Swedes, Norwegians, Poles, Bohemians, Serbo-Croats and Lithuanians than any other American city; it had the second largest number of Germans, Greeks, Slovaks, Jews and Negroes and the third largest number of Italians and Irishmen.

In Chicago immigrants displayed their usual tendency to congregate with their own kind. The result, according to the writer Mike Royko, was that the population of Chicago was a mosaic of ethnic neighbourhoods. 'To the north of the Loop was Germany. To the northwest Poland. To the west were Italy and Israel. To the southwest were Bohemia and Lithuania. And to the south was Ireland.' Of course, the boundaries of what were known as ethnic ghettoes, were seldom fixed or well defined; over the years the neighbourhoods occupied by particular groups expanded or contracted, such neighbourhoods never being occupied exclusively by a single ethnic group. As one contemporary observer put it, foreign residential quarters 'resemble a field; one growth – be it of wheat, rye or millet – gives it its character, but on close inspection we find much else growing there also.' Thus a typical block in South Chicago contained 558 Serbo-Croats out of a total of 733; but the remaining 175 people represented twelve different nationalities. More strikingly still, a five-block area in the heart of Little Italy on the Near North Side was found in 1912 to be in fact only fifty-three per cent Italian; the remaining forty-seven per cent were drawn from a variety of nationalities, chiefly Swedish, German and Irish.

There was also the phenomenon which sociologists have labelled 'population succession' – a process whereby a neighbourhood's ethnic character changed

Children at play in front of
a saloon in Chicago's
'Little Poland', 1903.

successively in the face of fresh waves of immigration. Take what happened, for example, in the neighbourhood of Hull House, the famous social settlement, opened in 1889 on Chicago's Near West Side. After the fire of 1871 the original American residents were displaced by Irish and German immigrants who within twenty years gave way to east European Jews and Italians. They in turn were pushed out by the Greeks and Bulgarians who crowded in after 1900. Finally, during and after the First World War, Mexicans and Negroes took over the neighbourhood.

Population succession was not always a harmonious process. Existing residents resented the intrusion of other nationalities. In James T. Farrell's trilogy *Studs Lonigan*, Old Man O'Brien sums up these feelings.

It used to be a good Irish neighbourhood, but pretty soon a man will be afraid to wear a shamrock on St Patrick's day, because there are so many noodle-soup drinkers around. We got them on our block. I even got one next door to me. I'd never have bought my property if I knew I'd have to live next door to that Jew, Glass's his name. But I don't speak to him anyway.

Sometimes hostility took uglier forms than simple ostracism. In Chicago it was the blacks who bore the brunt of the animosity of longer-established residents. In response to the demand for labour induced by the war, there was a huge influx of blacks from the South between 1910 and 1920. It precipitated a housing crisis. Attempts by more prosperous Negroes to move out of the black belt to adjacent neighbourhoods produced a hostile reaction from whites. So did attempts by Negroes to use parks, playgrounds and beaches, hitherto used only by whites. When Negroes attempted to use recreational areas in the Irish and Polish districts they were set upon by gangs of whites calling themselves 'athletic clubs'. The most notorious were the Regan Colts, a band of Irish youths said to enjoy the protection of a police force by then largely Irish. The Regan Colts were in the thick of the terrifying race riot of 1919, in which twenty-three Negroes and fifteen whites died and hundreds of both races were injured.

The Poles and the Italians reacted in similar fashion to the Mexican influx of the 1920s, the Poles with particular vigour. Physical assaults upon Mexicans and their property by Poles became an everyday occurrence. And if Italians reacted less violently they were equally hostile to the Mexican influx, despite the fact that the two cultures were fairly close. Colour-consciousness lay at the root of the trouble. Italians were reluctant to live alongside people with darker skins and tended to class Mexicans with Negroes. A social worker noted, however, that newly-arrived Italians got on well with Mexicans; only after they had been in the United States for some time did they refuse to associate with them. 'In Italy,' he said to one Italian, 'you would not be prejudiced against the Mexicans because of their colour.' The reply was: 'No, but we are becoming Americanized.'

National and cultural antipathies were equally evident elsewhere. They were largely responsible for the remarkable change of personnel that took place in American industry. Up until the nineties, for example, most Pennsylvanian miners were either native-born Americans or British, German or Irish immigrants; thereafter they were mainly Slovaks, Hungarians, Poles and Italians. Contemporaries accounted for this kind of replacement in economic terms and spoke of older employees being unable to compete with the lower standards of the newer arrivals. But wages were not the heart of the matter. Native-born Americans felt an aversion to working with the more recent arrivals from Europe; the contemptuous nicknames they bestowed upon the newcomers – Hunkies, Polacks and so forth – reflected a deep repugnance to their habits and modes of thought. 'You don't call . . . an Italian a white man?' a Californian construction boss was asked in 1891. 'No sir,' he replied, 'an Italian is a Dago.'

Ethnic snobbery was universal. In New England textile factories Irish girls objected to the introduction of French-Canadian girls; they in turn would not work alongside Polish and Italian women. Often these animosities had their roots in ancient rivalries – thus Poles and Lithuanians, Slovaks and Hungarians, Turks and Armenians would not work together if they could help it. Sometimes workmen even objected to the employment of people of the same nationality as themselves. When a southern Italian was taken on in a New Haven factory, his northern Italian workmates intimidated him into leaving. When the foreman asked what the objection was to the newcomer, he was told: 'We don't want no Dago here.' However, immigrants usually found that, whether they liked it or not, they had to work side by side with people of different backgrounds from their own. Employers tried to balance nationalities by hiring immigrants of diverse origin, hoping to check the growth of trade unions. Lack of communication, it was hoped, would keep employees divided among themselves and make it difficult for them to take concerted action. But employers sometimes found this a recipe for industrial confusion. Workmen could not always understand instructions and, apart from the resulting inefficiency, the disregard of warnings shouted in an alien tongue was a major cause of the appalling accident-rate in American industry.

But while all this impeded union growth, it did not prevent it. John Mitchell, president of the United Mine Workers, was told that ethnic antipathies were so strong that he could not hope to win the support of all the various ethnic groups; but by gaining the trust of priests and other community leaders, he was able to build an organization strong enough to hold out during the anthracite strike of 1902 – which ended in acceptance of the principle of collective bargaining. Indeed it was the Slav nationalities that contributed most to that success. Poles and Lithuanians, Slovaks and Ruthenians, put aside their mutual grudges and responded to a man to the strike call.

Nor did ethnic barriers prove an insuperable obstacle to union organization in the Chicago stockyards. At the time of the meat strike of 1904 forty per

Chicago's famous Union Stock Yards were a labyrinth of abattoirs extending over 250 acres. The meat-packing industry relied heavily upon immigrant labour, especially that of Poles, Lithuanians, Czechs, Germans and Irishmen. Though visitors were fascinated and astounded by the rapidity and efficiency of the slaughtering and packing processes, they were often horrified by the carnage they witnessed, by the stench that pervaded the entire stockyards area and by the conditions in which immigrants worked and lived.

cent of the workers were Irish or German; another forty per cent were Polish or Bohemian; the rest were a mixture which included Lithuanians, Slovaks, Ukrainians, Finns and Greeks. The newer groups, accustomed to associating only with their own kind, wanted to organize unions along strict lines of nationality. But the Irish and Germans who controlled the unions there were adamant in their opposition. They insisted that organization must be by trades and departments, regardless of nationality. Though they met great resistance from immigrant community leaders the Irish/German view prevailed. Thus at meetings of the Amalgamated Meat Cutters' Union, business was sometimes transacted in as many as five languages. The result, according to Carroll D. Wright, Commissioner of Labour, was a softening of ethnic antagonisms. In a letter to President Roosevelt in 1904 he reported that, 'the feeling of the Irish against the Dutch and the Polack is rapidly dying out. As the Irish in Chicago express it, "association together and industrial necessity have shown us that however it may go against the grain we must admit that common interests and brotherhood must include the Polack and the Sheeny".' However, the inherent prejudice displayed here does rather take the edge off the sentiments expressed.

American politics, too, bore the impress of ethnic rivalries. Though the claim that ethnic and religious affiliations have been the most important factors in voting behaviour since 1830 somewhat overstates the case, undeniably immigrants tended to vote in blocs. Broadly speaking Irish Catholics were Democrats, German Protestants, Republicans. Indeed, it could be argued that the main reason why the Germans were Republicans was that the Irish were Democrats. In the late nineteenth century the Irish came to enjoy, as we have seen, a remarkable pre-eminence in American politics. Their power rested on their ability to organize and meet the needs of later groups of immigrants. But when it came to sharing political power they behaved in the same exclusive way towards newcomers as the New England Yankees had behaved towards them. To French-Canadians or Italians or Jews, the Irish seemed a selfish and superior breed, which was why these newer groups gravitated towards the Republican Party. What brought this phase to an end was the Great Depression of the 1930s; shared poverty drove immigrants indiscriminately into Franklin D. Roosevelt's Democratic Party.

In city and state politics the diverse backgrounds of voters made it necessary for politicians to appeal to as wide a range of groups as possible. Hence the phenomenon of the balanced ticket, that is, the making of lists of candidates chosen, not for their qualifications for office, but for their ethnic appeal. Edward J. Flynn, the Democratic boss of the Bronx, illustrated how the choice of candidates was designed to reflect the ethnic make-up of the borough: 'Our ticket shaped up as a well-rounded one; Lyons and Foley were Irish, Joseph and Lyman were Jewish, Delagi and Loreto were of Italian descent.' But the number of places on the slate was rarely large enough to accommodate representatives of all the ethnic groups whose support was sought. Thus politicians

OPPOSITE Immigrants of many different backgrounds joined the picket lines during a New York clothing workers' strike of 1913.

had to see that jobs were fairly distributed and that each group's special interests were recognized.

The two politicians whose careers best exemplify the use of ethnic factors in American politics were Anton J. Cermak, mayor of Chicago, 1931–3, and Fiorello H. La Guardia, mayor of New York, 1934–45. Tony Cermak, born in Prague in 1873, was brought to Chicago as an infant. As early as 1906 he took the lead in organizing an anti-Prohibition campaign which drew support from a wide variety of ethnic groups. Prohibition, indeed, was to provide him with political cement for the next twenty-five years. It was an issue which aligned immigrants against the traditional elements in American society. Having risen steadily through the Democratic ranks, he carefully constructed a personal network of ethnic alliances. Their range was indicated in 1930 in the classically balanced ethnic ticket of Cermak, Kaindl, Brady, Allegretti and Smietanka, that is, Bohemian, Jewish, Irish, Italian and Polish respectively.

Born in New York in 1882, the son of an immigrant musician from Italy, Fiorello H. La Guardia was an outstandingly successful mayor of New York from 1934 to 1945. Here the 'Little Flower' launches into a passionate anti-Nazi speech at Madison Square Garden in 1941.

Cermak's opponent in the 1931 mayoralty election was William Hale ('Big Bill') Thompson, who had three times been mayor of Chicago. Thompson had earlier been notorious for the crudity of his ethnic appeals. In an effort to endear himself to German-Americans he had ostentatiously refused during the First World War to invite the French Marshal Joffre to Chicago. A few years later, partly in an effort to curry favour with the Irish, he threatened that if King George V ever set foot in Chicago he would 'punch him on the snoot'. But his neglect of most of the 'new' immigrant groups worked to his disadvantage in the 1931 campaign. So did his sneers at Cermak's foreign birth. With the forthcoming Century of Progress Exposition in mind, Thompson taunted his opponent with a piece of nativist doggerel:

> *Tony, Tony, where's your pushcart at?*
> *Can you imagine a World's Fair mayor with a name like that?*

Cermak's reply was one which all of Chicago's multifarious groups could have made: 'It's true I didn't come over with the Mayflower, but I came over as soon as I could.' Though Thompson retained the support of the Negroes, Irish and Italians, Cermak was swept to victory by nearly all the other ethnic groups.

La Guardia was a melting pot in himself. Half-Jewish and half-Italian, he spoke five languages, and, moreover, had Cermak's gift of being able to portray himself as the personification of ethnic groups generally as well as the representative of a particular one. He was even sensitive to the needs of the minority of New Yorkers of old American stock. All this meant that La Guardia was able to play what Arthur Mann has called 'tribal politics' to greater effect than his opponents. Thus every numerically important ethnic group in New York was represented on the Republican ticket in 1933; besides La Guardia there was an Irishman, a Jew, and an Anglo-Saxon Protestant. That proved to be a winning combination. For the first time New York got a mayor who was neither an Anglo-Saxon Protestant nor an Irishman.

The same problem of welding disparate groups into a unit became particularly acute in the Roman Catholic Church. Immigration transformed a weak and struggling Catholic Church into the largest single religious denomination in the country. But the diverse character of the influx created serious strains. The millions of newcomers who owed allegiance to Rome came from widely separated parts of Europe as well as from Mexico and French Canada. They each brought with them a distinctive set of practices and traditions which they were anxious to preserve in America. The American Catholic hierarchy, on the other hand, overwhelmingly of Irish origin, was determined to create religious unity by Americanizing their varied immigrant flocks.

As we saw in the last chapter, the first group of non-English-speaking Catholics to express discontent at the Irish dominance of the American Church were those from Germany. Italian Catholics were similarly hostile to the Irish hierarchy's Americanizing policies and so in turn were the Poles. During the 1890s, in fact, groups of Poles at Scranton, Buffalo and Chicago became so resentful of the disregard of their traditions that they founded a schismatic church of their own, the Polish National Catholic Church of America, which repudiated the authority of the Pope and substituted Polish for Latin in the mass, but whose dogmas and ritual were otherwise Catholic. In 1912 similar controversies led to the formation of the Lithuanian National Catholic Church. To prevent further schisms the Vatican was obliged tacitly to concede the demand of the dissident groups for national parishes under the control of their own priests. Rome also took steps to ensure a somewhat wider representation in the American hierarchy. Thus in 1908, Bishop Paul Rhode, the first American prelate of Polish origin, was consecrated auxiliary bishop of Chicago.

The bitterest Catholic conflicts of all, however, were those between the Irish and the French-Canadians. The Irish hierarchy found the French-Canadians who were settled chiefly in New England to be especially resistant to Americanization. The proximity of Quebec meant that they returned home frequently and thus looked to the Catholic hierarchy in Canada for leadership. Despite the opposition of the American bishops, separate French-speaking parishes were created throughout New England. So, too, were French-speaking parochial schools. By 1890, 21,000 children were attending French-speaking parochial schools in Massachusetts alone. The Catholic Church was proud of the way its schools were Americanizing Catholic children of different origin. But while Catholic children of Irish, Italian, German and Polish origin were being taught together in English, those of French-Canadian parentage were being taught separately, and in French. After decades of friction the school issue erupted in 1926 into violent controversy. When Bishop William Hickey of Providence, Rhode Island, attempted to raise funds for parochial schools by assessments on the different parishes in his diocese, a group of French-speaking parishioners in Woonsocket went to law to challenge his right to do so. They lost the case and, moreover, were excommunicated. Peace was restored to the diocese only after two years, when a compromise was agreed permitting the bilingual system in all French-speaking parishes.

School was easily the most effective Americanizing agency. Young children, easily identifiable on entry as little Italians, Poles or Greeks, emerged later talking, eating and behaving in ways that no longer distinguished them either from each other or from American children generally. Sometimes a great variety of ethnic types was represented in one school. Public School No. 1, at the corner of Catherine and Henry streets in New York's East Side, was one such. In 1903 an article in a New York journal indicated contemporary attitudes to immigrants. The author, A. R. Dugmore, is speaking of Public School No. 1:

Here are centred all the hopes of the miserably poor polyglot population of the surrounding district – for its pupils the scene of their greatest interest and endeavour, and for their parents an earnest of the freedom they have come far and worked hard to obtain. The child of American parentage is the exception in this school. The pupils are of the different nationalities ... that have their separate quarters in the immediate neighbourhood. If they were to be divided according to their parental nationality, there would be twenty-five or more groups ... it is a large task that schools of this kind are doing, taking the raw, low-class foreign boys of many nationalities and moulding them into self-supporting, self-respecting citizens of the Republic.

He ended: 'The most noticeable thing in the school is the perfectly friendly equality in which all these races mix; no prejudice is noticeable.'

The school day began with a salute to the flag, patriotic exercises of this kind probably helping to stimulate awareness of a common loyalty. So too did lessons on American national heroes. Mary Antin's famous autobiography, *The Promised Land*, testifies to the fervent American patriotism produced in a young immigrant girl from Polotzk. Here she recalls her feelings at school:

In a dingy New York street, baseball plays a part in Americanizing immigrant children, *c.* 1920.

When we began to study the life of Washington, it seemed to me that all my reading and study had been idle until then. . . . When the class read and it came [to] my turn my voice shook and the book trembled in my hands. I could not pronounce the name of George Washington without pause. Never had I prayed . . . in such utter reverence and worship as I repeated the simple sentences of my child's story of the patriot. I gazed in adoration at the portraits of George and Martha Washington till I could see them with my eyes shut. . . . Now I grew humble all at once seeing how insignificant I was beside the great. As I read about the noble boy who would not tell a lie to save himself from punishment, I was for the first time truly repentant of my sins. Even if I had never, never told a lie I could not compare myself to him. . . . But the twin of my newborn humility . . . was a sense of dignity I had never known before, for if I found that I was a person of small consequence I discovered at the same time that I was more nobly related than I had ever supposed – ,this George Washington! He and I were fellow citizens. . . . As I read how the patriots planned the revolution . . . it dawned on me gradually what was meant by *my country* . . . for the country was for all the citizens, and *I was a citizen*!

Children salute the Stars and Stripes, the Mott Street Industrial School, New York, *c.* 1889–90.

157

But what teachers were concerned with chiefly was not Americanization as such, but the three R's. This was so even in schools which were predominantly or wholly immigrant in composition. Except for the so-called 'steamer' classes, designed to teach newcomers English rapidly with a view to placing them later in appropriate grades, no other provision was made for immigrant children. They became Americanized as a result of the accumulated impressions received in the course of a normal academic and practical education. The Americanizing work of the schools had, however, some unfortunate consequences. By transforming immigrant children into Americans it sometimes drove a wedge between them and their parents. That was particularly the case, as we shall see later, among groups like southern Italians, whose concepts of the role of education was vastly different from those of Americans.

Older immigrants of course had to adjust to American ways as best they could. Americans themselves assumed that assimilation was an automatic process and that no special efforts were needed to assist it. But the 'new' immigration gradually undermined this comfortable belief. Alarmed by the great numbers pouring into the United States, and still more by their diversity, Americans became increasingly inclined to question whether the American environment would suffice to assimilate such outlandish newcomers. Critics pointed to the isolation of the 'new' immigrants, to their tendency to congregate in tightly-knit blocks in the great urban centres, to their unfamiliarity with the political system, and to the host of evils that had supposedly followed their arrival – slums, crime, disease. Some observers felt that these circumstances pointed to the need for restricted immigration, that 'new' immigrants menaced the nation's unity, others that a positive effort was needed to facilitate the process of assimilation. If the melting pot was not working fast enough, a vigorous stir might do the trick.

Thus in the decade of the First World War a formal Americanization movement developed. Both public and private agencies sought by means of classes, lectures and mass meetings to teach immigrants English, to instruct them in the fundamentals of hygiene and personal cleanliness, and to familiarize them with the American political system and with American history.

Of the numerous Americanization agencies the YMCA probably ran the most successful programmes. The organization's main emphasis at first was on English lessons, but its activities were subsequently broadened to include welfare work, citizenship classes and helping immigrants to become naturalized. But the facilities provided by public authorities were often totally inadequate. Immigrants were lumped together irrespective of age and previous education so that the same evening class included old men and boys, the well-educated and the illiterate. It was seldom appreciated that what the student most needed to acquire was conversational rather than written English. Without such instruction he was liable to fall into total confusion and bewilderment – like Hyman Kaplan, Leo Rosten's marvellously evoked immigrant. In one of

אַן איללוסטרירטער לעקטשור

"וויא אזוי צו ווערען אן אמעריקאנער ביטיזען"
בײ מר. א. אלפערט, (איש קאווא)
אידישער בעקרעטאר צו דיא נארטה אמעריקאן סיוויק ליעג פיר
איממיגראנטעס.

מיוזיק

מר. לעאנארד מ. פאטטאן, פרישידער פון דיא וואשינגטאן
איווינג סקהל וויעט פריידען.

פרייטאג אָבענד,
דעם 19 טען דזשענואָרי
אום 8.00 אזהר

וואשינגטאן סקהל
קאדנער סאומה מאָרדישין
און נארמאן סטריטם
וועקט ענד

אונטער דיא אויפזיכט פֿון דיא
נארטה אמעריקאן סיוויק ליעג
פיר איממיגראנטעס.

Conferenza Illustrata

Con Proiezioni di Lanterna Magica

"La Patria Adottiva e le Opportunita'
delle sue diverse regioni"
Per IL SIGNOR S. R. ROMANO

Musica Scelta,—Boston Music School Settlement

Il Signor EDWARD F. O'DOWD Direttore della Scuola
Serale Hancock, Presiedera

Martedi 6, Febbraio
ore 8.00 P. M.

Hancock School
Parmenter Street
North End

Sotto gli Auspici Della North
American Civic League
for Immigrants

Illiustruota Paskaita

"APIE ABRAHOMĄ LINCOLNĄ"
Skaitys DR. F. MATULAITIS

MUZIKA

Ponas JOHN W. LILLIS, Perdetinis Bigelow Vakarines
Mokyklos, bus vedeju to vakaro.

SEREDOJE
SAUSIO 24=tą d.
7:45 val. vakare
Bigelow
Morkykloje
E ir Fourth Sts.
SOUTH BOSTON MASS.

Po globa North American
Civic Leagua for Immigrants.

Temat Ilustrowanej Lekcyi:
"ŻYCIORYS JERZEGO WASZYNGTONA"
PRZEZ JANA SOKOŁOWSKIEGO
MUZYKA
Kornet i Fortepian
p. p. S. Kłosowoski i J. Zieliński.
Overtura: Panna Z. Drożyńska.
Pan Chester H. Wilbar, Pryncypał wieczornej Szkoły.

W czwartek wiecz
Dnia 29 Lutego,
O godzinie 7-45 wieczorem
W Sali Szkolnej
Bigelow.
Róg E. i Fourth str.
SO. BOSTON.
Pod egida Ligi dla
Emigrantów.

The illustrated lectures advertised in this handbill in Yiddish, Italian, Lithuanian and Polish – were part of an ambitious Americanization programme devised by the North American Civic League for Immigrants, an organization founded in 1908 by a group of Boston businessmen. The patriotic themes of the lectures reflect the League's concern that ignorance of American history and institutions exposed the newer immigrants to radical and revolutionary influences.

A naturalization ceremony at Pittsburgh Naturalization Court, *c.* 1912.

Rosten's stories (in his collection *The Education of Hyman Kaplan*) Kaplan, now living in New York, brings to his English class a phrase he hears repeatedly in the city's busy streets: what, he asks, does 'I big de pottment' mean? It takes a very long time, fraying of tempers and much writing on the blackboard before Hyman finally understands that passers-by had been merely apologizing when they bumped into each other: 'I beg your pardon.' The subject matter used in English lessons too, was frequently ill-adapted to the age or experience of the pupils. Text books were worse still. Classes for twenty-five to thirty-year-olds were given books about 'the squirrel with the long tail'. Not unnaturally results were poor and attendances fell.

The Americanization movement, which rose to a crescendo during the nationalist frenzy of the First World War, became increasingly coercive and intolerant. 'Employees of foreign birth who retain their foreign citizenship', ran an announcement of the Packard Motor Car Company in 1916, 'will not be discriminated against in their present positions of work, but they will not be promoted to positions of responsibility and trust.' Easily the most fatuous Americanization programme was that run by Henry Ford. At the compulsory English school he ran at his Detroit car factory, the first sentence immigrants were taught was, 'I am a good American' – this being illustrated by the melting pot pageant which employees enacted as part of their Americanization course. The performance consisted of a column of immigrants, clad in a variety of old world costumes, filing from one side of the stage into a giant melting pot placed in the middle. Simultaneously, from the opposite side another column emerged, dressed in identical suits and brandishing little American flags. That was not just symbolism. The more fervent Americanizers – the 'one hundred per cent Americans' as they were known – demanded that every vestige of foreign culture be stamped out. 'Still eating spaghetti,' ran a social worker's report on an Italian immigrant family. 'They have not yet become Americanized.'

Immigrants reacted angrily. Many felt deeply humiliated at the suggestion that their cherished ways of life were marks of inferiority. A typical reaction was expressed in 1921 by Carol Aronovici, a California state official:

To one who knows the soul and spirit of the immigrant, who has passed through the painful experience of analyzing, sorting and accepting American life, the spectacle of the rabid and ignorant Americanization efforts was disheartening. It did not represent America as the foreigner had pictured it before landing upon these shores. It flavoured more of Hungary where the Magyarization of several millions of people was attempted by means not consistent with American tradition, or of Russia in its Tsarist days with the persecution of the Jew and the denationalization of the Poles.

The failure of the Americanization crusade had a further consequence. It discouraged those who believed that the 'new' immigrants could, with a little help, be assimilated as readily as the 'old' and it gave a further crucial stimulus to the demands for immigration restriction.

8

THE NEW DIASPORA

MOST OF THE EUROPEANS who crossed the Atlantic in search of a new life had to pull up roots which were centuries old. They left places where for generations their ancestors had lived and died. But with Jews it was otherwise: emigration to America was but the latest in a long series of wanderings that stretched back to the diaspora. Scattering widely throughout Europe after having been driven out of their homeland in Palestine the Jews were never able to find more than a temporary resting place. Throughout the Middle Ages they were treated as outcasts and in times of crisis or public calamity, such as after the Black Death, they were cruelly persecuted and plundered. In the thirteenth and fourteenth centuries they were expelled successively from England, France and some German towns. Finally in 1492, they were also banished from Spain, where they had enjoyed some centuries of respite. Providentially 1492 was also the year that Columbus discovered America, the land which today holds five and a half million Jews – about twice as many as there are in Israel and over a third of the world total.

These persecutions resulted in the concentration of Jews in the eastern half of Europe. By the eighteenth century it was possible to distinguish three main groups of European Jews, each of which was in turn to contribute to the peopling of America: the *Sephardim*, a well-to-do group, Spanish or Portuguese in origin, who used a special, ancient form of worship; the *Ashkenazim* (Hebrew for 'German'), who included not only the Jews living in Germany but also those from Austria and Bohemia; and the eastern-European Jews, the latter comprising some eighty per cent of all European Jews.

The first Jewish immigrants to settle in America were twenty-five Sephardim who arrived at Nieuw Amsterdam on board the bark *St Charles* in September 1654. They came from the Brazilian port of Recife where they had lived peacefully under Dutch rule, enjoying a quarter of a century of prosperity and

OPPOSITE An Armenian Jew at Ellis Island, 1924.

162

religious freedom. But the Portuguese reconquest of Recife reopened the prospect of persecution. The Jews fled to the Dutch outpost on the Hudson where they got an unfriendly reception from Governor Peter Stuyvesant and were only allowed to stay after Jewish share-holders in the Dutch West India Company interceded for them. Within a decade they had become subjects of Charles II. The Dutch colony of New Netherland passed to the English crown in 1660 and was renamed New York.

Between then and the American Revolution New York's Jewish community grew slowly. Individual Jews arrived there from different parts of Europe, Sephardim from Spain and Portugal, and Ashkenazim from England and Holland, while lesser communities were growing up elsewhere along the Atlantic coast. Nevertheless there were still only about two thousand Jews in the American colonies in 1776. Some worked in the professions and in a variety of skilled occupations – as tallow-chandlers, watchmakers, engravers and so on. But most were engaged in commerce and trade. Some like Aaron Lopez of Newport, Jacob Franks of New York or Moses Lindo of Charleston made fortunes out of trade with the West Indies or with Europe. Others like Barnard and Michael Gratz of Philadelphia prospered as fur traders and land promoters.

Under English rule the colonial Jews enjoyed a greater degree of political and religious freedom than they did anywhere else in the world, including England itself. They were allowed to vote and to hold elective office; they could enter universities; they were allowed, after an act of Parliament of 1740, to become naturalized. Although in law Jews were not free to worship as they pleased they were in practice granted religious freedom. Each of the major settlements had a synagogue, the earliest being that built in 1729 by a congregation named 'Shearith Israel' in New York. By the middle of the eighteenth century the Ashkenazim were in a majority in all the colonial settlements. But their Sephardic predecessors constituted a distinct aristocracy and continued to set the tone for Jewish life generally. That, added to the desire to remain a united community, was why the Sephardic rite continued to be followed in most communities for several decades longer.

For nearly two centuries after the *St Charles* had brought her passengers to Manhattan the Jews remained a tiny minority. Then, around 1830, their numbers began to increase rapidly. In the next half century at least a quarter of a million Jews entered the United States, mainly from Germany, uprooted from the same general areas as other German emigrants by the same elemental forces. The majority were petty retailers and artisans, many of them quite poor.

The German Jews scattered widely. They lived along the Atlantic seaboard and in scores of towns in the South, the Middle West and the Far West. A sizable number began their American careers as itinerant peddlers. This was a calling they were familiar with in Europe and one which needed little capital. The Yankee peddler was already a familiar figure in America's rural regions. Now the Jews followed his example, trudging long distances with packs on their backs, selling such things as thread, lace, bonnets, knives and jewellery. Profit margins were low, but in a remarkable number of instances peddling proved to be the first rung on the ladder of commercial success. Some of the founders of America's great department store dynasties started out in this way. Lazarus Straus, who arrived in America in 1854, peddled with horse and waggon in the South until he had acquired enough capital to open a crockery and glassware business in a small Georgia town. His son Isidor moved to New York in 1874 and, before the end of the century, he and his brother Nathan had become owners of Macy's, which they subsequently developed into the largest store in the world. Peddling was also the seed from which other well-known American department stores grew: Gimbel's, Bloomingdale's and Altman's in New York, Filene's in Boston, Goldwater's in Phoenix, Arizona. By a similar process of evolution the son of a middle western peddler named Samuel Rosenwald became the owner of the Chicago mail order firm of Sears Roebuck.

The careers too of Nelson Morris in meat-packing, Meyer Guggenheim in mining, Isaac Friedlander in grain-exporting, demonstrate the variety of the business activities of German Jews. But it was above all in finance that the great German Jewish fortunes were made. After the Civil War some of the best-known investment banking houses on Wall Street were those headed by German Jews – Kuhn, Loeb and Co., Goldman, Sachs and Co., J. and W. Seligman and Co., and Lehman Brothers. Some German Jews began humbly. Joseph Seligman, arriving in 1837, poor and unknown, was at first a peddler, then with his brothers founded a clothing firm which was transformed in 1862 into the banking house of J. and W. Seligman and Co. Others were already well-to-do when they crossed the Atlantic. Jacob H. Schiff, the head of Kuhn, Loeb and Co., for instance, came from a Frankfurt family which rivalled the Rothschilds in wealth and distinction. Similarly the brothers Felix and Paul Warburg came from a very distinguished Hamburg banking family.

By the 1880s New York's great Jewish banking families constituted a tightly-knit and socially prominent elite. They lived in immense style in Fifth Avenue mansions, which ranged from Jacob Schiff's baronial castle to Otto Kahn's Italian Renaissance palace. Their summer villas in the Adirondacks or in Florida were hardly less grand. Some possessed yachts and, like other members of the international aristocracy, they visited Europe regularly to take the cure at Bad Gastein or Marienbad. Their success in making money was matched by their zeal in giving it away, while several of them became well-known as patrons of the arts. Adolph Lewisohn possessed the finest collection of French impressionists in America; Jesse Seligman was a notable patron of the Metropolitan Museum of Art and of the American Museum of Natural History; Otto Kahn, assuming virtual control of the Metropolitan Opera in 1903, was responsible for the first American performance of *Parsifal* and captured for the Metropolitan some of Europe's greatest musical figures, among them Toscanini.

Temple Emanu-El, corner of Fifth
Avenue and 43rd Street, New York,
built in 1867. From the moment it was
founded in 1845 Emanu-El was in the
van of the movement to reform Jewish
worship. Rapidly winning the support
of many of the more prosperous
German Jews it became the largest and
most influential of New York
congregations.

The economic status of the German Jews as a whole was extraordinarily high – certainly higher than that of any other group of immigrants. A federal government survey in 1890 revealed that about half of the German Jewish population were in business; one fifth were accountants, clerks and such like; one in eight were artisans, one in ten were salesmen, one in twenty doctors, lawyers and other professional men. Only one per cent were peddlers and half that proportion were labourers.

Back in Germany Jews had not lived in special areas nor possessed a distinctive culture; they spoke the same language as other Germans, had shared most of their customs and displayed the same provincial loyalties. True, German Jews had laboured under certain disabilities – the restrictive Bavarian marriage laws for instance – but they had been sufficiently well integrated to be able to regard themselves simply as a religious group like German Lutherans.

In the United States the Ashkenazim continued to be closely identified with Germany, many of them appearing more German than Jewish. They continued to speak German, to live in German communities, to read German newspapers. Deeply devoted to German culture they were as keen as other Germans to preserve it. In certain districts they did establish societies and lodges of their own – but for most of the nineteenth century they were accepted freely in societies founded by non-Jewish Germans. The result was that a sizable number of Ashkenazim ceased to affiliate with the Jewish community. Then, especially if marriage took place outside the faith, the second generation would tend to fall away from the Jewish heritage. Immigrants, anxious for acceptance, occasionally took the same path themselves. The most spectacular example was that of the New York banker August Belmont. Having changed his name from Schönberg upon leaving Frankfurt for New York in 1837, Belmont became a Christian and made a determined – and successful – effort to obscure his antecedents. He was soon a well-known figure in New York society; his marriage in 1848 in Grace Episcopal Church to the daughter of a distinguished American naval officer was a glittering occasion and marked the peak of his triumphant social career.

Most German Jews, however, clung to their religion – or at least to an Americanized version of Judaism known as 'Reform', the first stirrings of which had occurred in Germany early in the nineteenth century. It was an attempt to modernize orthodox Judaism, and to give its religious services a more dignified, more western air. Transplanted to America German Jews became more insistent in demanding such changes. Like other immigrants, their eagerness to be Americanized led them to demand a form of worship that differentiated them as little as possible from their neighbours. Hence there were calls for the abandonment of ancient rituals, the introduction of sermons, the addition of organs or mixed choirs, the translation of Hebrew prayers and the replacement of the curtained women's gallery by family pews.

By 1881, out of 200 or so major congregations in the United States only about a dozen were still orthodox. The rapid advance of Reform Judaism was largely due to the recognition that it might stem conversion and retain the allegiances of the second generation. In America conditions favoured Reform, for each congregation was free to act independently, unrestrained by the communal organizations that once controlled Jewish life in every European city.

By about 1880, the Reform movement had thus culminated in a brand of Judaism which had been stripped of much traditional orthodoxy. Ritual and belief became barely distinguishable from those of Christian denominations. The interior of the synagogue – now called a temple – looked very like that of a church. Some congregations even adopted a Sunday service, while German gave way to English as the language of worship. The practice of exchanging pulpits with Christian churches was on the increase.

The beginning of large-scale immigration from eastern Europe, however, changed the scene. Reform Judaism had no appeal to the two million Jews who arrived in the next forty years. Hence while the number of synagogues in the United States rose from 270 in 1880 to nearly 2000 in 1916, Reform itself declined to the position of a minority creed. Moreover, the new east-European influx transformed the entire position and outlook of middle-class American Jewry. Within a single generation German Jews found themselves vastly outnumbered by newcomers with whom they had little in common and to whom they at first felt a strong aversion.

The Jews of eastern Europe began to leave their homes in great numbers in 1881–2, soon after a wave of pogroms in southern Russia when the government embarked upon a calculated anti-Semitic policy. In Russia most Jews were confined to the Pale of Settlement, an area which extended along the western borders of the Tsarist empire. Even there Jews were restricted to certain occupations and forbidden to hold land, while education was largely denied to their children. During the reign of Alexander II the restrictions were relaxed somewhat, but the Tsar's assassination in 1881 set off a wave of anti-Jewish riots in which peasant mobs were officially encouraged to demonstrate their inherited prejudices and a year later the harsh measures known as the May Laws restored all the old disabilities and added new ones.

Despite the chorus of protest from abroad, worse was to follow. In 1891, about 20,000 Jews in Moscow, St Petersburg and Kiev were suddenly expelled. In 1897 a government monopoly on the drink trade deprived thousands of Jewish inn-keepers of their livelihoods. Then at the beginning of the twentieth century there were fresh outbreaks of popular violence. The first was the Kishineff massacre of 1903, sparked off by the revival of the ritual murder slander of the Middle Ages (it was said that Jews had ritually sacrificed Christian babies). But the worst pogroms of all came after the suppression of the Russian Revolution of 1905. In many towns and villages Jews were attacked and murdered, their bodies mutilated and their property pillaged and destroyed. The spectre of the pogrom constantly haunted Russian Jews. In her autobiography, *The Promised Land*, written in Boston in 1912, Mary Antin wrote:

I remember a time when I thought a pogrom had broken out in our street, and I wonder that I did not die of fear. It was some Christian holiday, and we had been warned by the police to keep indoors. Gates were locked; shutters were barred. If a child cried, the nurse threatened to give it to the priests, who would soon be passing by. Fearful and yet curious, we looked through the cracks in the shutters. We saw a procession of peasants and townspeople, led by priests, carrying crosses and banners and images. In the place of honor was carried a casket, containing a relic from the monastery in the outskirts of Polotzk. Once a year the Gentiles paraded this relic, and the streets were considered too holy for Jews to be about; we lived in fear till the end of the day, knowing that the least disturbance might start a riot, and a riot lead to a pogrom.

On a far grimmer note, Chaim Gross, a sculptor, who came from Russian-dominated Poland in 1919, recalls the experience of his family in the First World War when the Cossack army was on the rampage:

They broke up the door, they broke the window – three large Cossacks came in with their sabres and guns and so on. My mother jumped out of bed, and my father and brother and I, and the first thing, one of the Cossacks grabbed my mother – the idea was to rape her. My father tried to stop them, and they took a sabre, and as they were pulling my mother, one of the Cossacks, I don't know if it was the same one, started chopping at my father's head. And my mother put her hands over her head, and he chopped her fingers and then he started chopping my mother's head and my father put his hands out to her and they chopped his fingers again. . . . After the Cossacks had gone both my father and mother were unconscious for a long time . . . my mother for many, many weeks.

It is, however, an oversimplification to think of the mass exodus of east-European Jewry as being caused solely by persecution. Earlier pogroms like the one at Odessa in 1871 had not led to heavy emigration. It is also significant that Jewish emigration, when it did begin, was proportionately just as great from those areas in eastern Europe where there was little overt persecution – Austrian Galicia, for example – as from those where it was recurrent and systematic. Moreover, within Russia itself Jewish emigration did not come particularly from regions which experienced pogroms – that was the case, for instance, after the pogroms of 1905–6. Indeed, those outrages coincided with an economic depression, brought on by the Russo-Japanese War and the ensuing revolution, which caused the curve of non-Jewish emigration from Russia – Finns, Poles, Lithuanians and Ukrainians – to rise just as sharply.

Economic pressure was probably the main reason for Jewish emigration; the pogroms served only to strengthen the already formed conviction that there was no future for the Jews unless they emigrated. Like other Europeans the Jews were suffering the consequences of population increase and economic change. The number of Jews in Russia, for instance, increased and economic opportunities shrank for reasons unrelated to persecution. It is true that one of the major economic changes – the coming of large-scale farming – did not

Pogrom victims in
the Ukraine, 1918–20.

directly affect the Jews for they had not been farmers; but since they had served
the agricultural population as traders and peddlers, they were displaced along
with the peasants. Similarly, the growth of factories squeezed out Jewish artisans as it did those who were not Jews.

Some of the Jews threatened with economic suffocation did no more than
move about within the Pale; like other displaced Europeans they fled from the
poverty of the villages to nearby towns and cities, thronging into Polish industrial centres in particular. In these densely-packed cities they lived a life of
extreme hardship and squalor. 'The vast majority of them are in poverty', wrote
the American minister in St Petersburg in 1893, 'and a very considerable part
in misery – just on the border of starvation.'

Some Russian Jews made their way to Palestine, especially after the founding
of the Zionist movement in 1897. But restrictions imposed by the Turks kept
the numbers below 30,000. Rather more settled in Argentina, largely as a result
of the colonizing work of a German Jewish philanthropist, Baron Maurice de
Hirsch. There was also a sizable movement of Russian Jews to Great Britain.
This was how London's East End came by its large Jewish population. But
there was some hostility in Britain to the influx of Russian and Polish Jews

and the Aliens Act of 1905 brought it to an end. Britain in fact retained only about a third of the east-European Jews who arrived between 1891 and 1914, the rest moving on to America after longer or shorter intervals.

From the very beginning the United States was the favourite destination of east-European Jewry. The more Jewish emigration increased the more popular America became. In the decade before 1914 more than ninety per cent of all Jewish emigrants from eastern Europe settled in what they had come to regard as their *goldene medine* (golden land).

Jewish newcomers from eastern Europe were more literate and more skilled than the other 'new' immigrants of the period. They were not peasants or farm labourers but people who had experience of urban life, either in a city ghetto or, more commonly, in a *shtetl*, the typical Jewish small town in the Pale. Furthermore, their numbers included almost as many women as men, as well as a high percentage of children. It was significant, too, that in their old homes the east-European Jews had formed the majority of the population. Unlike German Jews they had not been assimilated by the people around them and had thus preserved their own language – Yiddish – and their own customs. Above all, they had clung to their traditional Judaism as a badge of identity. But this high orthodoxy was tempered by the political extremism which a minority of intellectuals had embraced. Thus east-European Jewry brought to America both an intense piety and a commitment to a variety of secular causes – socialism, trade unionism, anarchism and Zionism among them. One thing, however, they all agreed about: a determination to become American citizens at the earliest opportunity. What this meant to Moses Kirshblum, who emigrated from Bialystok, Poland in 1923, has recently been described by his son, a New York rabbi:

To my father it meant everything. . . . He knew well enough that a man who cannot speak English – how is he going to become a citizen? But he persevered and the day came when he went before a judge, who questioned him. I remember he was asked: 'Are you a bigamist?' He had never heard of the word, and he said 'yes' with great pride. 'Do you have any prison record?' and again he said 'yes'. He figured he can't go wrong by saying 'yes'. Then the judge began to ask him about certain American holidays: He said: 'Do you remember what the Fourth of July is?' And he said 'Labour Day'. But toward the end he turned pleadingly to the judge and says, 'Mr Judge, please do me a *taver* [a corruption of the Hebrew word *tovah*, meaning a favour] – Do me a *taver*. I want to be an American citizen.' And the judge – because he was deeply moved by this old man pleading for American citizenship – said tearfully, 'A citizen you shall be', and granted him papers.

Established Jews viewed this mass influx from eastern Europe with disdain and misgiving. They disliked both the orthodoxy and the radicalism of the newcomers and were repelled by their poverty and uncouth appearance. Also, they were worried that the arrival of these outlandish strangers might stimulate anti-Semitism and threaten their own middle-class status. Hence they sought to

The New Diaspora

dissociate themselves from the newcomers. The New York *Hebrew Standard* commented in 1894:

The thoroughly acclimated American Jew ... stands apart from the seething mass of Jewish immigrants and looks upon them as in a stage of development pitifully low. ... He has no religious, social or intellectual sympathies with them. He is closer to the Christian sentiment around him than to the Judaism of these miserable darkened Hebrews.

German Jewish charitable institutions tried hard to relieve the distresses of their *Glaubensbrüder* (co-religionists), but some leaders of the Jewish community sought to divert, if not to check, the inflow by means of rural colonization.

There had been attempts to establish Jewish agricultural communities even before the Civil War, though none lasted more than a few years. But in the early 1880s the rising tide of Jewish immigration gave fresh impetus to the movement. Some felt it was in the immigrants' own interests to move from crowded ghettos to farms, others that agricultural colonies would forestall anti-Semitism. Hence various Jewish relief bodies established about a dozen rural colonies at places like Sicily Island, Louisiana, Cotopaxi and New Odessa, Oregon. But these and other colonies founded in the West and the South were short-lived. Jewish settlers had no experience of agriculture and in any case preferred to live in cities, mainly because of the educational and religious opportunities they presented. The only successful agricultural colonies were those planted in southern New Jersey at Carmel, Woodbine, and Rosenhayn, settled by the Hebrew Emigrant Aid Society. But even they survived only with the help of large subsidies and because the colonists supplemented their earnings by working in nearby factories.

From about 1890, roughly two-thirds of America's Jews were concentrated in a handful of cities: New York, Chicago, Philadelphia, and Boston. The remainder settled in such cities as Cleveland, Baltimore, Los Angeles and Pittsburgh. Their poverty condemned them to live, initially at least, in the poorest and most densely-crowded districts – the Lower East Side of New York, the West Side of Chicago, the North End of Boston, the city centre in Philadelphia. Formerly these neighbourhoods had been inhabited by German and Irish immigrants. Now, in face of the Jewish invasion, they moved elsewhere.

The greatest magnet of all was New York City. By 1890 it held half of all the Jews in America. By the beginning of the First World War, 1,400,000 Jews lived there, a figure larger than New York's entire population in 1870. When large-scale immigration from eastern Europe began New York was being transformed into a modern city. At its very heart, in the shadow of Brooklyn Bridge, there grew up something resembling an old world ghetto. In time the Lower East Side contained the largest Jewish community in the world. Occupying a territory little more than one mile square, it extended eastward from the Bowery almost to the East River and southward from 14th Street as far as

A cartoon, published in a satirical Yiddish weekly, *Der Groyser Kundes (The Big Stick)* in 1909. A newly-arrived Russian-Jewish immigrant receives contradictory advice from Jacob Schiff, the German-Jewish banker, and William Randolph Hearst, the wealthy New York newspaper proprietor and politician.

Schiff: Go West, don't stay in New York. Don't endanger the position of the whole Jewish community by congregating here.
Hearst: No! Mr Schiff, you are mistaken. There is strength in numbers. If they are dispersed, they won't count for anything.
Immigrant: I wish I knew what they really want me to do.

Brooklyn Bridge. The thousands of Jews who lived there were a cosmopolitan crowd. They included Galicians, Lithuanians, Poles, Rumanians, Ukrainians, and Levantines, each grouped together in separate neighbourhoods. They looked with suspicion or disdain upon co-religionists who came from a different part of Europe. But, penned together in a narrow bridgehead, the different varieties of Jews became fused into a single community – a fusion best demonstrated in the way their different dialects became blended into an 'American' Yiddish.

By 1900 the Lower East Side had become one of the most densely settled places on the face of the globe. Statistics showed it to be infinitely more crowded than Paris or Berlin, more crowded even than Bombay. To add to the general *mêlée*, an observer described how:

It was a custom among all the immigrants to have boarders. A family with two children rents an apartment of three rooms and then goes ahead and rents out the kitchen and the living room to two or three boarders. Sometimes there would be shifts, people would sleep in the daytime, and the same place would be used by somebody else at night.

Things were worst in the Tenth Ward, which contained scores of factories and shops as well as tenements. Small wonder that Arnold Bennett, visiting America in 1912, should remark that on Rivington Street 'the architecture seemed to sweat humanity at every window and door'.

On Friday mornings the area around the Hester Street market was thronged with Sabbath shoppers. A seething mass of humanity completely blocked the street to traffic. Along both sides of the street the pavements were lined by a double row of pushcarts containing such things as fruit, vegetables, fish, poultry, clothing and soda water. Around the carts bewigged women swarmed and jostled, haggling with the traders in a variety of dialects. Peddlers, hoping to tempt passers-by with such merchandise as ribbons, shoelaces and buckles, filled the air with their cries. Only at sundown did the throngs disperse and the clamour subside.

Typical of the Lower East Side was the 'dumb-bell tenement', so called because the tenement buildings on one street were connected with those on the next by a narrower building containing an air-shaft. In 1888 such tenements were described as follows:

They are great prison-like structures of brick, with narrow doors and windows, cramped passages and steep rickety stairs. . . . In case of fire they would be death-traps, for it would be impossible for the occupants of the crowded rooms to escape by the narrow stairways, and the flimsy fire-escapes . . . so laden with broken furniture, bales and boxes that they would be worse than useless. In the hot summer months . . . these fire-escape balconies are used as sleeping-rooms by the poor wretches who are fortunate enough to have windows opening upon them. The drainage is horrible, and even the Croton as it flows from the tap in the noisome courtyard, seemed to be contaminated by its surroundings and have a fetid smell.

The Lower East Side
at the turn of the century.
LEFT The Jewish market,
Hester Street.
ABOVE Street vendors in
Hester Street.
RIGHT A pushcart peddler.

The New Diaspora

These grim, insanitary barracks, honeycombed with dark, tiny rooms might have been expected to be New York's worst hotbeds of disease. Astonishingly, they were not. The tenth ward, with the highest average density of occupants per house in the city, had one of the lowest death rates, a fact which public health officials attributed to high standards of personal cleanliness and the strict dietary laws required by orthodoxy. Nor, despite their poverty, did Jews add to the pauperism generally associated with immigration. Drunkenness, one of the main causes of pauperism, was rare among Jews, while the resources of Jewish philanthropy – the United Jewish Charities and the Hebrew Immigrant Aid Society, for instance – gave the kind of help that the taxpayers had to provide for other immigrants.

In New York the *shtetl* and ghetto Jews of eastern Europe became a proletariat. They supplied the bulk of the 'sweated' labour needed by the rapidly expanding garment industry. It was called 'sweated' because of the long hours, low wages and insanitary conditions prevailing in the manufacture of ready-made clothing under a contracting-out system. Although only about eleven per cent of Jewish immigrants had been tailors back in the old world, they flocked to the garment trade once they reached the shores of America. Despite its record of exploitation, the system of subcontracting and piecework had compensations. Families could work together under conditions that facilitated religious observance and also by working long hours and living frugally – sometimes on a diet of bread and pickles – they could accumulate the capital they needed either to set up on their own as clothing manufacturers or return to their more familiar pursuits.

Jacob Riis, the Danish-born police reporter and reforming journalist, described the system in his book, *How The Other Half Lives*, published in 1890:

The homes of the Hebrew quarter are its workshops also. . . . You are made fully aware of it before you have travelled the length of a single block in any of these East Side streets, by the whirr of a thousand sewing-machines, worked at high pressure from earliest dawn until mind and muscle give out together. Every member of the family, from the youngest to the oldest, bears a hand, shut in the qualmy rooms, where meals are cooked and clothing washed and dried besides, the live-long day. It is not unusual to find a dozen persons – men, women and children – at work in a single room.

Riis pointed out that although there was a law regulating factory labour, tenement working conditions were not included. In factories, ten hours was the legal work-day, forty-five minutes at least had to be allowed for dinner, and child labour was prohibited. But in the tenements, 'the child works unchallenged from the moment he is old enough to pull a thread. There is no such thing as a dinner hour; men and women eat while they work, and the "day" is lengthened at both ends far into the night.'

OPPOSITE Baxter Street Court on the Lower East Side.

ABOVE Moe Levy's
garment workshop, Lower
East Side, *c.* 1912.
RIGHT Taking work
home; a familiar Lower
East Side scene, *c.* 1910.

In 1899 New York followed the example of other states in adopting legislation governing tenement work. It introduced a system of licensing and inspection to ensure minimum standards of ventilation and sanitation. Its purpose was not to protect the workers but to prevent the spread of contagious and infectious diseases. Its effect, however, was to drive shopwork from the tenements. By 1901, although home finishing was still widespread, garments were no longer being completely manufactured in East Side tenements. Pauline Newman emigrated with her family to New York in 1907. She still works at the headquarters of the ILGWU and has described her early working experiences:

It was child's work, since we were all children. We had a corner in the factory which was like a kindergarten. The work wasn't difficult. The shirtwaist finished by the operator would come to us so we could cut off the thread left by the needle of the machine. You had little scissors because you were children. Somehow the employer knew when the inspector was coming. Materials came in high wooden cases and when the inspector came we were put in them and covered with shirtwaists. By the time he arrived there were no children.

In the busy season, we worked seven days a week. That's why the sign went up on the freight elevator: 'If you don't come in on Sunday, don't come in on Monday.'

By the time of the First World War the needle trades possessed two of the most powerful trades unions in America: the International Ladies' Garment Workers' Union and the Amalgamated Clothing Workers of America. Both were Jewish led and their members were mostly Jews. Early in the new century the garment workers staged a series of dramatic strikes. The first began in September 1909, and involved 20,000 female shirtwaist makers – the first great strike of women in American history. It was a largely spontaneous affair, caused by the company's dismissal of union labour. Female union members were even less popular than their brothers:

When they found out that you went to a meeting, you were fired the next day: 'Get the hell out of here'. In the beginning the employers were so confident that they would not have a union in their shop they didn't listen even to public-spirited people. It was after the 1909 strike when they realized that there was no use fighting them, they would have to try and get along with them.

During the strike company guards, police and passers-by assaulted picketing girls. But middle-class sympathizers and Jewish organizations gave them moral and material aid. In February 1910, arbitration ended the strike, the strikers winning wage increases and union recognition.

The victory encouraged the ILGWU to call a general strike in the summer of 1910. Their aims were a forty-eight hour week, the end of the 'inside' system which generated sweatshop conditions, and union recognition in the cloak-makers' industry. After a lengthy stoppage involving 60,000 workers the cloak-makers gave way and signed the 'Protocol of Peace'. This was a milestone in the history of the clothing industry for it not only conceded the strikers' demands, but set up machinery for resolving future industrial disputes.

Less than six months later, on 26 March 1911, the garment district was once more in the news because of the most terrible industrial tragedy in the history of Yiddish New York. At 4.35 on a Saturday afternoon, fire suddenly broke out on the eighth floor of the Triangle Waist Company's factory off Washington Place. Hundreds of employees, mainly girls, were inside. Most of them escaped, either by clambering on to the roof or by means of the elevator. But 146 lives were lost. Most of the bodies were charred beyond recognition but more than a third who died lost their lives jumping from windows into the street far below. The victims were interred in a common grave following a memorial parade of 50,000 mourners. The disaster did, however, have one good result: the state legislature set up a Factory Investigating Commission. Among its many recommendations which became law one was designed to eliminate fire hazards in factories.

The Lower East Side was much more than an agglomeration of crowded slums and sweatshops. Contemporary journalists, though appalled by the squalor of the tenements, were fascinated by the picturesqueness and vibrancy of the district. They drew an affectionate picture of a community pulsating with life and energy and possessing a special warmth and richness of texture – qualities that one Gentile observer, Hutchins Hapgood, was to call 'the spirit of the ghetto'. What impressed outsiders most was the variety and intensity of the cultural life of the Lower East Side – its learned Hebrew scholars ignoring their poverty to devote themselves to the study of an ancient language and literature; its coffee houses bursting with poets, writers, actors, revolutionaries; its Yiddish newspapers; and above all its celebrated Yiddish theatre.

Triangle Fire victims, 1911. The heavy death toll focused attention on the evils of the sweatshop in the garment trade.

The theatre was without question the best-loved venue for popular culture among the Jews of the Lower East Side. Around the turn of the century 1100 performances were given annually before audiences which were estimated at two million. Everyone went – sweatshop workers, rabbis, housewives, intellectuals. Playwrights like Jacob Gordin and actors like Jacob P. Adler and Boris Thomashevsky were, as Harry Golden has remarked, 'the folk-heroes of the ghetto'. Farce and melodrama were the staple offerings of the Yiddish theatre; nothing else would have appealed to predominantly uneducated and unsophisticated audiences. But the extraordinary popularity of the Yiddish theatre was due primarily to its realism; the situations and scenes depicted on stage were those with which the immigrant audience could identify, being drawn from everyday life in the ghetto.

The outstanding figure in Yiddish journalism was Abraham Cahan. Born in a Lithuanian village near Vilna in 1860, the son of a poor Hebrew teacher, Cahan was at once the most typical and the most influential member of the Jewish Lower East Side community. In turn, factory worker, lecturer, English teacher, trade union organizer, law student, socialist agitator and journalist, his life touched the Jewish immigrant experience at virtually every point. But it was as a newspaper editor that Cahan was best known. He transformed a struggling sectarian journal, the *Jewish Daily Forward*, into a mass-circulation daily. He did it by applying the style and methods of American journalism and by simplifying the paper's language. Instead of the usual highbrow Yiddish he substituted the Americanized Yiddish as it was currently spoken. This enabled him not only to reach the masses with the message of socialism but to urge upon them the desirability of Americanization. It was in fact Cahan's special purpose to interpret for his readers the strange new world to which they had been transplanted. This he accomplished both in his editorials and in the famous *Bintl Brief* (Bundle of Letters) column, in which the editor dispensed advice to immigrants seeking to come to terms with their new situation:

1908

Dear Editor,

I ask you to give me some advice in my situation. I am a young man of twenty-five, sixteen years in America, and I recently met a fine girl. She has a flaw, however, that keeps me from marrying her. The fault is that she has a dimple in her chin, and it is said that people who have this lose their first husband or wife. . . .

Respectfully,
The Unhappy Fool

Answer:
The tragedy is not that the girl has a dimple in her chin but that some people have a screw loose in their heads! One would need the knowledge of a genius to explain how a dimple in the chin could drive a husband or wife to the grave. Does the angel of death sit hiding in the dimple? It seems to us that it is a beauty spot, and we never imagined it could house the Devil . . . !

1939

Dear Editor,

... A short time ago I had occasion to ride on a train and I took the *Forverts* to read on the way. My brother-in-law said it wasn't nice, that it wasn't fitting to read a Jewish newspaper on the train. Even though I'm still a 'greenhorn' in America, my Americanized brother-in-law's statement didn't have any effect on me.

I know America is a free country and the Jew is not oppressed here as in other lands, so why should I have to be ashamed of my language here? I certainly would not read a Jewish paper in a train in Germany or Poland. And do you know why? Because there they would beat me up for such *chutzpa* (nerve). Here, in America, though, I don't have to be afraid of anyone.... I would like to hear your opinion about this.

With thanks,
The 'Greenhorn'

Answer:

No, people should not be ashamed to read a Yiddish newspaper in the train or subway. Many are not ashamed to do so. One should only be ashamed of something bad or not respectable. And something not respectable should not even be done in secret. The *Talmud* says, 'That which should not be done hidden in a closed room is also not permitted in the open.'

It is well known that our mother tongue has already gained an honourable position among the world languages. The writings of Yiddish authors and poets are being translated into various languages, including English, and have received their due recognition by literary critics. There is absolutely no reason to be ashamed of or to hide the Yiddish newspaper.

1962

Dear Editor,

The question came up in our family as to how religious parents who keep strictly *kosher* should act when they come to visit their children who do not keep *kosher* homes. Should religious people eat non-*kosher* meat when they are at their children's homes in order not to insult them? ...

With respect and thanks,
M.A.

Answer:

We cannot imagine that children would demand of their religious parents that they eat their non-*kosher* food. In such a case the parents do not have to adapt to the children's way, but just the opposite. Not the children but the parents should feel insulted when they come to visit and are served a non-*kosher* meal.

Until he died in 1951 at the age of ninety-one, Cahan was the foremost spokesman of the Lower East Side. He was also its leading interpreter, writing what is probably the most famous of all immigrant novels, *The Rise of David Levinsky*, published in 1917. It tells the story of a pious immigrant youth who, in the course of adapting to the American environment, abandons, step by step, all the practices of Judaism. He arrives in America determined to adhere to his strict orthodox training. But the moment he enters the garment trade his

ABOVE Abraham Cahan, editor of the *Jewish Daily Forward*, spokesman for and interpreter of the Lower East Side.

LEFT Boris Thomashevsky in his role of 'the cobbler'. Thomashevsky, born in Kiev in 1864, emigrated to the United States in 1877 and became a leading actor of the Yiddish stage and the matinée idol of Lower East Side girls.

183

A tenement dweller
prepares for the Sabbath,
c. 1890.

religious interest begins to decline. Within a short time he cuts off his earlocks and shaves his beard; his phylacteries and his prayer-book are no longer used; finally he stops going to the synagogue, first on weekdays, then on the Sabbath as well.

But not all east-European Jews abandoned orthodoxy as easily as David Levinsky. Many remained attached to the religion that had shaped their way of life in Europe. They did not feel at home in either the Reform or the Conservative synagogues they found in America, and insisted therefore on establishing their own. This determination was evident in the appearance on the Lower East Side of traditional religious functionaries: the *shohet*, (ritual slaughterer), the *mohel*, (circumcizer) and the *masgiach* (inspector of dietary regulations). The orthodox also made great efforts to re-create in America the European system of religious education, introducing first the *cheder*, not the basic school of east-European Jewry, but a one-teacher establishment meeting

after school hours in a basement. When that proved unsatisfactory it was replaced by the Talmud Torah, also a supplementary school, which taught
Hebrew classes in English.

A Talmud school in a
Hester Street tenement,
c. 1898.

Yet such efforts could do no more than slow down the flight from orthodoxy.
While older people continued to observe the Mosaic law, Jewish youth was
impatient to be done with it. Orthodoxy declined partly because only a small
minority of Jewish children were reached by the *cheder* and the Talmud Torah;
a 1908 survey showed that only twenty-eight per cent of the Jewish children
in New York had received even the most meagre Jewish education. More funda-
mentally the texture of life in America was hardly compatible with traditional
Judaism. What had held Judaism together for so long was persecution. Without
that spur religion flagged. Paradoxically, therefore, religious freedom produced
a reaction against religion. No longer treated as outcasts because of their religion
Jews found less need to cling to it. In any case, when they went out to work

second-generation Jews found that they had to live in a business world adjusted to a Christian rather than a Jewish calendar. That made religious observance inconvenient, if not impossible.

The urge to preserve orthodoxy first co-existed with, then was eventually replaced by, a yearning for the educational opportunities that Jews had been denied in eastern Europe. Jewish parents prized education highly and made great sacrifices to keep their children at school. Rabbi Usher Kirshblum of New York has recalled: 'I remember when I once took a job with a butcher delivering orders and my mother felt that I was taking too much time from my studies – she began to weep. She said, "I'll wash floors, but please keep studying, because if you won't study, you'll never get anywhere".' The son of another immigrant recalls:

Mama had a method that was called mama's remedial arithmetic, which meant simply this: one bicycle equals twelve books; cancel the bicycle to keep the books, right? Four ice cream cones equal one violin lesson. Cancel out the ice cream cones and you take the violin lesson. It wasn't easy. Everybody loves a bicycle. Everybody loves an ice cream cone too.

The effects of this kind of pressure were described in 1901 by Kate Claghorn, an investigator for the Industrial Commission:

One of the most striking social phenomena in New York City today is the way in which the Jews have taken possession of the public schools, in the highest as well as the lowest grades. The City College is practically filled with Jewish pupils, a considerable proportion of them children of Russian or Polish emigrants on the East Side. In the lower schools Jewish children are the delight of their teachers for cleverness at their books, obedience and general good conduct; and the vacation schools, night schools, social settlements and libraries . . . of the East Side are fairly besieged with Jewish children eager to take advantage of them.

This passion for education largely explained the extraordinary speed of Jewish social and economic advance. Within a single generation a community of garment workers and small traders lifted themselves into the middle class.

The children of the immigrants became white-collar workers, businessmen, doctors, dentists, teachers and lawyers; very few of them would be found in sweatshops. Not that education was indispensable in a country offering so many opportunities. Some immigrants reached the goal of prosperity without it. It was reported in 1901 that many tenements in the Lower East Side were owned by people who had formerly lived in them, and that 'many a Broadway merchant and professional man' had risen from the ghetto. It was a common saying that 'from Hester Street to Lexington Avenue is a journey of about ten years for any given family'. The second generation, too, demonstrated that the educational ladder was not the only one to the top. The rapidly expanding world of popular entertainment offered ample scope for Jewish musical and theatrical talents. The names of Irving Berlin and Eddie Cantor – both products of the

The crowded reading room of the Educational Alliance, c. 1898. Set up by German Jews to Americanize their co-religionists from eastern Europe, this community house offered a wide variety of cultural activities.

Lower East Side – symbolized the contribution Jews would make to popular music and the stage.

Perhaps the most striking manifestation of Jewish economic advance was the exodus from the congested ghetto areas. The migration from the Lower East Side began even before the influx of east-European Jewry had reached its peak and after the First World War the pace accelerated. The wealthiest stayed in the fashionable districts of Manhattan, but many favoured destinations further out, in Brownsville and the Bronx, Borough Park and Flatbush. Between 1914 and 1930 the Lower East Side lost half its Jewish population, as did other major Jewish cities. Yet in seeking better homes Jews were not moving away from their own kind. South Brooklyn, Williamsburg and Browns-ville were as distinctly Jewish as the Lower East Side had been.

However, the exodus from the ghetto did not at once unify American Jewry. The division between the long-settled German Jews and those who had arrived more recently from eastern Europe persisted. Social contacts were few and intermarriage rare. The welding of the two communities into one was to take several decades and would come about only as Jews learned that the challenges they faced had to be met together.

The strongest cement was to be provided by American anti-Semitism. German Jews were the first to be affected. The acceptance they had enjoyed was replaced in the years after the Civil War by a social discrimination which became increasingly blatant. The most publicized incident occurred in 1875 when Joseph Seligman, the well-known banker, was refused accommodation in the Grand Union Hotel in Saratoga Springs, where he had often stayed before. The action of the hotel was widely denounced, and not only by Jews, but it nevertheless established a pattern of social exclusion. By the 1890s many clubs and societies had adopted a consistent policy of barring Jews from membership; the same thing happened in summer resorts and private schools. Such snubs were a measure of the resentment provoked by the unusual speed with which Jews gained in earning power and social position.

Anti-Semites who sought to check this rapid climb at first justified their actions by alleging that the Jews were acquisitive vulgarians. But as the century ended the stereotype of the Jew as the personification of avarice acquired new and ominous overtones. In 1894 a magazine article ascribed the wealth of the Jews to the fact that they were: 'a parasitical race who, producing nothing, fasten on the produce of land and labor and live on it, choking the breath out of commerce and industry as sure as the creeper throttles the tree that upholds it.' The bitter controversy of the 1890s over the gold standard stimulated vague fears of Jewish financial power and of an international Jewish financial conspiracy. Such fantasies inspired a flood of anti-Semitic literature. One example was William H. Harvey's novel of financial conspiracy, *A Tale of Two Nations* (1894). It blamed the world's monetary difficulties upon the Rothschilds and other Jewish bankers, one of whom is told: 'You are very wise in your way, the commercial way, inbred through generations. The politic, scheming, devious way, inbred through generations also.'

Such effusions had their pictorial counterpart in the vicious caricatures appearing in such popular magazines as *Puck* and *Life*. These new and un-favourable conceptions, moreover, recognized no distinction between Jews of different origin; those who dwelt in Hester Street tenements and those who occupied Fifth Avenue mansions were lumped together as socially undesirable.

In the early years of the new century anti-Jewish prejudice became more acute and took on new forms. As the east-European Jews made their way out of the ghetto they ran full tilt into the barriers of discrimination. Restrictive

covenants debarred them from some apartment houses and certain residential areas. Their origin made it difficult for them to enter some occupations, newspaper advertisements specifying that only Christians need apply. Access to the professions was equally restricted. By the 1920s, almost every leading American college and university had, openly or otherwise, adopted a quota system for Jewish applicants. These steps were justified, ironically enough, on the same grounds cited earlier by the Tsarist authorities, namely, that without a *numerus clausus*, Jews would monopolize the high schools, universities and learned professions.

From the time of the First World War Jews increasingly became the target of hate-mongers who capitalized on the antipathies of the rural regions towards cities and banks, connecting Jews with both. Thus the lynching of Leo Frank in Georgia in 1915 was the result of the feeling whipped up against 'the libertine Jew' by the Southern Populist leader, Tom Watson. Convicted on dubious evidence of the rape and murder of a fourteen-year-old mill girl, Frank was taken from jail by a mob the day after the governor of the state had commuted his death sentence to life imprisonment. This incident proved to be the prelude to a more sustained anti-Semitic agitation. Its leader in the early 1920s was the automobile manufacturer, Henry Ford, who was obsessed with the notion of an international Jewish conspiracy. Ford seized upon the calumnies in *The Protocols of the Elders of Zion*, a crude fabrication by the Tsar's secret police

This anti-Semitic cartoon reflecting current stereotypes of the Jew was published in the popular magazine, *Life, c.* 1910. It conjured up the spectre of a Jewish conspiracy aimed at controlling the whole of New York's economic life.

earlier in the century, and used the columns of his newspaper, the *Dearborn Independent*, to publicize them. In the face of such assaults American Jewry drew more closely together. This tendency was enhanced in the 1930s by the concern all American Jews felt for the fate of their co-religionists in Nazi Germany. The rise of Hitler blurred the lines between Jews of different origins and strengthened Zionism. It might have been expected that the World Zionist Organization, founded in Basle in 1897, would quickly attract support from the Jewish community in the States. But in fact it was slow to take root there. As late as 1914 it had no more than 20,000 active American adherents and most American Jews were hostile to it. 'America is our Zion', they declared. Affluent Ashkenazim looked disdainfully upon Zionism as an old world movement, feeling it ran counter to the Reform tradition which had rejected the idea of a restored Jewish state. Even among east-European Jews Zionism was a minority creed. Socialists like Morris Hillquit dismissed it as irrelevant to the class struggle while to the orthodox it was a blasphemous anticipation of God's will.

Conflict between Zionists and anti-Zionists persisted for decades, mainly over the question of whether the bogy of divided loyalty would damage the standing of Jews with their fellow countrymen. But from the end of the First World War American Zionism steadily gained strength. It received a boost from the Balfour Declaration of 1917, which for the first time seemed to make a Jewish homeland in Palestine a practical possibility. The anti-Semitism of the 1920s also helped to overcome the apathy with which the Zionist movement was regarded. But it was the most terrible event in modern Jewish history that proved decisive: the murder of six million Jews by the Nazis. A Jewish congressman, Emanuel Celler, explained why he became converted to Zionism:

The Nazi terrors ... brought many Johnny-come-latelies into the Zionist fold. I suppose I could be counted among those. The reasons were of compelling force. No country would take the Jews. There was the historic association of the Jews with Palestine for two thousand years. There were the Jews already in Palestine who, before the turn of the century, were draining the marshes, reviving the tired, wasted soil, building for the day of statehood [and also] there was the virus of anti-Semitism, which no country in the world had yet succeeded in eradicating. . . .

Even as early as 1937 Nazi persecution had brought about a significant change. Reform Judaism, finding it impossible any longer to regard Jews simply as a religious group when German Jews were being persecuted regardless of their religious beliefs, adopted what was in effect a Zionist platform. And by the end of the Second World War, when the full horror of the holocaust had become known, American Jews had come to adopt a common position. While few envisaged returning to Palestine themselves they were fully prepared to stand solidly behind the Zionist demand for a Jewish state.

During the final years of the struggle for Israel, American Zionists became a cohesive and highly influential group. Their leaders included men who were prominent in American public life : Justices Brandeis and Frankfurter, Secretary of the Treasury Henry J. Morgenthau, Jr, Senator Robert F. Wagner, and Congressmen Sol Bloom, Jacob Javits and Emanuel Celler. Zionism also enjoyed the sympathy and support of an American public sickened by Nazi atrocities. Furthermore, the ability of Zionists to exert political pressure was enhanced by the number and location of Jewish voters. America's five million Jews were concentrated in a handful of politically sensitive states and cities; forty per cent of the total were in New York. Thus the arithmetic of American electoral politics proved vitally important at the moment of Israel's birth. Faced with a revolt of Jewish Democrats, President Truman reversed his previous stand and, in direct opposition to the State Department's advice, granted *de facto* recognition to Israel on 15 May 1948, just eleven minutes after the independence of the new state had been proclaimed.

The birth of Israel was a crucial event. At long last Jews had what every other immigrant group had always possessed – a homeland of their own. True, Israel was not a homeland in quite the same sense as, say, Ireland or Italy. Moreover the existence of Israel intensified the dilemma that had always lain at the heart of American Zionism, namely, whether America or Israel was the promised land. It gave new point to the old joke, as accurate as it was cruel: a Zionist is a Jew who gives money to a second Jew so that a third Jew can go and live in Palestine. Nevertheless the realization of the Zionist dream gave American Jews a special sense of pride. Asked recently what Israel has given the American Jew Rabbi Usher Kirshblum replied:

When I was a child, in my own mind I always thought a Jew was a person whose back is bent, who is always afraid, who is always on the run, who is always absorbing blows. Israel has straightened the backbone of every Jew – every Jew consciously or otherwise walks taller than he did before Israel was created. . . . He is serene and unafraid, the look of the persecuted has gone from his face.

True, almost no American Jews intended to emigrate there, but when Israel's blue and white flag took its place alongside those of other nations, the feelings of inferiority and of rootlessness that had so long oppressed them were at last dissipated.

9 THE ITALIAN EXODUS

IT IS IRONIC THAT ITALY, the classic land for expatriates, was the greatest of Europe's emigrating countries. While she was being discovered by a flood of foreign poets, painters and musicians in search of peace and inspiration, her own children were streaming away from her shores in search of bread. Foreign visitors settled for a season, a span of years, a lifetime; so too did the people who left. Italy's reputation as a haven for the artist rested on the example of a handful of famous people: Keats and Shelley, Robert and Elizabeth Browning, Wagner and Musset, Gogol and Ruskin. The mass exodus was composed of those unknown to history except as names on a steerage list. The transplanted foreigners settled mainly in the cities and if they did not all grace *palazzi* on the Grand Canal as did Ruskin, nor Medicean villas like the Brownings, they were usually found in prosperous and elegant neighbourhoods, near to Italy's priceless treasures. Most of the emigrants, on the other hand, were *contadini*, peasants who came from a primitive, rural Italy. Uninterested in the glories of their country's past, they were solely concerned with the task of wresting a living from a harsh and unyielding soil.

The basic cause of Italian emigration was that Italy was a land of chronic poverty. By the end of the nineteenth century she had become one of the most crowded countries in Europe – and one of the poorest. Less than a quarter of the land is flat and fertile, most of it being in the Po Valley – and even there huge efforts of irrigation and drainage have been needed since Roman times to make crops grow. During her history Italy has suffered severe deforestation, which denuded the Apennines and allowed streams to carry away the topsoil. Furthermore she has no coal or iron to meet the needs of heavy industry. In short, nature has been extremely niggardly to Italy. Her recent industrial growth springs from sources formerly untapped – water, volcanoes, natural gas – and from American aid.

Conditions were particularly bad in the Mezzogiorno – the southern half of the peninsula and Sicily. In the eighth century BC Greek colonists had made it the centre of a great civilization; during the Middle Ages too it had seen periods of greatness. But from then on the life of the region sank into torpor. The Spanish and Bourbon rulers were by turns neglectful and oppressive. (Bourbon rule was memorably described by Gladstone as 'the negation of God erected into a system of government'.) Bad administration did not cease after the unification of Italy in 1861, the new centralized government maintaining the tradition of neglect and exploitation. The Mezzogiorno remained a region where brigandage was endemic, religion was suffused with gross superstition and destitution was unique in the western world.

This was a parched region, desolate and almost barren; even the olive found it difficult to root in the heavy clay. Furthermore wholesale deforestation had created stagnant swamps which were breeding-grounds for the malarial mosquito. By the late nineteenth century malaria had become a widespread scourge, forcing the peasants to live in hills miles away from their infested plots. As

OPPOSITE New York's 'Little Italy', *c.* 1900.

193

The Italian Exodus

in Ireland, absentee landlords – the *latifondisti* – regarded their estates only as sources of income, operating a system of short leases and high rents which forced tenants to exploit the land. As for the plots owned by the *contadini* themselves, the laws of inheritance resulted in minute subdivisions of properties – *frazionamento* is the expressive Italian word – on such a scale that the peasants were always at near-starvation level. Farming methods had hardly changed since Biblical times. Most of the peasants had no ploughs, but relied on the *zappa*, a kind of hoe, which scarcely scratched the surface of the land.

How bad conditions were in southern Italy may be gauged by their persistence into our own times. Even today, more than a century after the unification of Italy, the Mezzogiorno is far from being integrated, economically or socially, with the rest of the country. Neither land reform, nor the conquest of malaria, nor lavish government expenditure on schools, roads and dams have succeeded in modernizing a primitive agrarian economy or in preventing a massive drain of the southern population to the factories of Turin and Milan.

The first Italian emigrants were, however, from the less poverty-stricken north. Even here the pressure of numbers was enough to generate a sizable outflow. Northern Italians at first went mainly to neighbouring lands, usually as construction workers. In the course of the 1880s, however, a double change occurred: southern Italy began to supply an increasing proportion of emigrants, and the new world overtook Europe as the popular destination. Departures rose from an annual average of 100,000 in the mid-1880s to 300,000 a decade later, to reach the staggering total of half a million annually between 1900 and

Italian emigrants arriving at the Emigrant Aid Society's Naples office before embarking for America.

1914. The exodus from southern Italy was essentially a belated response of conservative *contadini* to chronic hardship. They had begun to realize that Italian unification was not going to bring the promised reforms but that indeed Rome intended to continue treating them as a conquered colony. In the late 1880s came two further blows: competition from California and Florida almost closed the American market to Italian citrus fruit thus ruining thousands of growers in the south. At the same time France built a prohibitive tariff wall against Italian wines, depriving the southern grape growers of their chief export market. And while pressures to leave were growing the ease of transatlantic travel was increasing daily. By the end of the 1880s regular steamship services were running from Genoa and Naples to North and South America.

Of the three million Italians who crossed the Atlantic between 1876 and 1901, about two millions went to Argentina and Brazil – probably because they felt more at home there than in the United States. The climate was reminiscent of the Mediterranean and both countries were Catholic, with Latin civilizations similar to that of Italy. The bulk of the emigrants to Latin America were from Lombardy, Venetia and other provinces. Emigration from southern Italy followed a different course, because of the accident that, just as it was gathering momentum, conditions in Brazil and Argentina were temporarily uninviting. In Brazil the civil war of 1893–4 was followed by the cholera epidemic of 1895 in Espirito Santo which claimed many Italian victims and which led the Italian government to suspend emigration to Brazil for several months. Meanwhile in Argentina labour unrest had become endemic and a militant anarchist movement had emerged. In the city of Buenos Aires there were nineteen major strikes in 1895, sixteen the following year and a huge, anarchist-led general strike in November 1902.

Thus an increasing number of emigrants turned their thoughts towards North America. Lower costs must have been one encouragement; New York is only half as far from Naples as is Buenos Aires. Emigrants from southern Italy could reach Naples in a few hours by rail or, in the case of Sicilians, by an overnight steamer from Palermo. In 1893 an American offical, G. B. Young, was surprised at the healthy appearance of the crowds who had come to Naples to embark, remarking that they afforded a pleasing contrast to the way they looked after being herded for seventeen days on shipboard, or after becoming slum-dwellers in the States. Some Italians carried very little with them; Young remembered seeing a young man whose luggage consisted of 'a handkerchief full of lemons and a green umbrella'. On sailing day emigrants were ferried in small boats to the ships in the bay of Naples. Italian government officials, accompanied by police and health officers mustered the passengers on deck and inspected them as they filed past. This was usually a lengthy procedure, and for emigrants a trying one. As many as 1400 men, women and children had to stand on deck for hours in the full glare of the Italian sun, usually without food or water. Sometimes the medical officer fell asleep in his chair while the endless procession passed. As sailing time drew near the passengers passed by almost too fast to count. The police rapidly examined passports and checked the emigrants against their lists of wanted persons: absconding debtors, criminals with unfinished sentences, men of military age and so on. Finally came ticket inspection – often an occasion for argument about children's ages since those between one and eight travelled half fare while infants under one went free. Ages thus tended to be understated. As one observer remarked: 'the number of children under one who can walk on by themselves boasting full sets of teeth is astonishing.'

The tides of Italian emigration, however, remained complex. Large numbers of Italians continued to seek work in other European countries; in 1911 there were 400,000 in France alone, Marseilles claiming no fewer than 125,000. There was also a continuing trickle across the Mediterranean to North Africa, especially after 1911 when Tripoli and Cyrenaica became Italian colonies. But the United States had now become the Italian immigrants' first choice. After 1900 Argentina was a poor second and Brazil a bad third. Italian arrivals in the United States rose from 12,000 in 1880 to 52,000 a decade later, and to 100,000 in 1900. The flood tide occurred between the years 1901 and 1910 when more than two million Italians entered the United States – twice as many as in the previous eighty years. And between 1910 and 1916 another million were counted – though it must be remembered that these statistics include those who entered the States more than once. In turning to the United States Italian emigration remained as characteristically impermanent as it had ever been. Unlike other emigrants, the Italians who left home did not necessarily intend to become permanent residents elsewhere. Writing in 1920, Stefano Miele, by then a successful New York lawyer, described the motives, typical of many Italians, that had led him to emigrate seventeen years earlier:

If I am to be frank, then I shall say that I left Italy and came to America for the sole purpose of making money. Neither the laws of Italy, nor the laws of America, neither the government of the one nor the government of the other, influenced me in any way. I suffered no political oppression in Italy. I was not seeking political ideals: as a matter of fact, I was quite satisfied with those of my native land. If I could have worked my way up in my chosen profession in Italy, I would have stayed in Italy. But repeated efforts showed me that I could not. America was the land of opportunity, and so I came, intending to make money and then return to Italy. That is true of most Italian emigrants to America. . . .

Approximately forty per cent of the Italians who emigrated to the United States did in fact go back to Italy again. However, many of those who returned subsequently emigrated once more. An American investigating commission on board the White Star liner *Canopic* in 1907, interviewed returning Italians, asking why they were going back and whether they intended to return. Of the 108 interviewed, seventy-three said they expected to return, twenty-four did not

and eleven were undecided. The great majority said they were returning for a visit, or to get married, or to join the army; only three said they were going back because they disliked the United States: fourteen were returning because of illness and, of these, several were in advanced stages of tuberculosis, clearly returning home to die.

But in fact these returning Italians gave fresh impetus to emigration. One quayside observer remarked in 1906 that it was not difficult to pick out from the *contadini* those who had spent some time in the United States: 'To one side could be seen the returned passengers, all in neat attire, unfastening their well-filled trunks preparatory to the customs inspection, while to the other side were the thousand or so awaiting embarkation, but presenting a severe contrast to their brethren returning from the States.' A landowner, on being asked in 1884 why the *contadini* emigrated, replied: 'They see their countrymen returning well dressed, with an overcoat, a cigar in the mouth, and therefore they all wish to go away.'

An Italian shoeshine boy in New York, *c.* 1910. Shoeshine boys, imported from Italy by *padroni* or labour bosses, frequently worked twelve hours a day for little more than their keep.

The Italian Exodus

Newly-arrived immigrants, unable to speak any English, relied upon the services of the *padrone*, an Italian labour boss. The *padrone* system, previously unknown in the United States, passed through several phases. In Italy *padroni* were originally associated with the recruitment and exploitation of children. In the late 1870s they collected them from the hillsides of Italy and carried them to America for employment as bootblacks, wandering musicians and street acrobats. The practice was stamped out about 1880 when public outcry forced the authorities to introduce stricter controls. Next, *padroni* recruited unskilled labourers on contract, usually paying their fares. When that practice too was prohibited the system assumed its final form: it functioned as a special kind of employment agency. Though he no longer recruited or imported labour the *padrone* supplied immigrants in gangs to work in mines, on the railroads and in agriculture. He advanced the money to transport immigrants to the places where they were needed, acted as their interpreter and provided them with food and lodging. The system gave *padroni* ample opportunity to cheat and exploit their gullible and ignorant countrymen. They misled labourers about the nature of the work they were to do, deducted large commissions from their wages and charged exorbitant prices for food and accommodation. Those they deceived found it impossible to obtain redress. Indeed they seldom thought of obtaining it. On one occasion in the States, when a travelling inspector sent by the Italian government informed a group of southern Italians that they were being cheated, they accepted the news resignedly. 'Signorino,' they said, 'we are ignorant and do not know English. Our boss brought us here, knows where to find work, makes contracts with the companies. What should we do without him?' Fortunately, however, the system only flourished during the early stages of Italian immigration. As they learned to make their own way in America, immigrants dispensed with the *padrone*'s services; the system had had its day by 1900, though it survived for some time longer among such newcomers as the Greeks and the Syrians.

In its earliest phases Italian emigration was predominantly male. That reflected the fact that many *contadini* went to the United States to earn rather than to settle. They shared the attitude of a group of Italian labourers building the Simplon Tunnel in Switzerland. Asked by the historian Pasquale Villari whether they loved their native land they replied: 'For us Italy is whoever gives us our bread.' But as time passed they found, as all immigrants did, that the ties that bound them to their new lives grew stronger and the desire to return diminished. Even those who went back sometimes found it difficult to fit in, having become accustomed to American wages and standards. As late as 1910 two-thirds of all Italian emigrants were men, though that was less than ten years before. The growing proportion of women and children demonstrated that the Italian movement was gradually becoming a genuine emigration.

To an extraordinary degree Italian immigrants duplicated the experience of the Irish half a century earlier. They settled in the same parts of the United

States, dominated the same unskilled occupations, occupied the same over-crowded slums. The Italians too were fated to become a despised minority.

As immigration increased and the predominance of southern Italians became greater its concentration in the industrial north-east became more marked. By 1910 more than four-fifths of the Italian population lived north of the Ohio and east of the Mississippi. New York State alone held nearly half a million and Pennsylvania, New Jersey and Massachusetts a further 400,000. An extremely high proportion was to be found in the cities, especially the larger ones. New York, with 340,000, was in a class of its own but there were large numbers in places like Philadelphia, Chicago, Boston and Newark.

Italians could be found in a variety of industrial employments. In Massachu-setts they worked in the shoe factories at Brockton and in the Lawrence woollen mills. In New Jersey they were silk dyers, in Pennsylvania and Illinois miners. From 1890 Italians of both sexes invaded what had hitherto been a Jewish pre-serve, the garment industry of New York and Philadelphia. Within a decade Italians were rivalling the Jews in this branch of manufacture; Italian women, indeed, were soon to form the bulk of New York's home-finishers.

Nevertheless, the great mass of Italian workers were still pick-and-shovel labourers, thousands being scattered throughout the country in railroad con-struction camps. As early as 1893 one observer remarked that 'the Irish have ceased building railroads. . . . The Italians have taken their place.' Public works

Italian rag-pickers in New York.

Italian labourers in a New York lodging house; a bed there cost fifty cents a night.

afforded an equally striking example of ethnic displacement. In all the great cities Italians came to hold an undisputed monopoly of excavation, surfacing and grading streets, laying gas and water pipes, digging sewers, building bridges, harbour works and subways. Italian labour helped rebuild Galveston after the hurricane of 1900, and played the same role in San Francisco after the earthquake and fire of 1906. Even on the New York waterfront Irish supremacy met a growing Italian challenge, for although the Italians were less physically strong than the Irish, they would work for lower wages.

Living conditions in the construction camps were abominable. Labourers slept and ate in dilapidated, windowless railroad cars or in shanty bunk-houses, roughly constructed of corrugated iron. Domenick Ciolli, an Italian-born student who spent some time as a railroad labourer in 1916, was appalled at accommodation which must have been reminiscent of the worst kind of steerage. The bunk-house was filthy, the atmosphere foul. Labourers slept on boards with bed-bugs and cockroaches as their companions; their only hot meal was supper which they cooked themselves in rusty tin boxes. Yet these men worked ten hours a day, seven days a week in all weathers.

200

In each city where Italians congregated there was a district identified as 'Little Italy'. Italian loyalties were narrowly circumscribed; they could have been summed up in the word *campanilismo*, a sense of fellow-feeling that encompassed only those within range of the village bell-tower. Hence in American cities immigrants settled according to origin in separate streets or blocks. In New York about 1900, Neapolitans and Calabrians congregated around Mulberry Bend; Genoese grouped themselves along nearby Baxter Street; Sicilians colonized part of Elizabeth Street; Piedmontese and Ligurians predominated west of Broadway in the Eighth and Fifteenth Wards; and a tiny outpost of Italian-speaking Tyrolese was located on Sixty-ninth Street, near the Hudson River.

Italian neighbourhoods were uniformly decayed and congested; more so, indeed, than those inhabited by any other group of immigrants. In New York, for example, the most notorious slums lay around Mulberry Bend, where the city's worst examples of overcrowding and its highest death rates were found. In 1890 the Danish-born journalist, Jacob A. Riis, described the district in his book, *How The Other Half Lives*:

There is but one 'Bend' in the world and it is enough. . . . Around it cluster the bulk of the tenements that are stamped as altogether bad, even by the optimists of the Health Department. Incessant raids cannot keep down the crowds that make them their home. In the scores of back alleys, stable lanes and hidden byways, of which the rent collector alone can keep track, they share such shelter as the ramshackle structures afford with every kind of abomination rifled from the dumps and ashbarrels of the city. . . . Corruption could not have chosen ground for its stand with better promise of success. The whole district is a maze of narrow, often unsuspected

An Italian organ grinder, New York, *c.* 1910.

Italian immigrants in the New York tenements
The Italian quarter of New York, *c.* 1920. Because of their
poverty Italians sought out the cheapest – and consequently
the worst – tenements.

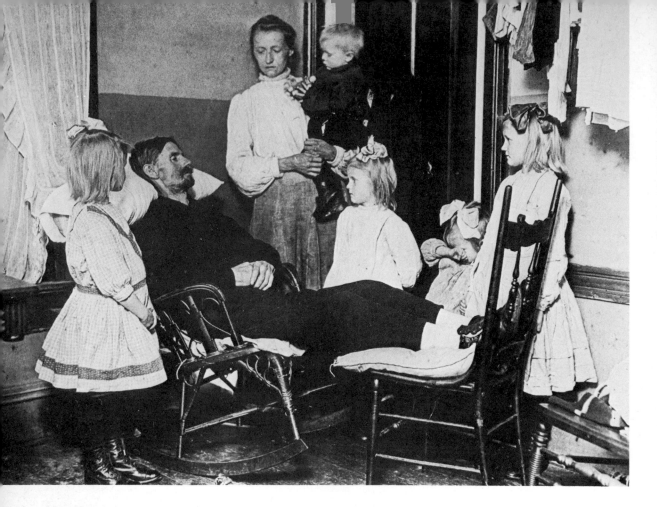

A family gathers anxiously
at the bedside of
a tubercular father.
Overcrowding, poor diet
and back-breaking toil
combined to make Italians
easy prey to tuberculosis.

passageways – necessarily, for there is scarce a lot that has not two, three or four tenements upon it, swarming with unwholesome crowds.

At the Elizabeth Street police station he was told that a few days earlier a dead goat had been reported lying in Pell Street. By the time the offal-cart came to take it away, 'an Italian had carried it off in his sack to a wake or feast of some sort in one of the back alleys.' The insanitary condition of the district was reflected in its heavy infant mortality rate. Riis learned that in one tenement, 'No. 59½, next to Bandit's Roost', there had been fourteen deaths in 1882, eleven of them children. In 1888, when that same tenement housed a total of thirty-nine people, five children died out of nine in one year.

Slum conditions were responsible too for the high rate of tuberculosis among newcomers. Native-born Americans believed that immigrants brought the disease with them. In fact it was far less common in Italy and in some regions it was said to have been unknown until *Americani* brought it back with them. The main cause of tuberculosis was the abrupt passage from an open air life to the close confinement of an American slum. Dr Antonio Stella, a New York physician, commented in 1904:

Six months of life in the tenements are sufficent to turn the sturdy youth from Calabria, the brawny fisherman of Sicily, the robust women from Abruzzi and Basilicata, into the pale, flabby, undersized creatures we see dragging along the streets of New York and Chicago, such a painful contrast to the native population. Six months more of the gradual deterioration, and the soil for the bacillus tuberculosis is amply prepared.

Sweatshop conditions, Dr Stella added, greatly increased the danger of contracting the disease. Italian women, already weakened by excessive child-bearing, used up their remaining energy by working long hours in factories or as home-finishers. That was why, he explained, there was a higher death rate from tuberculosis among Italian women than among their menfolk.

Changes of diet did little to help Italian immigrants' waning health; milk, cheese and eggs which had cost nothing but labour in Italy, were often beyond the means of immigrants in America while vegetables cost too much to supply the quantities they had been accustomed to. Hence Italians tended to live largely on starches which, according to a 1893 Chicago report, was why there was so much rickets among Italian children. The continuance of the practice of giving infants an adult diet before they were out of swaddling clothes was

An Italian family works at home making artificial flowers for which they were paid four to eight cents a gross. The youngest child is under five.

205

especially damaging. An Italian mother who brought her sick baby to a clinic insisted that she had only given the child what she and her husband had had themselves. But questioning revealed that the family diet of soup and butter-milk in Italy had been replaced by beer and coffee.

Like the Irish, and for the same reasons, few Italians settled on the land. Of those who had been in farming, only about seven per cent took up agricultural work in the United States. However, Italians did find seasonal work on farms since no capital was required; this gave alternative – and healthier – employment to those who lived most of the year in cities. Simple operations like fruit-picking, weeding and hoeing vegetables could be performed by women and children as well as by men. Thus in summer, when the schools were closed, Italian families from Philadelphia and Baltimore would take to the fields for months at a time. They would follow the berry crops northward, beginning with strawberries in Delaware in May and ending with cranberries in Massachusetts in September. In December, when construction work was at a standstill, Italians would move southwards to Louisiana for *la zuccarata*, the sugar harvest.

Italians who settled on the land generally chose branches of agriculture where lack of capital was less of a handicap and where their gregarious instincts could be satisfied. They took up market gardening along the Atlantic coast, cotton- and fruit-growing in the South, and vine-growing in California. Large groups of market-gardeners settled in the states of New York and New Jersey. Most of these settlements were made on poor land; hundreds bought abandoned or semi-abandoned farms in the New Jersey pine barrens, for example, and by sheer hard work brought the land back into production. At such places Italian growers united to buy fertilizers and to found co-operative marketing associations.

But it was in California that Italians made their greatest mark in agriculture. From an early date they were prominent in a variety of agricultural enterprises. Considerable numbers of Ticinese – that is, Italian-speaking Swiss – became dairy farmers along California's coastline, especially around San Luis Obispo. Thousands of northern Italians, especially Ligurians, went into market-gardening and fruit-growing, while California's vast wine industry was largely of Italian origin. It received a boost in 1881 when Andrea Sbarbaro, a Genoese banker who had been in California since gold-rush days, founded the Italian-Swiss Agricultural Colony at Asti in the Sonoma Valley. After early setbacks these vineyards prospered, eventually coming to dominate the American wine market. One of the most celebrated vintners was Louis M. Martini, who arrived in San Francisco from Pietra Ligura in 1900 at the age of thirteen to join his father. After some years in the family fish business he went back to Italy to study the science of wine-making at the celebrated enological and vini-cultural school at Alba. The Prohibition interlude between 1920 and 1933 was a severe blow to his career but today the Cabernet Sauvignon and Pinot Noir produced by the Martini vineyards are considered to be among California's finest wines.

While their everyday adjustments closely paralleled those of their Irish predecessors, the same can hardly be said of their religious life. Between 1820 and 1920 the volume of immigration from Italy was greater than that from any Catholic country save Ireland. It seemed to bring to the Catholic Church a massive and welcome reinforcement. Yet from the 1880s onwards American Catholics were gravely concerned at what became known as the 'Italian problem'. It was commonly alleged that millions of Italians and their children were falling away from the church in America and were either relapsing into religious indifference or falling victim to Protestant proselytizers. The charge that they lacked religious conviction came most frequently from the Irish bishops and

Italians picking and packing grapes at Guasti, California.

Italian fishermen mending their nets on the wharf at the foot of Union Street, San Francisco. Most of San Francisco's Italian fishermen were Neapolitans and Sicilians. Boats and gear were frequently owned in common and all shared in the profits of the catch.

clergy who dominated the Catholic Church in the United States. A typical indictment was in a letter in the Jesuit weekly *America* in 1914; it was commenting on an article by Father Joseph Sorrentino on religious conditions in Italy:

The Italians who come to this country are to a large extent uninstructed in the knowledge of the very elements of their Faith. Thousands upon thousands of boys and girls beyond the age of sixteen know nothing of their prayers, nothing of their catechism and have never been instructed for or made their First Communion or Confession. The Italian, as a rule, will work on Sunday ... and outside of a display at baptisms, marriages and funerals, a large proportion of them have little attachment to the Church, its services or its sacraments. Father Sorrentino says that at home the bulk of the Italian people are good, practising Catholics.... In that case their religion must be dropped root and branch in the Bay of Naples, for 99 per cent of them stay away from Mass when they come to this country.... In fact the Italians ... come ... not infrequently with a hatred of the Church and the priesthood in their hearts.

Such criticisms betray an ignorance of the religious background of Italian immigrants. The *contadini* were in fact profoundly religious but their religion had little in common with American Catholicism. Nominally Catholic, theirs was a folk religion in which pagan rituals and beliefs were fused with Christian doctrines and sacraments. Southern Italians believed themselves to be surrounded by a host of supernatural beings with powers of good or evil who had to be propitiated. This involved both a recourse to sorcery and magic and the worship of madonnas and saints who were associated, as ancient deities had been, with particular localities. Thus the *contadini* would seek to offset the power of the evil eye (*mal'occhio*) by means of amulets, potions and magical rites, at the same time invoking the aid of a particular 'madonna' known for her power to cure headaches or produce a good harvest.

Italian Catholicism did not, as in the case of the Irish or the Poles, define a national identity; on the contrary Italian nationalism was strongly opposed by the Catholic clergy. The fact was that Catholicism retained its hold on the *contadini* by providing a vehicle for popular religious sentiments. The most important Church festivals were the holidays dedicated to saints, especially the local patron saint. An elaborate mass was followed by a procession in which a gorgeously attired statue of the saint was borne through the streets. Such *feste* were only in part religious: they were also secular holidays characterized by dancing and other forms of revelry that were anything but solemn or reverent.

Small wonder, then, that the *contadini* found the church in America a cold and puritanical institution, irrelevant to their needs. They resented Irish domination and the efforts of Irish priests to Americanize them. Their demands for clergy of their own nationality were not easily met for Italian priests did not generally accompany their flocks across the Atlantic. Controversy within the Catholic Church over the 'Italian problem' encouraged Protestant proselytizers to focus their attention on Italian neighbourhoods. But the results of their labours were meagre: only about 25,000 Italians could be persuaded to join the Methodists, Baptists and Presbyterians.

However, in time the *contadini* set up their own parishes and built churches like those in Italy. Meanwhile, though casual in attendance at mass they were zealous in observing church holidays and saints' days. An immigrant *festa* followed traditional patterns and generally bore a local or provincial character. The great Neapolitan *festa* honoured the martyred San Gennaro; Sicilians from Palermo feted Santa Rossilia; those from Catania Sant' Agata. On such occasions Italian neighbourhoods such as New York's East Harlem were transformed. Altars were erected on the sidewalks, the streets were decorated with flags and illuminated arches and dense crowds led by a brass band followed the image of the saint as it was paraded through the streets. Dollar bills showered down from tenement windows to be pinned to the saint's robes. As in the old country, the bands played tunes from Verdi and Rossini, pizza-sellers did a roaring trade and the day ended with dancing and a display of fireworks.

If Italian immigrants were cool toward the church they were violently antagonistic toward the American public school. In education as in religion an 'Italian problem' emerged, which left the native-born baffled. As early as 1883 the teacher in charge of the West Side Italian school in New York outlined the problem to the Children's Aid Society.

One very perplexing feature of our work among these poor Italians is the avarice of the parents. Children of tender age are compelled to work, often at night as well as during the day, thus preventing them from attending school, and were it not for

the aid of the truant agent, who visits the parents and threatens them with the law (of which Italians as a rule, are in great dread) a great proportion of the children who are now forced into school would be growing up in total ignorance. When the parents are not avaricious, they are too often perfectly unconcerned as to a child's education. When spoken to on the subject they reply, with the characteristic shrug of the shoulders: 'I cannot read or write, and I earn my own money just as easy; why should my children know any more than I do? I don't want them to go to school!'

In *contadini* society the basic social and economic unit had been the family; the need to preserve it had guided every endeavour. In such a society there was no place for the notion of parental responsibility; children were seen as sources of material benefit, prized for the contribution they could make to the family economy. Italians felt there was no need for more than a smattering of education since the basic arts and skills could be learned at home. So could the moral code. These notions, carried to America, ensured the immigrant's antagonism to the public school. In his eyes education beyond a certain age was not only unnecessary but damaging, and doubly so: in the first place it meant the loss of the children as economic assets for years after they had become capable of earning; in the second it proved a threat to the family since children might pick up at school ideas hostile to those of their parents. The New York school attendance law of 1903, which raised the school-leaving age from four-teen to sixteen, was particularly unpopular. One Italian declared it had 'ruined all our hopes of a decent living, kept us poor and destroyed the sanctity of the home.' At bottom it was not avarice that led Italian families to complain bitterly that 'America took our children'. It was the fear that education was the enemy of *la famiglia*.

Such apprehensions were all too often well-founded. The school came to rival the parents as a source of authority, inculcating a different and more indivi-dualistic set of values. It also enabled the child to speak English fluently which gave him a practical superiority over them, making it impossible to hold him to traditional ideas of subordination and propriety. Parental control was in any case difficult to maintain because traditional social patterns did not have the legal sanctions in America that had sustained them in Europe. In many cases things went beyond mere indiscipline. In their anxiety to be accepted as Ameri-cans by their school-mates the children of the *contadini* often rejected both their old world heritage and their parents who symbolized it. Immigrant parents found that their values were belittled by their offspring, their loyalties scorned, their speech and appearance made a matter for ridicule. The pressures which led the second generation into such attitudes and the painful tensions which resulted were poignantly described in a celebrated short story, *The Odys-sey of a Wop*, by the Italian-American novelist John Fante. It tells of the cruel dilemma in which Italian immigrant children were placed when forced to choose between the two opposing sets of values; of the self-hatred and shame produced by denial of one's origins.

By 1900 or so the Italian barber was a familiar figure in every American city. In some places barbering virtually became an Italian monopoly. Members of the Squadrito family shown here emigrated from the Sicilian village of Gualtieri between 1898 and 1904, and in time came to own a chain of barber shops in Stonington, Connecticut. Such photographs were often enclosed in letters home and, suggestive as they are of American prosperity, proved a powerful stimulus to emigration.

The Italian Exodus

I am nervous when I bring friends to my house: the place looks so Italian. Here hangs a picture of Victor Emmanuel, and over there is one of the cathedral of Milan, and next to it one of St Peter's, and on the buffet stands a wine-pitcher of medieval design; it's forever brimming, forever red and brilliant with wine. These things are heirlooms belonging to my father, and no matter who may come to our house, he likes to stand under them and brag.

So I begin to shout at him. I tell him to cut out being a Wop and be an American once in a while. Immediately he gets his razor-strop and whales hell out of me, clouting me from room to room and finally out the back door. I go to the woodshed and pull down my pants and stretch my neck to examine the blue slices across my rump. A Wop! that's what my father is! Nowhere is there an American father who beats his son this way. Well, he's not going to get away with it; some day I'll get even with him.

I begin to think that my grandmother is hopelessly a Wop. She's a small, stocky peasant who walks with her wrists criss-crossed across her belly, a simple old lady, fond of boys. She comes into the room and tries to talk to my friends. She speaks English with a bad accent, her vowels rolling out like hoops. When, in her simple way, she confronts a friend of mine and says, her old eyes smiling, 'You lika go the Seester scola?' my heart roars. *Mannaggia*! I'm disgraced; now they all know that I'm an Italian.

My grandmother has taught me to speak her native tongue. By seven I know it pretty well, and I always address her in it. But when friends are with me, when I am twelve and thirteen, I pretend to ignorance of what she says, and smirk stiffly; my friends daren't know that I can speak any language but English. Sometimes this infuriates her. She bristles, the loose skin at her throat knits hard, and she blasphemes with a mighty blasphemy.

Conflict between generations was the common experience of immigrant families generally. Yet it was exaggerated among the *contadini*, who attached special importance to the primary family group. The same may have been true of conjugal ties. The fluidity of American society, the existence of divorce, the greater equality between the sexes, the absence of the social and religious restraints that had existed in Europe – these were among the reasons why marriage partners were more readily cast off in America. At the same time the male character of Italian emigration placed greater strains upon marriages than among groups emigrating as families. Protracted separations often led to the involvement by one or both partners in irregular sexual liaisons. The reports of Italian consuls in the United States to the government at Rome cited numerous cases of abandoned spouses and matrimonial tangles:

Nicola Del P., from Taranta Peligna, a resident of Rock Springs, Wyo., killed himself on 28 June 1910 on discovering that his wife, who had deserted him, was living at Louisville, Ky., with another Italian, Augusto P. di Mafalda from Campobasso, who had a wife in Italy and who was living in Louisville under the name of Camillo di D.

Family disorganization had serious consequences. In the great cities problems of crime and juvenile delinquency were closely associated with the children of immigrants. Those engaged in immigrant welfare work were agreed that the waywardness of immigrant children was traceable, not to an inherited lawlessness, but to the circumstances of immigrant life, and especially to broken homes and the erosion of parental authority.

The relationship between immigration and crime has excited a good deal of controversy in America. And while immigrants generally were associated in the popular mind with lawlessness, a special stigma of criminality came to be attached to Italians. It was widely believed by Americans that a large proportion of Italian immigrants were criminals, that newcomers from southern Italy and Sicily in particular possessed an innate leaning towards personal violence. Such impressions originated from the frequent murders – especially stabbings and bombings – in Italian neighbourhoods. Yet the crime statistics did not bear out these impressions. A Massachusetts enquiry in 1912 revealed that the Italian-born, who comprised eight per cent of the population of the state, made up only 4.2 per cent of those confined in penal institutions. Children of Italian origin may have contributed disproportionately to crime, yet the immigrants themselves did not. But to be Italian was to be regarded as a dangerous desperado, as a second-generation immigrant, Professor Francis Ianni, has shown:

On one occasion my father had bought a candy bar and was clutching it in his pocket. He was stopped by the police, and since he couldn't speak English and they couldn't speak Italian they assumed it was a gun or a knife of some sort because he was Italian, and they arrested him because he had a candy bar and couldn't explain where he got it.

However, as reports multiplied of blackmail and violent crime in America's Little Italys, the image was conjured up of a mysterious criminal organization, usually known as the Mafia or the Black Hand. It was thought of as a vast international conspiracy, controlled from Sicily and extending to every sizable American city with an Italian community. This notion, originating in the 1890s, was firmly established by the time of the First World War. That the older stereotype took on gangster overtones during the 1920s and 1930s was due to the fact that many of America's best-known gangsters, such as Big Jim Colosimo, Johnny Torrio, Al Capone and Lucky Luciano had Italian names. In the past twenty years the Mafia concept has been revived. In the 1950s it was dramatized by the Kefauver investigation into organized crime. Senator Kefauver paraded Italian-American gangsters in front of the television cameras and alleged that the Mafia was the 'shadowy international organization that lurks behind much of America's organized criminal activity'. A decade later another Senate subcommittee heard melodramatic stories from a convicted murderer named Joseph Valachi concerning the structure and operations of the organization he referred to as *Cosa Nostra*. More recently the immense success of books and films such as *The Godfather* have helped disseminate the Mafia stereotype still more widely.

The Italian Exodus

Such popular conceptions are, however, far removed from reality. Like all myths that of the Mafia has some foundation in fact. A secret criminal society of that name undoubtedly existed in the United States. Moreover the techniques of extortion and blackmail it employed were patterned upon those of the Sicilian Mafia. But most of the Mafia stereotype is based on misconception or hearsay. There is no proof that the highly organized international conspiracy in which many people believed has ever existed. Between the Sicilian Mafia and American criminals of Sicilian descent there is certainly a network of informal relationships, but the organization whose headquarters is in Palermo has never controlled the American underworld. As Luigi Barzini has pointed out, its writ did not even run in Catania, a few miles away, still less in Chicago. When Lucky Luciano, the reputed mastermind of the American narcotics ring, was deported to Sicily he was allegedly welcomed by the local Mafia not as a blood brother but as a chicken to be plucked; the story is that they swindled him out of fifteen million lire.

Even within the United States the Mafia has not been the tightly-knit crime syndicate of popular imagination; all that has ever been proved is the existence of a small group of criminals behaving in similar ways but operating independently. The Black Hand, for example, was not a centralized, cohesive organization. Nor was it responsible for more than a fraction of the violent crimes committed by Italians. In fact Black Hand crime flourished only when local conditions favoured it. It was unknown in Boston and Milwaukee, for example. In Chicago a combination of a frontier mentality, official corruption, and police venality produced a situation conducive to the spread of crime. That was why Chicago was a magnet for such a large number of Italian-born criminals.

Yet the most notorious of Chicago's Italian-American gangsters in the 1920s were the product of American rather than Italian conditions. Moreover, few of them were of Sicilian birth or descent. Al Capone was born in Brooklyn of Neapolitan parents; James Colosimo was born in Calabria but arrived in Chicago as a boy; Johnny Torrio, born in the province of Naples, was taken to the United States as a child of two by his parents and grew up in Brooklyn. Gangsters such as these had very little in common with the Sicilian *onorata società*, and the same can be said of more recent Italian-American Mafia leaders. They made fortunes out of activities which old world *mafiosi* would have considered unworthy: prostitution, gambling and drugs. There was another difference too. In Sicily the Mafia had employed violence, ostensibly at least, as a means of providing justice for the oppressed. In the United States, on the other hand, the Mafia has never pretended to be anything but an association of self-seeking criminals. Its members would not have shown any of the paternal concern for the weak that is characteristic of Don Corleone, the fictional American Mafia leader depicted in Mario Puzo's best-seller *The Godfather*.

Fear of the Mafia, together with the reputation Italians had acquired as bloodthirsty criminals, accounted for the frenzied character of the anti-Italian

OPPOSITE The Italian-language newspapers shown here represented only a fraction of the total. Such newspapers were widely read in immigrant communities. They reflected and expressed in a familiar tongue the attitudes and aspirations of their readers, informed them about group activities and introduced them to American ways.

LA FOLLIA DI NEW YORK.

LA TROMBA

LA SENTINELLA
GAZZETTA DEI LAVORATORI ITALIANI

LA GAZZETTA
DEL MASSACHUSETTS

L'INTERNAZIONALE
THE INTERNAZIONAL

La Gazzetta Comm
E POLITICA

L'ITALIA
CORRIERE D'ITALIA

The most influential Italian Newspaper in the State of R. I.

CORRIERE DI ROCHESTER

La LIBERTÀ,
UNIONE, BENEVOLENZA E CONCORDIA.
GIORNALE SETTIMANALE

La Luce

la Montagna

L'ECO DEL RHODE ISLAND

IL VESUVIO
THE MOST INFLUENTIAL PAPER

L'UNIONE

Il Corriere del Connecticut

LA GAZZETTA DEL BANCHIERE
E REPORTER D'EMIGRAZIONE

il Messaggero

IL MESSAGGERO

L'AVVENIRE
GAZZETTA DELLA COLONIA ITALIANA

La Gazzetta Medica

LA FRUSTA

Le Unione
RAGIONE NUOVA
PERIODICO MENSILE SOCIALISTA

La Questione Sociale

LA TRIBUNA ITALIANA

Il Proletario

LA SENTINELLA
GIORNALE SOCIALISTA

CRONACA SOVVERSIVA

SECOLO NUOVO

Tempi

I Nostri

L'ITALIANO IN AMERICA

LA NUOVA NAPOLI

LA LUCE.

LA SCINTILLA ELETTRICA

LA FAMIGLIA

RIVISTA COMMERCIALE

SECOLO DI FABRICA

L'INDIPENDENTE

BOLLETTINO COMMERCIALE

L'ORA

Rassegna Commerciale

LA RAGIONE
IL CORRIERE ITALIANO.

Il Popolo
ITALIAN INDEPENDENT NEWSPAPER

sentiment that developed in the 1890s. Italians now joined Negroes as the principal victims of American popular violence. Time and again native-born mobs administered rough justice to Italians charged with crime. In March 1895 at a time of labour unrest in the southern Colorado coalfields, a group of miners lynched six Italian labourers accused of the murder of a saloon keeper. A year later, in the small Louisiana town of Hahnville, a mob dragged six Italians from gaol and hanged them. The best-known incident occurred at New Orleans in 1890. On 20 October, the New Orleans superintendent of police, David O. Hennessey, who had been waging war upon Italian gangs, was ambushed and shot. Before dying Hennessey was said to have murmured, 'The Dagoes did it'. Orders went out to the police to comb Italian neighbourhoods; they rounded up and arrested hundreds of Sicilians believed to have associations with the Mafia. But when nine of the suspects were put on trial the jury refused to convict. Public opinion was outraged and there were allegations of bribery and of intimidation of witnesses by the Mafia. With newspapers calling for action to remedy 'the failure of justice', a mob forced its way into the parish prison and lynched eleven Italian prisoners.

The New Orleans incident had international repercussions. The Italian government demanded the punishment of the lynch mob and financial compensation for the families of the victims. When the United States returned an unsympathetic answer there was talk of war, but early in 1892 Italy accepted an American offer of an indemnity. No steps were taken, however, to punish the murderers. Nor did the authorities take effective action on the many other occasions when Italians charged with murder were summarily executed by vigilante bodies. Mob violence against Italians continued well into the twentieth century, most of it occurring in the rural South and West. One of the worst incidents took place in August 1920 in the mining town of West Frankfort, Illinois. After a series of bank robberies, followed by the kidnapping and murder of two boys, suspicion fell on the Black Hand. Mobs swarmed into the Italian quarter, attacking anyone in sight and setting fire to homes. The rioting went on for three days and was quelled only when 500 state troopers were sent to the town.

Even in the comparatively peaceful later decades of this century the Italian-American writer, Angelo Pellegrini, bitterly recalls his youthful feelings about his fellow Americans:

Many of them had come maybe a generation before us, maybe they were second generation immigrants – Norwegians, Irish and Germans – and yet they soon made us understand that the attitude of the 'native American', as we called them, towards us was roughly what the attitude of the American has been toward Negroes. We young men were forbidden to associate with American girls. And if one of us ventured to go out with one she would have to be of a poor-white-trash derivation. Otherwise she wouldn't be going with him; and being such a girl, she would surely have a brutal brother to clobber the hell out of the wop who dared!

The popular tendency to see Italians as a menace to the stability of American society was intensified by the belief that they were steeped in revolutionary radicalism. It is certainly true that before the First World War men of Italian origin were among the most prominent activists in American left-wing movements, especially anarchism and syndicalism. The silk-weaving city of Paterson, New Jersey, where Luigi Galleani founded one of the first American anarchist papers, was a leading centre of anarchism; Gaetano Bresci, the anarchist who assassinated King Umberto I of Italy at Monza in 1900, also came from there; Enrico Malatesta, the famous Italian anarchist, was shot at in Paterson during a tour of the United States – proof that the city contained more than one kind of Italian-American radical. The leadership of the Industrial Workers of the World, the revolutionary syndicalist trade union popularly known as the 'Wobblies', was also in part Italian. It included such figures as Giuseppe Ettor and Arturo Giovannitti, who organized the violent strike of textile workers at Lawrence in 1912. Giovannitti, an Italian-born poet, was the editor of the New York labour paper *Il Proletario*, to which Mussolini, during his Socialist phase, had contributed fiery articles. In the course of the Lawrence strike Ettor and Giovannitti were arrested and charged with having been responsible for the death of a striker who was killed during a clash between the police and pickets. Among those who campaigned to free them was the anarchist, Carlo Tresca, who had emigrated to the United States from Italy in 1904. By the time Tresca was mysteriously assassinated in a New York street in 1943 he had become the leading folk hero of the Italian-American Left.

The Italian anarchists, Nicola Sacco (left) and Bartolomeo Vanzetti (right), in prison awaiting execution for allegedly murdering a bank paymaster in Massachusetts in 1922.

Italians, along with the Jews, bore the brunt of the anti-foreign hysteria that characterized the Red Scare of 1919. Intolerance also marked the *cause célèbre* of the 1920s, the Sacco-Vanzetti case. The paymaster and his guard at a shoe factory in South Braintree, Massachusetts, were murdered on 15 April 1920. The murderers escaped by car, taking with them $15,000 in cash. Three weeks later the police arrested two Italian immigrants, on suspicion of having committed the crime. They were Nicola Sacco, a shoe factory worker, and Bartolomeo Vanzetti, a fish peddler. Both were anarchists, active in radical movements and both had been draft dodgers in the First World War. The evidence against them was inconclusive, but they were convicted and sentenced to death. Both men pleaded their innocence and the more articulate Vanzetti told the court that he believed he was being punished, not for the crime, but for his origins and his radicalism. World-wide public protest was inspired by the belief that the convicted men had been victims of prejudice. But the commission set up after years of argument to hear the case, concluded that they had been rightly convicted and they were electrocuted on 23 August 1927. Their death provoked anti-American demonstrations throughout the world.

Until the rise of Mussolini, Italians had not been particularly concerned with what was going on in Italy. While they had become less village-minded, their loyalties were still provincial, and they thought of themselves not as Italians but as Sicilians, Neapolitans or Piedmontese. But the victory of Mussolini's Fascism reverberated in every Italian-American community, blurring regional loyalties and generating a bellicose Italian-American nationalism. Soon after the march on Rome in 1922 Italian-Americans had become enthusiastically devoted to the Duce, their press being overwhelmingly pro-Fascist. Radicals like Carlo Tresca and political exiles like Gaetano Salvemini loathed Mussolini and waged an incessant campaign against him. But they cut no ice with the immigrant masses.

The Fascist sympathies of Italian-Americans were in part the result of Mussolini's attempts to woo them. He was anxious to counter anti-Fascist agitation in the United States and even believed that many of the four million Italians living in America might return to fight for Italy if war broke out. Hence propaganda emanating from Rome attempted to indoctrinate Italian-Americans with Fascist ideas and to encourage them to remain Italian in thought and feeling. But propaganda was less influential than the social pressures generated in the United States. Italian-American Fascism was essentially an attempt by an unpopular alien minority to derive from across the Atlantic the security and the status they were denied in America. Mussolini came to power when the morale of Italian-Americans was at its lowest. The Sacco-Vanzetti case had revealed to them the full extent of the hostility they faced; it had left them feeling inferior and rejected, while the immigration restriction law of 1924, which virtually halted Italian immigration, seemed to brand them as undesirable elements.

In these circumstances Mussolini, by making Italy respected abroad, conferred respectability upon Italians everywhere. To quote Angelo Pellegrini: 'Mussolini had made America understand that Italy had had a great civilization ... and that he was going to return the glory of Rome to Italy, re-establish the Roman Empire, so every Italian stuck out his chest, saying: "That's my boy, you know, that's my boy".' Italian-Americans took enormous pride in Fascist achievements, especially those which were widely publicized in the United States: Marshal Balbo's mass formation flight from Rome to Chicago in May 1933, for instance, and the capture of the Atlantic Blue Riband by the Italian liner *Rex* the following August. Devotion to Fascist Italy reached its peak with the Ethiopian War of 1935–6. Huge crowds turned out to express their support; men contributed money to the Italian war effort, many women answered Mussolini's appeal to send their wedding rings. A few hundred Italian-Americans left to fight in the Italian Army, despite warnings that they would lose their American citizenship if they took the Fascist oath. In 1936 Italian-American organizations staged an effective campaign against changes in the Neutrality Act which would have hampered Italian military operations. The campaign produced a remarkable display of political solidarity. Even Fiorello La Guardia, the Italian-American mayor of New York, who was privately anti-Fascist, found it expedient to support it.

For more than a decade after the march on Rome Mussolini enjoyed a remarkable vogue in the United States. Conservative businessmen praised him as a bulwark against Communism; some of the most prominent people in America – they included William Randolph Hearst, Cardinal O'Connell, Will Rogers and Ezra Pound – were his warm admirers. So long as that situation continued Italian-Americans felt free to express Fascist sympathies untroubled by the problem of reconciling divergent loyalties. But as American opinion turned against Mussolini and relations between the United States and Italy deteriorated, Italian-Americans were obliged to reconsider their attitudes. The need to do so became more urgent with the formation of the Rome-Berlin Axis and the vicious anti-American campaign in the Italian press in 1938.

From that point on Italian-American views of Mussolini became increasingly ambivalent. As late as June 1940 he was still sufficiently admired for Roosevelt's 'stab-in-the-back' speech, criticizing Italy's entry into the war, to be angrily resented in Italian-American neighbourhoods. But thereafter it became increasingly evident that support for Fascism was inconsistent with American patriotism. Once the issue came to be thus defined there was no doubt that Italian-Americans would discover that they were more American than Italian and that their ultimate loyalty could only be to the United States. It could be argued that the United States, having treated Italian immigrants with singular disdain, had not much deserved that loyalty. But she was given it just the same.

An Italian *festa* in the North End of Boston, 1959.

219

"What Happened To The One We Used To Have?"

10 THE NARROW GATE

IN THE AFTERMATH of the First World War the United States made a sharp break with the past. Congress passed restrictive laws designed not only to reduce drastically the volume of immigration but to discriminate against particular nationalities. Of course immigration had never been wholly free from restriction. Undesirables had long been barred and, after 1882, as we have seen, the list of excluded classes was steadily extended. Thus thousands of would-be immigrants got no further than Ellis Island. But before 1914 America had not tried to limit immigration quantitatively. Restrictions had been designed mainly as police and health measures and had not seriously checked the inflow. Thus, despite the grim reputation of Ellis Island, it had been poss-ible to claim that the asylum tradition, which stretched back to the earliest days of the republic, was still being observed. In the early 1920s however, that tradition was directly repudiated.

America was not alone; after the war the barriers were going up all over the world. By 1930 countries such as Canada, Argentina and Australia had abandoned the liberal immigration policies of the nineteenth century. To an extent previously unknown human beings would now be confined within national boundaries. In future those who wished to emigrate would have to acquire passports, visas and work permits.

Nevertheless the decision grew out of American conditions. America was now a mature industrial nation. Indeed, by 1890, when the superintendent of the census announced the disappearance of the frontier, the settlement of the continent could be said to be complete. The empty West, which Jefferson had believed would suffice to meet the needs of settlers 'unto the hundredth genera-tion', was now an historical curiosity – no longer was it possible to feel that America had room for all.

The new restrictions were also part of the general revulsion against Europe that followed the collapse of Wilsonian internationalism in 1919-20. America

OPPOSITE After the Second World War millions of displaced persons sought admission to the United States but Congress, fearing an influx of criminals and subversives, clung to the restrictive immigration policy established in the 1920s. This eloquent 1946 cartoon by Herblock shows President Truman and Dean Acheson rebuking a Congressman for forgetting America's long tradition of asylum.

had found its involvement in European power politics profoundly disillusioning. Having taken up arms in the belief that the war was a crusade for international righteousness, by 1919 Americans had come to believe that all the European powers were equally greedy and cynical; in short, the war had bred a distrust of all idealisms and a hostility to all foreigners. The new isolationist mood which led the United States to reject the Treaty of Versailles in 1919 and to stay out of the League of Nations led it also to erect barriers that would keep Europeans at home.

There was, however, nothing sudden about the decision. Agitation for immigration restriction had been gaining strength for decades – ever since the 1880s in fact. One might suppose that it originated in the huge increase in immigration then taking place. Arrivals in the 1880s reached the unprecedented total of five and a quarter millions, more than double the figure for the previous decade. Yet in the 1890s, though immigration fell to three and a half millions, the drive for restrictions continued to gather momentum. In fact it was not so much the volume of immigration that was worrying Americans, but its changed character. With so many unfamiliar types now arriving from southern and eastern Europe – and indeed from further afield – it was feared that American society was being radically altered, and for the worse, by a motley band of foreigners speaking strange languages and following strange customs. As Thomas Bailey Aldrich put it in 1892 in this poem, 'The Unguarded Gates':

> Wide open and unguarded stand our gates,
> And through them presses a wild, motley throng –
> Men from the Volga and the Tartar steppes,
> Featureless faces from the Hoang-Ho,
> Malayan, Scythian, Teuton, Kelt and Slav,
> Flying the Old World's poverty and scorn;
> These, bringing with them unknown gods and rites,
> Those, tiger passions, here to stretch their claws.
> In street and alley what strange tongues are these,
> Accents of menace alien to our air,
> Voices that once the Tower of Babel knew!
> O Liberty, white Goddess! Is it well
> To leave the gates unguarded?

Nativist fears took several forms. One was that, as a result of immigration, America was ceasing to be a Protestant country. When the United States became independent it was recognizably a child of the Reformation. Nearly all the white population – and all the blacks, for that matter – belonged to one or other of the Protestant sects. A century later immigrants had added hugely to Catholic strength and, to a lesser extent, to that of the Jews. While Protestants were still in a majority their relative strength was declining and in the cities they were already outnumbered. The revival of anti-Catholic agitation in the 1880s and the growth of anti-Semitism a decade later were proof of Protestant

disquiet at the changes immigration had brought about. All the same no one seriously suggested that Catholics and Jews should be excluded.

Perhaps even more widespread was another ancient fear – immigrant radicalism. The stereotyped picture of immigrants as dangerous revolutionaries dated back to the period of the French Revolution, when a variety of foreign radicals had sought refuge in the United States. The fear was recharged a century later by the Haymarket Affair in Chicago in May 1886, when seven policemen were killed and sixty injured, the violence growing out of a demonstration for an eight-hour day. It was blamed on a group of German anarchists led by August Spies, editor of the *Arbeiter Zeitung*, who had been preaching class warfare and publishing instructions on how to manufacture dynamite. Seven of the accused were convicted on dubious evidence of complicity in the crime and were sentenced either to death or to terms of imprisonment. The affair sent a wave of fear throughout American society, seeming to confirm the suspicion that the violent strikes and riots of recent years were the work of foreign agitators. Even trade-union leaders joined in the chorus of denunciation. 'The anarchist idea is un-American, and has no business in this country,' declared a leader of the Knights of Labor. A more extreme reaction, however, was that of a Middle Western newspaper editor who fulminated against 'long-haired, wild-eyed, bad-smelling, atheistic, reckless foreign wretches, who never did

Immigration from Ireland produced a virulent anti-Catholicism among the native-born. They blamed the Irish for the growth of municipal corruption and of boss rule, and denounced as unpatriotic priestly efforts to ensure that Catholic children attended parochial rather than public schools. In this Thomas Nast cartoon Boss Tweed of Tammany Hall and Irish politicians combine to destroy the American public school system, where all children are educated together.

Popular fears of foreign radicals and revolutionaries owed much to the Haymarket Affair of 1886, when a bomb was thrown into a group of policemen on Chicago's West Side. Eight anarchists, most of them German, were found guilty of murder and five of them were executed. But doubts persisted as to their guilt and, as this illustration by Flavio Constantini shows, revolutionaries have continued to cherish the memory of the 'Chicago martyrs'.

an honest day's work in their lives. . . . Crush such snakes . . . before they have time to bite.'

In fact the mass of immigrants had no interest in radicalism. But only an occasional act of foreign extremism was needed to keep the stereotype alive. Leon Czolgosz, for example, the anarchist who assassinated President McKinley in 1901, was in fact born in America but his foreign origin was so apparent from his name as to cause another hysterical flare-up. A few years later the strikes led by the Industrial Workers of the World produced a similar reaction. Though most of the Wobbly leaders were native-born, some were not. The legendary Joe Hill, for example, was born in Sweden and christened Joel

Haglund. Executed for murder in Salt Lake City in 1916, he was destined to become an international working-class martyr.

Old stock Americans were not alone in their fear of imported revolution. The Irish and other elements in the 'old' immigration were equally alarmed. The irony of the fact that a group who had themselves been victims of nativist intolerance should now join in the clamour for restriction was not lost on Mr Dooley, Finley Peter Dunne's famous fictional bartender of Chicago:

As a pilgrim father that missed the first boat, I must raise me claryon voice again' the invasion iv this fair land be th' paupers an' arnychists of Europe. Ye bet I must – because I'm here first. In thim days America was th' refuge iv th' oppressed in the wurruld. . . . But as I tell ye, 'tis diff'rent now. 'Tis time we put our back again' th' open dure an' keep out the savage horde.

Yet the most potent fear of all was that conjured up by the spectre of racial degeneration. Towards the end of the nineteenth century Americans became acutely sensitive to problems of race. The failure of the attempt after the Civil War to grant equality to the freed Negro seemed to confirm that there were innate racial differences. Oriental immigration, too, stimulated virulent racial feelings in California and other west coast states. Then the imperialism of the 1890s focused attention upon what Kipling called 'lesser breeds' and on the white man's duty towards them. The Darwinian theory of natural selection had accustomed people to divide mankind into biological types, each with its own distinctive physical and cultural characteristics. By the beginning of the twentieth century scientists had reached the conclusion – which half a century later they would reverse – that racial differences were fixed and immutable. Heredity counted for everything; environment for nothing. That was a startling conclusion for Americans to have to come to terms with, being completely at variance with the melting pot concept, till then regarded as an article of national faith. Hitherto it had been believed that while Europeans might have had the misfortune to have been born in an effete, corrupt part of the world, they could shrug off its stunting effects by breathing the air of American freedom. That had been a delusion, the scientists now said; instead, racial characteristics would persist from one generation to the next.

Thus America was becoming increasingly race-conscious. Nowhere was this more true than in New England, a region which had long prided itself on its English ancestry and on what it called its Anglo-Saxon tradition. The cream of New England society, the 'Boston Brahmins', feared that the Anglo-Saxon element, which in their view had made America what it was, would be submerged by inferior races from southern and eastern Europe. Thus in 1894 they founded the Immigration Restriction League. It singled out the 'new' immigrants for special condemnation, regarding them as a collective entity, different from and inferior to the 'old'. To one of the League's founders the essential question was this: 'Do you want this country to be peopled by British, German or Scandinavian stock, historically free, energetic, progressive, or by Slav, Latin and Asiatic races, historically down-trodden, atavistic and stagnant?' The League drew up a lengthy indictment. The new immigration, it claimed, was not a spontaneous movement but one artificially induced by steamship companies and American big business. New immigrants were less literate and less skilled than the old and did not spread out across the country as earlier immigrants had done, but congregated in urban ghettos. Indeed, it was said, they were hardly immigrants at all – they came to America simply to make money and then returned home.

These generalizations, though not entirely unfounded, were, nevertheless misleading. They drew too sharp a distinction between 'new' immigrants and 'old'. In any case, to lump together as a single group people who varied as much as the new immigrants did in literacy, skills and permanence of settlement was absurd. As for the assumption that the new immigrants came to an Anglo-Saxon country, Mr Dooley again provided the best commentary. As he explained to his friend, Hennessy:

An Anglo-Saxon, Hinnissy, is a German that's forgot who was his parents. They've a lot of thim in this country.... Mack [President McKinley] is an Anglo-Saxon. His folks come fr'm the County Armagh, an' their naytional Anglo-Saxon hymn is 'O'Donnell Aboo'. Teddy Rosenfelt is another Anglo-Saxon. An' I'm an Anglo-Saxon. I'm wan iv th' hottest Anglo-Saxons that iver come out iv Anglo-Saxony. The name of Dooley has been th' proudest Anglo-Saxon name in th' County Roscommon fr many years.

Impervious to irony, however, the League could now cite leading anthropologists and sociologists in support of its views on race. It could also use concepts drawn from the heady new science of eugenics. This taught that the vigour of a society depended upon breeding from the best human stock and upon restricting the offspring of the worst. A document prepared by the League in 1910 argued:

We should exercise at least as much care in admitting human beings as we exercise in relation to animals or insect pests or disease germs. Yet ... we are today taking actually more care in the selection ... of a Hereford bull or a Southdown ewe ... than we are taking in the selection of the alien men and women who are coming here to be the fathers and mothers of future American children.... We should see to it that we are protected, not merely from supporting alien dependents, delinquents and defectives, but from ... 'that watering of the nation's lifeblood', which results from their breeding after admission.

A considerable proportion of immigrants now coming are from races and countries ... which have not progressed, but which have been backward, downtrodden and relatively useless for centuries.... There is no reason to suppose that a change of location will result in a change of inborn tendencies.

Soon after its inception the Immigration Restriction League launched a campaign to alert the American public to the dangers of unrestricted immigration. To exclude paupers, convicts, anarchists and so on was not enough, they argued. They were, however, reluctant to be openly discriminatory towards the allegedly inferior races. Hence they hit upon the literacy test as a device which would achieve their object, but more indirectly. The ability to read a simple passage in any language ought, they argued, to be a condition of entry.

Even before this trade unions had been campaigning – with some success – for restrictions of a different kind. In the 1880s they had persuaded Congress to adopt two new measures: the Chinese Exclusion Act of 1882 and the Foran Act of 1885 prohibiting the importation of contract labour. The latter was adopted in the mistaken belief that the new immigrants were being imported in huge numbers on contract by American employers to hold down wages and break strikes. Since few immigrants were imported thus, the Foran Act had no appreciable effect on immigration. The Chinese Exclusion Act, on the other hand, lived up to its name. The Chinese were concentrated on the west coast, especially in California. Their critics in the labour unions alleged – correctly as it turned out – that they were not free immigrants but coolies, that is, a slave clement whose presence degraded American labour. But the anti-Chinese movement was not simply a reaction to economic competition: critics alleged that the Chinese were a filthy and depraved people whose racial characteristics constituted a permanent bar to assimilation. The Act of 1882 suspended the immigration of Chinese labourers for ten years; a similar prohibition followed in 1892 and in 1902 the ban was made permanent.

Given their history it was only to be expected that trade unions would add their voices to the clamour for a literacy test. In 1897 after several years of hesitation the American Federation of Labor came out in favour. It complained that the new immigrants lowered wages, added to unemployment and displaced native-born workers. Meanwhile the literacy test won support from patriotic and fraternal societies. Progressive reformers, too, fell into line. Leading Progressives like the economist, John R. Commons and the sociologist, Edward A. Ross, concluded that immigration was exacerbating, if not causing, many of the nation's social and political ills and that, without restriction, there was little hope of elevating the tone of American political life or of solving crime or slum housing problems. Even people who stopped short of supporting the demand for restriction took it for granted that the new immigrants were inferior. Woodrow Wilson, not yet embarked upon a political career, could refer in 1904 to newcomers from the south of Europe as being drawn from 'the more sordid and hapless elements' of the population, and as a 'coarse crew' less to be desired than the Chinese.

A bill providing for a literacy test was passed by Congress in 1897 but was vetoed by President Cleveland who rejected the racial distinctions of the bill's advocates and stressed the need to uphold America's asylum tradition. Although a similar bill was passed by Congress in 1913 and another in 1915, both were vetoed. President Wilson, now more sympathetic to immigrants, stated in his veto message:

The Narrow Gate

This bill embodies a radical departure from the tradition and long established policy of this country.... It seeks to close all but entirely the gates of asylum which have always been open to those who could find [it] nowhere else ... and it excludes those to whom the opportunities of elementary education have been denied without regard to their character, their purpose or their natural ability.

However, on the eve of America's entry into the First World War the restrictionists finally mustered enough support to override a second Wilsonian veto.

The Immigration Act of February 1917 provided for the exclusion of those unable to read a forty-word passage (in English or some other language). Exceptions were made for religious refugees and the illiterate relatives of admissible aliens. The law contained other restrictive provisions. It doubled the head tax on immigrants to $8 and added chronic alcoholics, vagrants and persons of 'constitutional psychopathic inferiority' to the list of excluded classes. Finally the act established a 'barred zone' in the southwest Pacific. That was aimed at Asian immigration. It was all of a piece with the Chinese Exclusion Acts and the Gentlemen's Agreement of 1907 between the United States and Japan designed to keep out Japanese labourers.

The adoption of the literacy test was due to the anxieties engendered by the European war. That conflict opened the eyes of Americans to the strength of immigrant attachments to the old world. Far from responding to Woodrow Wilson's appeal to be neutral in thought as well as in action, millions of American citizens sided with the countries from which they or their forebears had come. German immigrants went out of their way to express sympathy with the Fatherland; Irish and Jewish immigrants, who remembered their mistreatment at the hands of Great Britain and Russia respectively, were also pro-German. On the other hand, British, Italian, Polish and Czech immigrants were just as committed to the success of the Allies.

The persistence of these ancestral loyalties came as a great shock to Americans. Leading politicians denounced those they nicknamed 'hyphenated' Americans – people of divided loyalty. Wilson asserted that some Americans needed hyphens to identify their nationality because only part of them had crossed the Atlantic. Theodore Roosevelt believed that hyphenates threatened the survival of the nation. 'The question', he declared, 'is whether we are to continue as a nation at all, or whether we are to become merely a huge polyglot boarding-house and counting-house, in which dollar-hunters of twenty different nationalities scramble for gain, while each really pays his soul-allegiance to some foreign power.'

However, soon after the war it became evident that the literacy test was failing to achieve its purpose. Arrivals showed every sign of equalling pre-war levels: of the one and a half million immigrants who arrived in the United States in the four years 1918-21, only 6142 (or 0.4 per cent) were excluded because of inability to read. A large proportion of the rejects were from Mexico and French

OPPOSITE By the end of the nineteenth century the rising tide of immigration included such an assortment of peoples as to create doubts about the wisdom of the open gates policy. This *Harper's Weekly* cartoon which appeared in 1888, showing Uncle Sam surrounded by a variety of foreign types, expressed the growing fear that unrestricted immigration would ultimately make the old-stock Yankee a curiosity in his own country.

Canada. The south and east Europeans, whom the act had been intended to keep out, quickly became literate once literacy was a condition of entry.

Inevitably, there was a demand for more stringent legislation. In the immediate post-war years, a sharp economic depression hit the United States. Those thrown out of work feared that unless immigration was curbed jobs would be harder to find. They were particularly alarmed at reports that millions of people in war-torn Europe were preparing to cross the Atlantic as soon as shipping was available. There was also an upsurge of xenophobia resulting from the 'Red Scare' of 1919, a wave of labour unrest and a crop of bomb outrages. Immigrants played a prominent part in the violent strikes of that year in the textile and steel industries, and there were large numbers of foreign-born in the newly-formed American Communist Party and other radical organizations. In the notorious Palmer raids of 1919–20 thousands of immigrant radicals were arrested and hundreds were deported.

That the intolerant nationalism of wartime had not died away was apparent in still other ways. There was a marked revival of anti-Catholicism and anti-Semitism which found expression in the Ku Klux Klan, the secret society founded in Georgia in 1915. The Klan spread like wildfire throughout the South and the Middle West. By 1923 it had a membership of two and a half millions. In contrast to the Ku Klux Klan of the nineteenth century, this order combined an anti-Negro with an anti-foreign stance and admitted only native-born Protestant whites. 'What were the dangers which the white man saw threatening to crush and overwhelm Anglo-Saxon civilization?' asked Colonel William J. Simmons, the Klan's Imperial Wizard, rhetorically. '[They lay] in the dangerous influx of foreign immigration, tutored in alien dogmas and alien creeds, flowing in from all countries and slowly pushing the native-born white American population into the center of the country, there to be overwhelmed and smothered.'

The post-war debate on immigration gradually took on a racialist tone. Politicians, newspaper editors and popular writers tended more and more to reflect the views of the Immigration Restriction League. Like the characters in some of Jack London's novels they spoke of a race war in which the 'Nordic' element in America was threatened with being swamped. In 1921 the *Saturday Evening Post* published a series of articles on immigration by the popular novelist, Kenneth Roberts, who contended that a continuing deluge of immigrants would inevitably produce 'a hybrid race of people as worthless and futile as the good-for-nothing mongrels of Central America and south eastern Europe.' A book written in 1916, Madison Grant's *The Passing of the Great Race*, now enjoyed a great vogue. Grant, the curator of the New York Zoological Society, concluded from his studies of the Rocky Mountain goat and the caribou that a mixture of animal species resulted in the degeneration of the stock. The same thing, he contended, applied to human beings. America's greatness depended upon preserving the purity of its old 'Nordic' stock. Unless the inferior Alpine,

Mediterranean and Jewish breeds were excluded, the 'great race' would be replaced by 'the weak, the broken and the mentally crippled'.

In response to this restrictionist clamour Congress passed an Emergency Quota Act in 1921, though it is possible that, even if Congress had not acted, immigration would soon have dwindled. The appalling casualties of the First World War, along with a declining birth-rate, meant that Europe had fewer people to spare. But in the event, this new measure was the first to impose a numerical limit on immigration. It set a limit of 357,000 a year and prescribed quotas for all eligible national groups. The quota for each nationality was fixed at three per cent of the foreign born already resident in the United States at the time of the 1910 census. That meant a drastic reduction in the proportion of new immigrants. During the three years the emergency law was in operation, immigration was halved, mainly because arrivals from southern and eastern Europe dropped to the same annual level – about 155,000 – as those from northern and western Europe. Next, the National Origins Act of 1924 laid down a permanent immigration policy which tilted the balance still further against new immigrants. The purpose of the measure was to stabilize the ethnic composition of the American population. As well as reducing to 150,000 the number of immigrants to be admitted annually, it laid down a plan for allocating quotas to each nationality in proportion to its contribution to the existing population. That was a formula which experts needed time to work out. Until they had done so, each country would be allowed a quota equivalent to two per cent of the number of its nationals in the United States in 1890 – that is, before the new immigrants had become preponderant. Under this interim arrangement eighty-six per cent of the total quotas was allocated to the countries of northern and western Europe, only fourteen per cent to others. Peoples within the western hemisphere – the Americas – were exempt.

The national origins system, which went into force on 1 July 1929, changed these quotas only slightly. That system, despite numerous later changes in the law, was to remain the basis of American immigration policy until 1965. It did not work out in practice quite as its authors had intended. Immigrants from north-western Europe fell below expectations as favoured countries failed to take up the whole of their quotas. Great Britain, for example, though permitted forty-four per cent of the allotted total contributed only twenty-two per cent of the immigrants admitted between 1930 and 1965. After the Second World War, moreover, the quota system was repeatedly breached by legislation which permitted the entry of non-quota groups.

But during the long economic depression of the 1930s the system was rigidly adhered to. The Hoover administration, in response to demands, imposed even more obstacles to entry. In September 1930 the State Department instructed American consuls to refuse visas to prospective emigrants unless they were able to support themselves on arrival. In practice that meant having $50 in cash – a requirement that few could then fulfil. Not that many Europeans wanted to emigrate to a country where millions were out of work. During the Depression decade the total European immigration amounted to 350,000 – a figure only slightly higher than that of people who returned to Europe in the same period.

During the election campaign of 1932 Hoover claimed that there was no longer any need for America to act as an asylum. Only a few months later Hitler's rise to power showed how wrong Hoover had been. The Jewish exodus from Germany really got under way after the Nuremberg Laws of 1935, becoming a panic-stricken flight after the *Kristallnacht*, an organized pogrom in November 1938. Immediately before the outbreak of war European Jews were fleeing in every direction. But the world seemed to have little room – or sympathy – for refugees at that time. Nations everywhere were more ready to urge others to open their doors than to do so themselves.

Nevertheless, the United States finally admitted more refugees than any other country: about a quarter of a million between 1933 and 1945, about two-thirds of them Jews, though that figure was proportionately lower than the numbers admitted by such countries as Britain, France, Belgium and Switzerland. President Roosevelt made a number of sympathetic gestures but adamantly refused to contemplate changing the quota system. He was, however, powerless in the face of Congressional and public hostility. Feeling ran so high that even a proposal to admit 20,000 German refugee children as non-quota immigrants was killed. Opponents took the view that charity should begin at home. The United States, they argued, should take care of its own needy millions before importing others from abroad. Isolationism, now at high tide, was another reason for the lack of sympathy. But anti-Semitism was probably the crucial factor. At all events Congress made no difficulty about admitting refugee children from Great Britain a year later.

Among the refugees who arrived between 1933 and 1945 were many distinguished and famous names in science, scholarship and the arts. They included Albert Einstein, Thomas Mann, Walter Gropius, Bruno Walter, and Paul Tillich. Hundreds of others were people of scarcely less distinction. But the great majority consisted of businessmen, teachers, lawyers, doctors and white-collar workers. They came, that is to say, from very different backgrounds from the peasant immigrants of an earlier period. In some respects they were better equipped to make the necessary adjustments, being much better educated than the average immigrant and more accustomed to living in cities. But life was still hard for them. They had lived for years in the shadow of fear; many had suffered humiliation, physical abuse and imprisonment; they frequently left close relatives behind in Europe. All this meant that they arrived under great emotional strain. After 1937 they were only allowed to take out of Germany property to the value of RM. 10. Without the help of voluntary agencies like the National Refugee Service their plight would have been even more desperate. As it was, jobs were hard to find. Fluency in English was imperative and even that was sometimes not enough. Doctors, for example, faced

The Hebrew Sheltering
and Immigrant Aid
Society, set up in the
1880s to meet the needs of
an earlier wave of
immigrants, continues to
minister to newcomers; in
this case, refugees after the
Second World War.

various restrictive rulings which prevented or delayed them from practising
their profession. In the end most found a niche but it was often the work of
years rather than of months.

Since the Second World War there has been an uninterrupted flow of immigrants – seven million people having entered the United States in the last thirty
years. That is a small figure compared with the mass movements of the nineteenth and early twentieth centuries. Small, too, when set against an American
population now in excess of two hundred millions. Nevertheless, it means that
the United States has easily remained the largest immigrant-receiving country
in the world.

After the war the national origins quota system came under increasing
attack. 'The idea behind this discriminatory policy,' declared President Tru-

233

man in 1952, 'was, to put it baldly, that Americans with English or Irish names were better people and better citizens than Americans with Italian or Greek or Polish names.' He condemned such a concept as 'utterly unworthy' of American traditions and ideals. But Truman, in spite of his veto, was unable to prevent Congress from passing the Immigration and Nationality Act of 1952, which preserved the national origins principle in all its essentials. Its supporters no longer invoked the Nordic supremacy argument, but they felt that abandonment of the quota system would breach the principle of numerical limitation, and might open the door to a flood of Communists. That was a telling argument during the hysteria of the McCarthy era.

Truman's successors continued to press for change. Just before he became president, John F. Kennedy remarked that until 1921 American society had accurately reflected the words of Emma Lazarus' poem: 'Give me your tired, your poor, your huddled masses yearning to breathe free.' But under the 1952 Act, he declared, it would be necessary to add: 'as long as they come from Northern Europe, are not too tired or too poor or slightly ill, never stole a loaf of bread, never joined any questionable organization and can document their activities for the past two years.'

The national origins quota system was not in fact repealed until 1965, two years after Kennedy's death, though it was much diluted by the many special exceptions made by Congress. The first exceptions were made immediately after the war for GI brides – the women whom American servicemen had married while overseas. The War Brides Act of 1946 relaxed quota requirements so as to enable them to enter. In the five years after the war 150,000 wives and fiancées, 25,000 children and a few hundred husbands were brought from Europe, large numbers of them travelling in specially-chartered ships. A supplementary law of 1947 permitted the first sizable Oriental immigration for over a quarter of a century; it opened the gate to 5000 Chinese and 800 Japanese wives.

The European refugee problem was not so speedily dealt with. It had grown to vast proportions by the end of the war. Most of the 'displaced persons' (DPs) were those imported by Germany as forced labourers, chiefly from Poland and the Baltic states – areas now under Soviet control. There were also those who had fled westward to escape the advance of the Red Army in the last phases of the war. Those Jews who had escaped the gas chambers constituted a third, relatively small, category. The great majority of the DPs ultimately returned to their native lands, but about one million refused to go back to eastern Europe because of their distaste for Communism.

The Truman administration acknowledged that the United States could not solve the problem alone, but felt that it should set an example of generosity. America's moral obligations, its tradition of asylum and its wish to see stability restored to Europe were all invoked. Nevertheless, it took a major effort on the part of the administration to get Congress to pass the Displaced Persons Act of 1948. It provided for the admission of some 410,000 people over a four-year period. Despite the controversy and the delay the United States did more than any other country to solve the DPs problem, taking one-third of all those in need of re-settlement, though Australia and Israel – the two next largest receiving countries – both proportionately took as large a share.

By 1952 most of the people uprooted by the war had been re-settled; yet the refugee problem persisted, chiefly because of the continued flight of refugees from behind the Iron Curtain. Congress responded, somewhat more readily than before, providing for the admission of 214,000 refugees during a forty-one-month period. Both in 1948 and in 1953 Congress was willing to suspend the quota system temporarily yet sought at the same time to preserve the quota principle by insisting upon a kind of mortgage system: every refugee admitted was charged aginst his country's future quotas. This produced some absurdities: Latvia's quota was at one time mortgaged as far ahead as the year 2250.

Nevertheless, the United States managed to meet every new refugee problem with an act of humanitarianism. Sometimes as in the case of the Hungarian Freedom Fighters in 1956, the exodus was so sudden that there was no time for new legislation. But the Eisenhower administration discovered an obscure provision which enabled it to admit 30,000 Hungarian refugees. Special laws were passed in the next few years allowing entry to various groups of refugees – Chinese, Dutch-Indonesians, Slavs, Italians, Portuguese, Cubans. The Cubans were easily the largest group – 650,000 fled to the United States after Castro took power. In all more than one million refugees entered the United States between 1945 and 1965 – one-fifth of the total immigration of the period. Since a substantial number came from Asia and southern and eastern Europe it was clear that in practice the national origins quota system, designed to exclude such people, was being undermined.

In recent years the United States has not relied so heavily upon Europe for its immigrants as it did in the past. Since 1945 about forty per cent of the total immigration of seven millions has come from within the western hemisphere, especially from Canada and Mexico. Indeed if one takes into account Puerto Rican immigrants – a group not included in the official statistics because they are American citizens – and also the very large number of Mexicans who enter the country illegally, it seems clear that well over half of America's newcomers since the Second World War have come from the western hemisphere.

The unique feature of Mexican immigration is that the number of legal entrants is only a fraction of the total. The 'wetback' – so called because of the practice of swimming across the Rio Grande at isolated spots – first appeared in the 1920s. By entering thus he evaded the literacy test and the delay and expense of obtaining a visa. It was not until after the start of the government *bracero* programme (for the importation of Mexican *braceros*, farmhands), however, that the wetback invasion became a tidal wave. Substantial though the programme was it fell short of the needs of the American economy. Hence employers connived at, even encouraged, illegal immigration. They often preferred wetbacks to the legal *braceros*; it meant less red tape and they were under no necessity to conform to legally agreed wages, hours of work and contracts. Well over five and a half million wetbacks were apprehended in different parts of the United States between 1924 and 1969. Over a million were caught and sent back in 1954 alone. But even today the border patrols round up only a fraction of those who enter illegally, whether by swimming or travelling on foot overland or concealed in a car. As illegal immigrants wetbacks have no rights before the law. They are cruelly exploited by their employers in many ways, especially in regard to wages and housing. Mexican migratory labourers were for long one of America's most neglected and poverty-stricken minorities. But the grape-pickers' movement (*la huelga*) led by Cesar Chavez, has captured public sympathy and support throughout the country and has resulted in union recognition.

The campaign to abolish the national origins quota system finally reached its goal on 3 October 1965 when, in a ceremony at the Statue of Liberty, President Lyndon Johnson signed a comprehensive bill which Congress had overwhelmingly approved. A change in the law was undoubtedly overdue for the system had become increasingly unfair and unworkable, and gave offence to millions of Americans whose forbears had come from the countries discriminated against. The new measure meant that henceforth all applicants for entry would be treated equally, regardless of national origin, or for that matter, race, creed or colour. For that reason it was widely welcomed as a return to the best American traditions. But it did not contemplate any substantial increase in immigration. An annual limit of 170,000 was placed on arrivals from the eastern hemisphere and no more than 20,000 immigrants a year were to be admitted from any one country. The act established a system of priorities and preferences: of the seven preference categories, four were for relatives of American citizens, two for people possessing skills needed in the United States, and one for refugees. Immediate relatives were exempt from the numerical limitation. Moreover, for the first time, a ceiling was placed on immigration from within the western hemisphere; the annual limit of 120,000 was meant to keep the flow from rising above its existing level.

The priority given to relatives has increased immigration from Italy, Greece and other southern European countries formerly discriminated against. But the act's greatest impact has been on Asian immigration which has risen by 500 per cent. In recent years doctors, engineers, scientists and other skilled people from countries like India, Iran, Korea and the Philippines have flocked to the United States. For in sweeping away one evil the act has created another; it has accelerated the 'brain drain' from the poorer countries to the richer and thus widened the gap between them.

That does not alter the fact that the United States is still more hospitable

ABOVE Cuban refugees at Miami, Florida, 1962. Since Castro came to power in 1959, more than 650,000 Cubans have found their way to the United States, some escaping in open boats. Though many belonged to the wealthier classes of Cuban society, they arrived penniless since they were allowed to take very few possessions. Most Cubans have settled in Miami, though New York, Chicago and Los Angeles have absorbed sizable numbers.

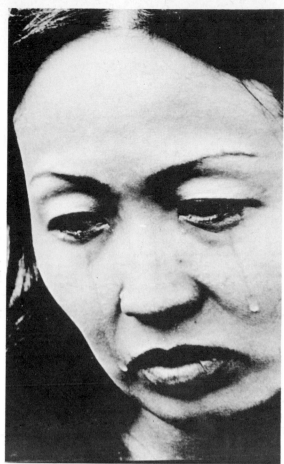

ABOVE RIGHT Tears
stream down the face of a
young Vietnamese woman
after her arrival at Eglin
Air Force Base, Florida, in
May 1975. She was one of
the 125,000 Vietnamese
refugees who fled to the
United States after the end
of the Vietnam war.

to immigrants in general than any other country in the world. Even today immigrants are still entering the country at the rate of about 400,000 a year. Moreover they are ethnically more diverse than ever before. In 1973 there were 173,000 arrivals from the western hemisphere, 124,000 from Asia, 93,000 from Europe and 7000 from Africa. Despite the fact that refugees are allotted only six per cent of eastern hemisphere preferences, ways are generally found to admit more when sudden emergencies arise. Thus, when the Saigon regime collapsed in the spring of 1975, President Ford was able to admit 'on parole' about 125,000 Vietnamese refugees, sixty per cent of them children. Coming as it did at a time of economic recession, the decision was criticized, not least by the liberals whose hostility to the Vietnam War extended to its victims. But most Americans, accepting that an obligation existed, regarded the President's action as one in keeping with the country's long established tradition of asylum.

Now in truth America can be called, in the words of one nineteenth-century poet, 'half-brother to the world'.

11
THE IMMIGRANT HERITAGE

A souvenir postcard issued to commemorate
the visit of the most famous of Irish-Americans
to his ancestral home in 1963.

THE HISTORY OF EMIGRATION to America is often told as a simple success story. The struggles of successive waves of newcomers, their triumphs over adversity and prejudice, their gradual rise to the level of their predecessors – these are the recurrent themes. But as this book has tried to show, the experiences of immigrants have been too varied to be summed up in a simple formula. Distinctions have to be made. What befell immigrants depended upon a whole range of variables: nationality, religion, age, language, education, wealth, skill. It varied with circumstances of departure, time of arrival, whether they travelled alone or with their families, the ease or otherwise with which it was possible to return home. It also depended upon sheer luck. Success did not come in equal measure to everyone. Sometimes it did not come at all. Of one thing they could be sure: it would be unlikely to come save by their own efforts. The point is admirably illustrated by the story of the three discoveries made by the Russian Jewish immigrant from Minsk. On arrival in the United States he found that the streets were not paved with gold; that they were not paved at all; and that he was expected to pave them.

It seems beyond dispute that the great mass of immigrants were ultimately better off in America than they had been in Europe. Only an exceptional and fortunate few – an Andrew Carnegie, a John Jacob Astor, an Alexander Graham Bell – rose from obscurity to the heights of wealth or fame. But most were able to improve their condition. It was generally agreed that immigrants were better fed, better clothed, better housed and of course better paid than they had been in Europe. That verdict is borne out by the overwhelmingly favourable tone of emigrant letters and, even more, by the golden stream of remittances that kept the tides of immigration flowing.

Great though the gain often was to the immigrant, it was greater still to his Americanized children. Unrestrained by the rigidities of the European social system they were free to take advantage of the opportunities offered by a more open society. President Kennedy perhaps overstated the case on his sentimental visit to Ireland in 1963. Standing on the spot from which his great-grandfather, Patrick Kennedy, had embarked for America, he declared: 'If he hadn't left, I would be working at the Albatross Company across the road.' That may not have been meant seriously, but if it was, it was based upon the delusion that opportunities in Ireland had not increased in the intervening three generations. Happily, a few days later when he was addressing the Irish Parliament in Dublin, he speculated that if his great-grandfather had stayed in Ireland, he himself might have been a member of the Dail. That was far nearer the probable reality. The educated and economically comfortable men he addressed that day were, by and large, descended from the same poverty-stricken peasant class as Patrick Kennedy. The aspect and character of its members were proof that the poor of Europe did not always stay poor.

According to the American ideal it should have been possible for everyone who started at the bottom to rise as high as their talents and energies would

The Immigrant Heritage

allow. But in practice those groups who got a head start by arriving in America early have tended to stay on top. An immigrant's time of arrival in the new world still influences his descendants' place in society. Though there are obvious exceptions, it remains the case that America's social and economic elite consists disproportionately of the descendants of seventeenth- and eighteenth-century colonists, most of whom were English. The white working-class, on the other hand, still largely consists of people of Slavic, Italian and Greek descent (i.e. those who arrived less than a century ago) – a fact which, as we shall see, has added to the political and social turmoil of recent years.

To discuss the experiences of immigrants solely in economic terms is, of course, to tell only part of the story. For while there was undoubtedly material gain there was also psychological and spiritual loss. While immigrants appreciated the advantages of American society they were not unaware of the price exacted. One who tried to calculate it was the novelist Ole E. Rölvaag, author of *Giants in the Earth*. Born in Norway, the son of a fisherman, Rölvaag spoke to a group of fellow immigrants in Minnesota in 1911 about the spiritual impoverishment of the immigrant. He singled out as the worst loss the fact that in leaving his homeland, the immigrant had ceased to belong. 'We have become strangers,' he declared, 'strangers to the people we forsook, and strangers to the people we came to.'

Crèvecoeur oversimplified, therefore, when he characterized the American as a European who, 'leaving behind him all his ancient prejudices and manners receives new ones from the new mode of life he has embraced . . . and the new rank he holds.' In practice old identities were not so easily exchanged for new ones. Americanization might indeed mean a new birth of freedom, but it also meant a change of name, the abandonment of language, indeed the renunciation of a former self. For countless immigrants, those sacrifices were a source of continuing anguish and frustration.

Nor was it any solution to return home. Those who did so generally found that they had grown too far away in outlook to be able to resume their former lives smoothly. The Swedish pastor, Gustaf Unonius, who returned to his homeland after seventeen years in Chicago, summed up the problem:

Though we could not but admit that the country where we had spent so many years had ... many advantages over the country we had left, still we longed for ... our fatherland ... and thither we were driven by our longing, without realizing that it might no longer have a place for those who had once despised its poverty and might now come to stand as strangers at its threshold. . . . Among my numerous missteps in life, there are two for which I may properly blame myself: one, that I ever emigrated to America; [two], that after I had made my home and found my field of service there, I returned from that country.

The ambivalence of the immigrant experience was equally characteristic of the impact of immigration on America. There can be no doubt about the enormous benefits that the United States has gained from immigration – benefits

Carl Schurz (1829–1906). Escaping to the United States after the failure of the German revolution of 1848, Schurz had a dazzling American career as politician, Civil War general, diplomat, historian and newspaper editor.

Born in Edinburgh in 1847, Alexander Graham Bell emigrated to Canada in 1870 and in the following year moved to Boston and became a teacher of the deaf. Within a few years he had developed the first practicable telephone.

that often went unrecognized. Without its immigrants the United States could hardly have advanced from colony to world power in less than two centuries. Immigrants were prominent in settling the West and building the canals and railroads that bound an expanding country together. Apart from supplying the technological know-how that gave industry its start and the endless reservoir of labour that helped America to become the most advanced industrial nation in the world, the names of even a handful of immigrants demonstrate the wide range of gifts the foreign-born have brought to America: Albert Einstein and Enrico Fermi in science; Edward Bok and Joseph Pulitzer in journalism; Victor Herbert and Irving Berlin in music; Albert Gallatin and Carl Schurz in politics; Michael Pupin and Charles P. Steinmetz in invention; Augustus Saint-Gaudens in sculpture; Emanuel Leutze and Mark Rothko in painting.

Ethnic diversity may have given to American life a richness and variety that are lacking in countries with more stable populations. But it has also placed enormous strains upon the American social fabric. It deprived America, for example, of the social coherence it had possessed when it became independent. In 1787 John Jay had thought it fortunate that 'Providence [had] been pleased to give this one connected country to one united people – a people descended from the same ancestors, speaking the same language, professing the same religion, attached to the same principles of government, very similar in their manners and customs.' Ever since the beginning of mass immigration there have been lacking those instinctive sympathies which create a sense of community among people who share a common culture. Thus much energy has had to be devoted to mediating ethnic differences. As we have seen, the consequences have been apparent in religion, politics, industry, education, entertainment. The schools have had to concentrate on Americanizing immigrant children as well as – sometimes instead of – educating them in the strict sense. Ethnic considerations have often taken precedence over fitness for office in the selection of party candidates. The formulation of a coherent foreign policy has been complicated by the need to propitiate powerful ethnic interests.

To draw attention to these problems is, however, only to suggest the magnitude of the American achievement. While the melting pot ideal may not have been fully realized in the way it has traditionally been invoked, the United States has been extraordinarily successful in getting people of vastly different backgrounds to live together in harmony. When one considers that most of America's immigrants have come from a continent divided for centuries by national rivalries, one is astonished, not that there has been so much ethnic discord, but that there has been so little. To have made a nation out of so many disparate elements is an accomplishment which has no historical parallel.

The United States nevertheless remains a nation of immigrants. Awareness of ethnic origin continues to influence the way that American society functions. To be sure, some of the more prominent marks of ethnic distinctiveness have now disappeared: many churches have lost their ethnic character; immigrant

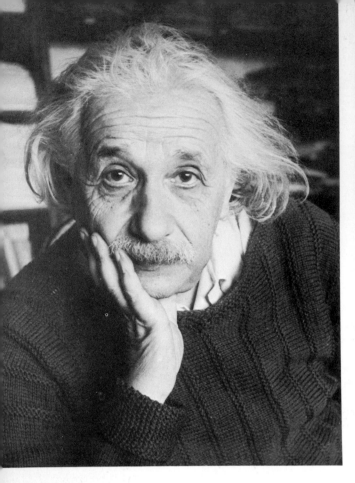

ABOVE The physicist
Albert Einstein emigrated
to the United States in
1933 as a refugee from
Nazism.
ABOVE RIGHT The song-
writer Irving Berlin, born
in Russia in 1888,
emigrated with his parents
to the United States at the
age of five.

mutual aid societies no longer flourish as they once did; the foreign-language press has long been in decline, and though by 1970 there were still 440 ethnic newspapers in thirty-eight different languages, that was only about one-fifth of the number that existed in 1914. However, there are still ethnic enclaves in most large American cities: the Irish neighbourhood in South Boston, the Polish district on Chicago's West Side, the Italian colonies in South Brooklyn and the south side of Philadelphia. Here old world foods and foreign language newspapers are sold and old country religious festivals are a feature of summer Sundays. But the flight to the suburbs, the impact of highway construction and urban renewal have drained away the vitality of most of the old ethnic ghettos. This is the natural consequence of the ending of large-scale European immigration. Immigrants now constitute a smaller proportion of the population than at any time since the United States became independent. From a peak of 14.7 per cent in 1910 the foreign-born population declined to only 4.7 per cent in 1970. The proportion born in Europe was barely 2 per cent.

Thus, in the face of this rapid falling-away, the results of a United States Census Bureau survey in 1972 are startling. They show that sixty per cent of the population still identify themselves as having a single ethnic origin, mostly European. They all think of themselves primarily as Americans, of course, but are nevertheless conscious of having another affiliation. That finding is hard to interpret but at least it suggests that indiscriminate intermarriage between ethnic groups is not yet the norm and confirms the impression that for certain purposes and on certain occasions many second- or even third-generation immigrants still think of themselves as, say, Irishmen, Englishmen, Italians or Jews.

For it is still a fact that many areas of American life reverberate to the sound of ethnic conflict. French-Canadians and Italians resent Irish dominance of the Catholic Church. Irish and Italian youth gangs fight for territory in parts of Philadelphia. Increasingly such conflicts have taken on a racial character. The bitter Ocean Hill-Brownsville education controversy of 1968 was one between black parents and the largely Jewish teachers' union. The school-busing issue produced violence in South Boston in the autumn of 1974 when black children were introduced to schools in a largely Irish neighbourhood.

But it is in politics that the ethnic factor remains supremely important. Ethnic appeals have been a feature of American politics for well over a century and they remain the stock-in-trade of many local and national politicians. While it seems unlikely that ethnic groups vote as tightly-knit blocs, they are undoubtedly influenced by the candidates' ethnic background and by his readiness to satisfy their group aspirations. Hence in cities like New York the balanced ticket is still the rule, as is the celebrated 'three I's tour' – the politician's obligatory visit to Ireland, Italy and Israel.

Both the major political parties maintain Nationalities Divisions whose job it is to woo voters belonging to the different ethnic groups. This is done by means of nominations and appointments and by attendance at nationality parades – for example, those on St Patrick's Day, Columbus Day and Pulaski Day. Frequently attempts are made to capitalize on ethnic attachments to the homeland. Thus the Republican party has made great efforts in the past quarter of a century to win the votes of Americans who have links with countries behind the Iron Curtain.

Nevertheless, at rock bottom, American foreign policy is far less responsive to ethnic pressure than is alleged. Irish-American organizations may have succeeded in raising considerable sums of money to help the IRA, but they have not so far induced the administration to put pressure on Great Britain to withdraw her troops from Ireland. Nor did a massive Greek-American demonstration in front of the White House in 1974 result in any change in Dr Kissinger's Cyprus policy. American support of Israel is frequently cited as proof of the strength of the Jewish lobby, but it is doubtful whether such support would be forthcoming if it did not coincide with what are considered to be the national interests of the United States.

In the last decade or so there has been a remarkable resurgence of ethnic awareness and pride. One of its manifestations (and one that also occurred in Europe) has been the heightened self-awareness of Jews, especially since the

The Immigrant Heritage

1967 Six-Day War. This has shown itself in the formation of such organizations as the Jewish Defence League which has sought by various means to force the Soviet Union to relax its harsh Jewish emigration regulations.

However, the new awareness has been equally associated with the descendants of non-Jewish immigrants from southern and eastern Europe – Italians, Greeks, Poles, Croats and other Slavs, mainly blue-collar workers living in the Middle West and north-eastern cities.

The most immediate cause of their new assertiveness was the rise of Black Power, the black agitation for equal rights in the late 1960s. The feeling that the blacks were advancing at their expense was a source of deep resentment among the poorer white ethnic groups. Henry Cygan who worked most of his life as a postman, now acts as a guide in Chicago's Polish Museum of America. Discussing Polish culture, he said 'It was really the drive for Black Power that started all this. They were trying to find their own identity and the Poles and other groups looked at their own culture and thought, my God, we have a far richer heritage than this – so everybody started digging.' While federal money was being poured into programmes for blacks, severe problems in white ethnic neighbourhoods were being neglected. Once Black Power was seen to result in conspicuous gains for the blacks, white ethnics decided to employ the same militant rhetoric and behaviour – as indeed did other minority groups like the American Indians and the Chicanos (Mexican-Americans). The surprisingly large vote George Wallace obtained in white working-class neighbourhoods in the North in the 1968 presidential election was due to his ability to tap the wellsprings of ethnic discontent. While not really poor, the ethnics were far from well-to-do. They felt themselves to be squeezed between the blacks and the dominant middle-class culture from which they were excluded. In the late 1960s ethnic community organizations began to appear, their aims being to press for reforms to improve the quality of life in ethnic neighbourhoods and to demand more ethnic political appointments.

The white ethnics had, however, an even older grievance, namely, the patronizing attitude of the dominant WASP (white Anglo-Saxon Protestant) community. They had long resented 'ethnic jokes', which poked fun at such groups as the Poles, the Greeks and the Italians. Strong feeling has been generated by the mass media's habit of portraying Italians invariably as criminals. One popular television series of the 1960s, *The Untouchables*, set in the Prohibition era, tirelessly typecast Italians as bootleggers and gangsters. Others rang the changes on the Mafia syndrome, giving the impression that the entire Italian-American community was a hotbed of organized crime. Protest became increasingly vehement in the 1960s, culminating in the formation of the Italian-American Civil Rights League in 1970. Its founder was Joseph Colombo, Senior, who had been named by the Justice Department as a Mafia leader. At a mass rally in 1970 at Columbus Circle, New York, speakers declared that the Italian community would no longer submit to discrimination and insult.

Ethnic demonstrations in America
The last decade has witnessed a resurgence of ethnic consciousness.

RIGHT A pro-Israel rally outside UN headquarters in New York in November 1974 against the participation of the Palestine Liberation Organization in the Middle East peace talks.
BELOW Violent scenes in front of the FBI office in New York during a demonstration on 'Italian-American Unity Day' in June 1970 as a protest against alleged FBI harassment of Americans of Italian descent.
BELOW RIGHT Irish-Americans march on the British Consulate in San Francisco in February 1970 to protest against the killing of thirteen Londonderry civilians on 'Bloody Sunday'.

244

The seventieth birthday
of Federal Judge John
J. Sirica, US District
Court Building,
Washington, 1974.
This son of Italian
immigrants was lifted
from obscurity
while presiding over
the Watergate case.

In a short time the League had enrolled more than 60,000 members, raised two million dollars and had picketed offending institutions.

The campaign produced spectacular results. The Nixon administration ordered the Justice Department to stop using the terms Mafia and Cosa Nostra as synonyms for organized crime. The National Broadcasting Company and the *New York Times* followed suit. The Paramount Picture Corporation agreed to delete all references to the Mafia in the film then being made from Mario Puzo's novel, *The Godfather*. Soon afterwards the Italian-American Civil Rights League disbanded. Its victories were, perhaps, more symbolic than real. But it had shown how acute resentment was among Italian-Americans. It had also shown that they could be mobilized into a political force.

Today the melting pot ideal is out of favour, not because Americans reject the notion of intermingling, but because in practice it has often meant narrow conformity to a WASP standard. Nowadays Americans are much more ready to tolerate diversity of every kind, ethnic and otherwise. Most of them now accept that the United States is in fact an ethnically diverse society, that its peoples have the right to preserve their distinctive cultural heritage and that ethnic group identity is perfectly compatible with loyalty.

Whatever happens in the future it seems unlikely that the present ethnic awareness will either disappear or experience a massive revival. American society will probably retain its ambiguous character, neither completely integrated nor ethnically divided. Some Americans, as at present, will live out their lives wholly within their own ethnic group; they will constitute a tiny minority. At the other extreme there will be the considerably larger number who have little or no sense of ethnic affiliation. And in between there will be the great majority, the people who, while thinking of themselves primarily as Americans, will nevertheless find it convenient to have an alternative identity in reserve. A descendant of Cornish immigrants, who lives in a Wisconsin community where others share a similar background to her own, was recently asked how she felt about her ancestors and whether being Cornish was important to her. She replied:

Yes, it's important because it's our roots. It's where we came from and why we're here.... Of course, we're Americans, there's no question of that.... It's just that our heredity is Cornish. I think its still the Cousin Jack feeling because there's a strong sense of family and cousinship among the Cornish in this area, and the fact that we're all related and share the same roots makes for a happy neighbourhood.

Most Americans, one might say, regard their ethnic heritage in the way one does an old but comfortable jacket – as something that is no longer worn very often, but equally as something one would never think of discarding, if only because it remains part of one's personality. Out of sight most of the time it is nevertheless constantly at hand, ready for use should time and occasion demand.

NOTES ON SOURCES

References are identified by folio number (bold type) and by line number (italics).

14/*16* *Third Report from the Select Committee on Emigration from the United Kingdom, 1827*, P.P. 1826–7, V, p. 7

15/*40* Samuel Gompers, *Seventy Years of Life and Labor*, (New York, 1925) I, pp. 18–19

18/*29* Alexis de Tocqueville, *Democracy in America*, (London, 1946) p. 32

24/*15* *Illustrated London News*, 21.12.1850

24/*22* *Ballou's Pictorial*, (Boston) VIII, p. 152; cited in Terry Coleman, *Passage to America*, (London, 1972) p. 82

24/*37* *Morning Chronicle*, 15.7.1850

26/*12* Robert H. Billigmeier and Fred A. Picard, *The Old Land and the New*, (Minneapolis, 1965) p. 191

26/*33* *The Times*, 8.1.1852, quoting the *Liverpool Albion*

29/*11* *Report from the Select Committee on the Passengers' Act, 1851*, P.P. 1851, XIX (632) p. xxviii

29/*18* *Ibid.*, evidence of Sir George Stephen, Q.2889

29/*25* *Ibid.*, pp. xxix–xxx

29/*34* William Hancock, *An Emigrant's Five Years in the Free States of America*, (London, 1860) pp. 9–10

30/*1* *Report on the Affairs of British North America from the Earl of Durham*, P.P. 1839, XVII (3) Appendix A, pp. 86–7

30/*29* *A Copy of a Letter addressed to the Land and Emigration Commission*, P.P. 1851, XL (198) pp. 2–7

30/*39* *Ibid.*

32/*1* William Bell, *Hints to Emigrants*, (Edinburgh, 1824) p. 26

32/*14* *Report on the Affairs of British North America . . .*, P.P. 1839, XVII (3), Appendix A, pp. 87–8

32/*33* C.O. 384/88, Frederick W. Hart to Mure, 29.3.1851

32/*39* *Ibid.*, Mure to Palmerston, 4.2.1850

33/*3* *Congressional Globe*, 36th Congress, 1st session, 29, 2, p. 955

34/*4* Quoted in Edwin C. Guillet, *The Great Migration*, (Toronto, 1937) pp. 136–7

35/*22* Quoted in Robert G. Albion, *The Rise of New York Port, 1815–1860*, (New York, 1939) p. 346

37/*8* *Papers Relative to Emigration*, P.P. 1847–8, XLVII (932) p. 5

37/*20* William Smith, *An Emigrant's Narrative; Or, A Voice from the Steerage*, (New York, 1850) p. 17

40/*34* Quoted in Roy Anderson, *White Star*, (Prescot, Lancs., 1964) p. 17

42/*10* *A Report on Emigrant Ships by the Sanitary Commission of The Lancet*, (London, 1873) p. 26

42/*15* *Letter from the Secretary of the Treasury . . .*, 43rd Congress, 1st session, Senate Ex. Doc. 23, p. 12

42/*40* *Report with regard to the Accommodation and Treatment of Emigrants . . .*, P.P. 1881, LXXXII (2995) pp. 3–5

43–4 *passim* *Congressional Record*, 47th Congress, 1st session, 13, 3, pp. 3016–19

48/*3* Quoted in Albion, *op. cit.*, p. 336

50/*27* *Report of the Select Committee to Investigate Frauds on Emigrant Passengers*, New York Assembly Document 46, (1848)

50/*33* John F. Maguire, *The Irish in America*, 4th edn, (New York, 1876) p. 190

53/*18* *New York Times*, 27.2.1874

54/*18* *Report of the Select Committee . . . to Inquire into . . . the Importation of Contract Laborers . . .*, 50th Congress, 2nd session, House Report 3792, p. 2

57/*4* Stephen Graham, *With Poor Immigrants to America*, (London, 1914) pp. 41–2

59/*10* Thames Television interview

61/*8* Willard A. Heaps, *The Story of Ellis Island*, (New York, 1967) pp. 82–3

63/*3* Elia Kazan, *America, America*, (London, 1961) p. 185

63/*32* *Reports of the Industrial Commission on Immigration*, XV, (Washington, 1901) p. 647

64/*4* *Annual Reports of the Commissioner General of Immigration for . . . 1908, 1915*, (Washington, 1908, 1915)

69/*15* *Kerry Evening Post*, 5.5.1847, quoting the *Southern Reporter*; cited in Oliver MacDonagh, 'Irish Overseas Emigration during the Famine', in T. D. Williams and R. D. Edwards, *The Great Famine*, (Dublin, 1956)

70/*38* Marie Anne de Bovet, *Three Months' Tour in Ireland*, (London, 1891) p. 280

70/*43* *The Times*, 7.4.1847, quoting the *Tuam Herald*

71/*9* 'Irish Crisis', *Edinburgh Review*, LXXXVII, (Jan. 1848) pp. 289–97

72/*3* *Appendix (C) to the First Report . . . on the Condition of the Poorer Classes in Ireland*, I, P.P. 1836, XXX, 35, pp. 76–7

72/*15* *Third Report . . . on Colonization from Ireland, 1848*, P.P. 1849, XI (86) Appendix X, p. 131

72/*18* *Ibid.*, p. 129

73/*4* *Ibid.*, p. 129

75/*21* Philip H. Bagenal, *The American Irish and their Influence on Irish Politics*, (Boston, 1882) p. 74

75/*31* Isabel Skelton, *The Life of Thomas D'Arcy McGee*, (Gardenvale, N.Y., 1925) pp. 259–60

76/*1* *Belfast News Letter*, 17.4.1821; cited in William F. Adams, *Ireland and Irish Emigration to the New World*, (New Haven, 1932) pp. 341–2

76/*14* Bagenal, *op. cit.*, p. 73

76/*38* *Report of the Committee on Internal Health on Asiatic Cholera*, Boston City Documents, (1849) pp. 12–15

78/*23* *Boston Pilot*, 25.9.1886

79/*3* Quoted in William V. Shannon, *The American Irish*, (New York, 1963) p. 29

79/*13* Rev. John O'Hanlon, *The Irish Emigrant's Guide for The United States*, (Boston, 1851) p. 81ff

79/*32* Thames Television interview

80/*32* *New York Observer*, 6.9.1841; cited in Vincent P. Lannie, *Public Money and Parochial Education*, (Cleveland, Ohio, 1968) p. 178

80/*41* Quoted in George Potter, *To the Golden Door*, (Boston, 1960) p. 440

81/*33* *The Citizen*, (New York), 19.7.1856

81/*41* Quoted in Potter, *op. cit.*, p. 372, 386–87

84/*7* *Correspondence relating to Kingwilliamstown*, Quitrent Office Collection, P.R.O. Dublin; cited in Arnold Schrier, *Ireland and the American Emigration 1850–1900*, (Minneapolis, 1958) p. 24

85/*3* *The Times*, 14.5.1850

85/*22* Thomas Colley Grattan, *Civilized America*, 2 vols, (London, 1859) II, pp. 3–5

85/*26* Thomas D'Arcy McGee, *A History of the Irish Settlers in North America*, 2nd edn, (Boston, 1852) p. 196

87/23 Thames Television interview

90/15 William L. Riordon, *Plunkitt of Tammany Hall*, (New York, 1963) p. 3

91/14 Bagenal, *op. cit.*, p. 124

91/31 *Irish World*, 13.11.1880; cited in Thomas N. Brown, *Irish-American Nationalism, 1870–1890*, (Philadelphia, 1966) p. 24

91/38 Charles C. Tansill, *America and the Fight for Irish Freedom, 1866–1922*, (New York, 1957) p. 363

92/24 Milo M. Quaife, ed., *An English Settler in Pioneer Wisconsin*, (Madison, 1918) p. 184

94/17 William Cobbett, *Rural Rides*, 2 vols, (London, 1893) pp. 335–6

94/28 J. Knight, ed., *Important Extracts from Original and Recent Letters Written by Englishmen in the United States of America to their Friends in England*, 2nd series, (Manchester, 1818) pp. 6–7

94/41 *Report from the Select Committee on Agriculture*, P.P. 1833, v (612), Q. 2552

96/2 Philip Taylor, *The Distant Magnet: European Emigration to the USA*, (London, 1971) pp. 71–3

97/4 William A. Baillie-Grohman, *Camps in the Rockies*, (New York, 1882) pp. 321–2

97/18 J. Knight, *op. cit.*, pp. 4–5

99/4 Alan Conway, ed., *The Welsh in America: Letters from the Immigrants*, (Minneapolis, 1961), pp. 115–16

102/15 *Ibid.*, pp. 315–16

103/7 *Ibid.*, p. 318

103/14 *Ibid.*, p. 315

106/18 Ms. letter in possession of Mr Donald Robbins, Lawrence, Massachusetts.

106/25 *America and the Americas by a Citizen of the World*, (James Boardman), (London, 1833) p. 2

106/31 *The Times*, 7.8.1865, 5.4.1866

107/13 Charlotte Erickson, 'Encouragement of Emigration by British Trade Unions, 1850–1900', *Population Studies*, 3, (1949) pp. 248–73

107/43 James Burnley, *Two Sides of the Atlantic*, (London, 1880) pp. 62–6

108/2 Benjamin Brierley, *Ab-o'th'-Yate in Yankeeland*, (Manchester, 1885) p. 135

108/7 Thames Television interview

108/15 *American Manufacturer*, 16.12.1881; cited in Rowland T. Berthoff, *British Immigrants in Industrial America*, (Cambridge, Mass., 1953) p. 59

111/24 *New York Bureau of Statistics of Labor, Third Annual Report*, (1885) pp. 488–9

111/40 *Pennsylvania Bureau of Industrial Statistics, Thirteenth Annual Report*, (1885) p. 174

113/1 *Third Annual Report of the*

113/1 *Massachusetts Bureau of Statistics of Labor, 1872*, (Boston, 1872) pp. 388–400

113/19 George Jacob Holyoake, *Among the Americans*, (Chicago, 1881) pp. 219–20

113/32 *Druid*, (Scranton) 24.4.1913; quoted in Rowland T. Berthoff, *op. cit.*, p. 58

114/35 *Western British-American*, (Chicago) 5.6.1915; quoted in Berthoff, *op. cit.*, p. 140

117/5 John Spargo, 'On Becoming an American Citizen', *The Independent*, LXV, (1908) pp. 994–1000

117/9 Thames Television interview

117/14 Thames Television interview

117/38 Charles W. Stubbs, 'Some Impressions of America', *Outlook*, LXV, (1900) p. 448

120/2 *Deutsch-Amerikanischer Hecker Denkmal Verein*, (Cincinnati, 1881) pp. 22 3; cited in Hildegard B. Johnson, 'Adjustment to the United States', in A. E. Zucker, ed., *The Forty-Eighters*, (New York, 1950) p. 48

122/20 Thames Television interview

123/6 Harry H. Anderson, ed., *German-American Pioneers in Wisconsin and Michigan: the Frank-Kerler Letters, 1849–1864*, (Milwaukee, 1971) p. 56, 72

124/14 Frederick Law Olmsted, *A Journey Through Texas: or A Saddle-Trip on the South Western Frontier*, (New York, 1857) pp. 184–7

124/32 Lewis W. Spitz, Sr., *The Life of Dr. C. F. W. Walther*, (St Louis, 1961) p. 44

124/36 Mack Walker, *Germany and the Emigration, 1816–1885*, (Cambridge, Mass., 1964) pp. 78–9

125/2 Henry S. Lucas, ed., *Dutch Immigrant Memoirs and Related Writings*, 2 vols, (Seattle, 1955), I, p. 17

126/12 Friedrich Münch, Sonst und Jetzt ...', *Der deutsche Pionier*, IV, 7, (Cincinnati, 1872) pp. 226–31

127/5 E. D. Kargau, 'Missouri's German Immigration', *Missouri Historical Society Collections*, II, (1900) pp. 23–4

127/13 Olmsted, *op. cit.*, p. 430

127/23 Benjamin Rush, 'An Account of the Manners of the German Inhabitants of Pennsylvania', *Essays, Literary, Moral and Philosophical*, (Philadelphia, 1798) p. 226

127/40 George M. Stephenson, ed., 'Typical America Letters, 1859–1869', *Year-Book of the Swedish Historical Society of America*, VII, p. 58–61

129/23 Theodore C. Blegen, ed., *Land of Their Choice: The Immigrants Write Home*, (Minneapolis, 1955) p. 427

130/18 *Ibid.*, pp. 406–7

130/35 Ole E. Rölvaag, *Giants in the Earth*, (New York, 1927) pp. 101–2

131/13 Theodore C. Blegen, *Norwegian Migration to America: The American Transition*, (Northfield, Minn., 1940) pp. 53–4

133/26 Fredrika Bremer, *The Homes of the New World*, (London, 1853) II, p. 359

136/21 Thames Television interview

139/2 Charles Follen Adams, *Yawcob Strauss and Other Poems*, (London, 1910) p. 269

139/23 *Illinois Staats-Zeitung*, 14.2.1889

143/6 J. Hector St John de Crèvecoeur, *Letters from an American Farmer*, (Philadelphia, 1793) p. 46

143/12 Quoted in Merle Curti, *The Growth of American Thought*, 3rd edn, (New York, 1964) p. 225

143/24 Israel Zangwill, *The Melting Pot*, (New York, 1909) pp. 37–8

143/35 Joseph Leftwich, *Israel Zangwill*, (London, 1957) p. 252

144/37 *Report of the Commission on the Problem of Immigration in Massachusetts*, (Boston, 1914) p. 134

145/2 Peter Roberts, *The New Immigration*, (New York, 1920) p. 309

145/30 Carl Sandburg, *Chicago Poems*, (New York, 1916)

145/40 W. T. Stead, 'My First Visit to America', *Review of Reviews*, IX, (Jan.–June 1894) p. 414–17

146/2 Rudyard Kipling, 'How I Struck Chicago, and how Chicago Struck Me', *From Sea to Sea: Letters of Travel, Part II*, (New York, 1906) pp. 230–48

146/13 Monsignor Count Vay de Vaya and Luskod, *The Inner Life of the United States*, (London, 1908) p. 172

146/26 Mike Royko, *Boss: Richard J. Daley of Chicago*, (London, 1971) p. 24

146/32 Peter Roberts, *op. cit.*, p. 160

148/12 James T. Farrell, *Young Lonigan*, (New York, 1958) p. 79

148/40 Cited in Paul S. Taylor, *Mexican Labor in the United States: Chicago and the Calumet Region*, (Berkeley, Calif., 1932) p. 235

149/12 *Chinese Immigration*, 51st Congress, 2nd session, House Report 4048, (1891) p. 44, 55

153/12 *Final Report of the Commission on Industrial Relations*, IV, (Washington, 1915) pp. 3470–5

153/39 Edward J. Flynn, *You're the Boss*, (New York, 1947) p. 223

154/26 John M. Allswang, *A House for All Peoples: Ethnic Politics in Chicago, 1890–1936*, (Lexington, Ky., 1971) pp. 105–7

156/11 A. R. Dugmore, 'New Citizens for the Republic', *World's Work*, (April 1903) p. 3326

157/1 Mary Antin, *The Promised Land*,

Notes on Sources

(Boston and New York, 1912)
pp. 222–5
160/9 H. H. Wheaton, 'Survey of Adult Immigrant Education', *Immigrants in America Review*, I, 2, (June 1915) pp. 42–55
161/3 *Senate of the State of New York . . . Report of the Joint Legislative Committee Investigation Seditious Activities*, IV, (Albany, 1920) p. 3717
161/22 Carol Aronovici, 'Americanization', *American Academy of Political and Social Science Annals*, XCIII, (Jan. 1921) p. 134
169/1 Mary Antin, *op. cit.*, pp. 8–9
169/15 Thames Television interview
170/9 Andrew Dickson White to Walter Q. Gresham, 6.7.1893, *Foreign Relations of the United States, 1894*, (Washington, 1894) pp. 525–35
171/27 Thames Television interview
171/3 *Hebrew Standard*, 15.6.1894; quoted in Moses Rischin, *The Promised City; New York's Jews, 1870–1914*, (Cambridge, Mass., 1962) p. 97
173/13 Thames Television interview
173/20 Arnold Bennett, *Your United States*, (New York, 1912) p. 187
173/35 Allen Forman, 'Some Adopted Americans', *The American Magazine*, 9, (Nov. 1888) pp. 51–2
176/28 Jacob A. Riis, *How The Other Half Lives*, (New York, 1975) p. 80
176/39 *Ibid.*, p. 91
179/10 Thames Television interview
179/28 Thames Television interview
181/30 Isaac Metzker, ed., *A Bintel Brief: Sixty Years of Letters from the Lower East Side to the Jewish Daily Forward*, (Garden City, N.Y., 1971) pp. 73–4, 165–6, 181
186/8 Thames Television interview
186/13 Thames Television interview
186/20 *Reports of the Industrial Commission on Immigration*, XV, (Washington, 1901) p. 478
186/38 *Ibid.*, p. 477
188/25 Quoted in Oscar Handlin, *Adventure in Freedom: Three Hundred Years of Jewish Life in America*, (New York, 1954) p. 182
188/33 William H. Harvey, *A Tale of Two Nations*, (Chicago, 1894) p. 289
190/26 Emanuel Celler, *You Never Leave Brooklyn*, (New York, 1953) pp. 113–14
191/24 Thames Television interview

195/33 *Annual Report of the Supervising Surgeon-General of the Marine Hospital Service of the US for the fiscal year 1893*, 2 vols, (Washington, 1895) II, p. 121
195/36 *Ibid.*, p. 122
196/8 *Ibid.*, p. 126
196/28 Stefano Miele, 'The Differences between Americans and Italians', *World's Work*, (Dec. 1920)
196/40 *Reports of the Immigration Commission*, IV, 'Emigration Conditions in Europe', 61st Congress, 3rd session, Senate Doc. 748, pp. 230–1
197/7 *Ibid.*, p. 231
197/13 *Ibid.*, p. 232
198/22 Adolfo Rossi, *Un italiano in America*, 3rd edn, (Treviso, 1907); quoted in Robert F. Foerster, *The Italian Emigration of Our Times*, (Cambridge, Mass., 1919) p. 326
198/34 Quoted in Foerster, *ibid.*, p. 22
199/20 G. F. Parker, 'What Immigrants Contribute to Industry', *The Forum*, (Jan. 1893) p. 602
200/11 Domenick Ciolli, 'The Wop in the Track Gang', *Immigrants in America Review*, II, (July 1916) pp. 61–6
201/18 Riis, *op. cit.*, pp. 42–3
204/5 *Ibid.*, p. 44
204/8 *Ibid.*, p. 47
205/1 Antonio Stella, 'Tuberculosis and the Italians in the United States', *Charities*, (7.5.1904) pp. 486–9
206/1 Michael M. Davis, Jr., *Immigrant Health and the Community*, (New York, 1921) pp. 249–50
208/4 *America: A Catholic Review of the Week*, XII, 3, (New York, 31.10.1914) p. 66
209/41 *Thirty-First Annual Report of the Children's Aid Society*, New York Senate Docs, (Albany, 1884) p. 44
211/21 Leonard Covello, *The Social Background of the Italo-American School Child*, (Leiden, 1967) p. 295
211/24 *Ibid.*, p. 296
212/1 John Fante, 'The Odyssey of a Wop', *American Mercury*, XXX, 117, (September 1933) pp. 89–97
212/39 *Bollettino dell' Emigrazione, 1911*, 1, (Rome, 1911) p. 169
213/19 Thames Television interview
216/36 Thames Television interview
218/26 Thames Television interview

222/22 Thomas Bailey Aldrich, 'The Unguarded Gates', *Atlantic Monthly*, LXX, (1892) p. 57
223/17 Terence V. Powderly, quoted in Henry David, *The History of the Haymarket Affair*, (New York, 1963) p. 182.
223/19 *Albany Law Journal*, 15.5.1886; quoted in David, *ibid.*, p. 188
225/8 Finley Peter Dunne, *Observations by Mr Dooley*, (New York, 1902) pp. 49–50
225/42 Quoted in Barbara M. Solomon, *Ancestors and Immigrants*, (Cambridge, Mass., 1956) p. 111
226/17 Finley Peter Dunne, *Mr Dooley in Peace and War*, (London, 1899) pp. 54–5
226/30 *Reports of the Immigration Commission*, 61st Congress, 3rd session, Senate Doc. 764, 41, pp. 103–110
227/35 Woodrow Wilson, *History of the American People*, (New York, 1902) V, pp. 212–14
228/1 Henry Steele Commager, ed., *Documents of American History*, (New York, 1946) 404
228/33 Theodore Roosevelt, *Fear God and Take Your Own Part*, (New York, 1916)
230/22 Quoted in David M. Chalmers, *Hooded Americanism*, (New York, 1965) p. 113
230/36 Kenneth Roberts, *Why Europe Leaves Home*, (Indianapolis, 1922) p. 22, 230–1
231/2 Madison Grant, *The Passing of the Great Race*, (New York, 1916) p. 7, 64–5
233/12 John F. Kennedy, *A Nation of Immigrants*, (London, 1964) p. 78
234/15 *Ibid.*, p. 77
237/14 Philip James Bailey, *Festus: A Poem*, 7th edn, (London, 1884) p. 97
239/15 I owe this anecdote to Mr Louis Kushnick of the University of Manchester
239/32 Kennedy, *op. cit.*, p. x
240/18 Quoted in Theodore Jorgenson and Nora O. Solum, *Ole Edvart Rölvaag: A Biography*, (New York, 1939) pp. 153–6
240/33 *A Pioneer in Northwest America, 1841–1858: The Memoirs of Gustav Unonius*, translated by Jonas O. Backlund, and edited by Nils W. Olsson, (Minneapolis, 1960) II, p. 320, 322
244/13 Thames Television interview
247/21 Thames Television interview

FURTHER READING

1 The Golden Door

Davie, Maurice R., *World Immigration, with Special Reference to the United States*, (New York, 1936)

Handlin, Oscar, *The Uprooted*, 2nd edn, (Boston, 1973)

Hansen, Marcus L., *The Atlantic Migration 1607–1860*, (Cambridge, Massachusetts, 1940; London, 1961)

Jones, Maldwyn A., *American Immigration*, (Chicago and London, 1960)

Taylor, Philip, *The Distant Magnet: European Emigration to the USA*, (London, 1971; New York, 1974)

Wittke, Carl, *We Who Built America: The Saga of the Immigration*, 2nd edn, (Cleveland, Ohio, 1964)

2 The Journey

Bowen, Frank C., *A Century of Atlantic Travel*, (London, 1932)

Coleman, Terry, *Passage to America*, (London, 1972; New York, 1973)

Guillet, Edwin C., *The Great Migration: The Atlantic Crossing by Sailing-Ship since 1770*, (Toronto and London, 1937)

Hyde, Francis E., *Cunard and the North Atlantic 1840–1973*, (London, 1975)

MacDonagh, Oliver, *A Pattern of Government Growth 1800–1860: The Passenger Acts and their Enforcement*, (London, 1961)

Tyler, David B., *Steam Conquers the Atlantic*, (New York, 1939)

3 Guardians of the Gate

Albion, Robert G., *The Rise of New York 1815–1860*, (New York, 1939)

Novotny, Ann, *Strangers at the Door: Ellis Island, Castle Garden and the Great Migration to America*, (Riverside, Connecticut, 1971)

Pitkin, Thomas M., *Keepers of the Gate: A History of Ellis Island*, (New York, 1975)

4 Flight from Hunger

Adams, William F., *Ireland and Irish Emigration to the New World from 1815 to the Famine*, (New Haven, 1932)

Brown, Thomas N., *Irish-American Nationalism*, (Philadelphia, 1966)

Greeley, Andrew M., *The Most Distressful Nation*, (Chicago, 1972)

Potter, George W., *To The Golden Door*, (Boston, 1960)

Shannon, William V., *The American Irish*, 2nd edn, (New York, 1965)

Wittke, Carl, *The Irish in America*, (Baton Rouge, 1956)

Woodham-Smith, Cecil, *The Great Hunger: Ireland 1845–49*, (London and New York, 1962)

5 Cousins and Strangers

Berthoff, Rowland T., *British Immigrants in Industrial America 1790–1950*, (Cambridge, Massachusetts, 1953)

Conway, Alan, ed., *The Welsh in America*, (Cardiff, 1961)

Erickson, Charlotte, *Invisible Immigrants: The Adaptation of English and Scottish Immigrants in Nineteenth-Century America*, (London, and Coral Gables, Florida, 1972)

Rowe, John, *The Hard-Rock Men: Cornish Immigrants and the North American Mining Frontier*, (Liverpool and New York, 1974)

Taylor, Philip A. M., *Expectations Westward: The Mormons and the Emigration of their British Converts in the Nineteenth Century*, (Edinburgh and London, 1965)

Thomas, Brinley, *Migration and Economic Growth*, (Cambridge, 1954)

6 The Way West

Blegen, Theodore C., *Norwegian Migration to America*, 2 vols, (Northfield, Minnesota, 1931–40)

Faust, Albert B., *The German Element in the United States*, 2 vols, (Boston, 1909)

Hawgood, John A., *The Tragedy of German-America*, (New York, 1940)

O'Connor, Richard, *The German-Americans: An Informal History*, Boston, 1968)

Walker, Mack, *Germany and the Emigration 1816–1885*, (Cambridge, Massachusetts, 1964)

Wittke, Carl, *Refugees of Revolution: The German Forty-Eighters in America*, (Philadelphia, 1952)

7 The Myth of the 'Melting Pot'

Gleason, Philip, 'Melting Pot: Symbol of Fusion or Confusion', *American Quarterly*, XVI, (Spring, 1964), pp. 20–46

Gordon, Milton M., *Assimilation in American Life*, (New York, 1964)

Hartmann, Edward G., *The Movement to Americanize the Immigrant*, (New York, 1948)

Herberg, Will, *Protestant – Catholic – Jew*, (New York, 1955)

8 The New Diaspora

Birmingham, Stephen, *Our Crowd: The Great Jewish Families of New York*, (New York, 1967)

Handlin, Oscar, *Adventure in Freedom: Three Hundred Years of Jewish Life in America*, (New York, 1954; Folkestone, 1971)

Higham, John, *Send These to me: Jews and Other Immigrants in Urban America*, (New York, 1975)

Rischin, Moses, *The Promised City: New York's Jews 1870–1914*, (Cambridge, Massachusetts, 1962)

Sanders, Ronald, *The Downtown Jews*, (New York, 1969)

Schoener, Allon, ed., *Portal to America: The Lower East Side 1870–1925*, (New York, 1967)

Silverberg, Robert, *If I Forget Thee, O Jerusalem: American Jews and the State of Israel*, (New York, 1970)

9 The Italian Exodus

DeConde, Alexander, *Half Bitter, Half Sweet: An Excursion into Italian-American History*, (New York, 1971)

Diggins, John P., *Mussolini and Fascism: The View from America*, (Princeton and London, 1972)

Foerster, Robert F., *The Italian Emigration of Our Times*, Cambridge, Massachusetts, 1919)

Nelli, Humbert S., *The Italians in Chicago 1880–1930*, (New York and London, 1970)

Williams, Phyllis H., *South Italian Folkways in Europe and America*, (New Haven, 1938)

10 The Narrow Gate

Bernard, William S., ed., *American Immigration Policy – A Reappraisal*, (New York, 1950; Folkestone, 1970)

Davie, Maurice R., *Refugees in America*, (New York, 1947)

Divine, Robert A., *American Immigration Policy 1924–1952*, (New Haven, 1957)

Higham, John, *Strangers in the Land: Patterns of American Nativism 1860–1925*, (New Brunswick, New Jersey, 1955)

Solomon, Barbara M., *Ancestors and Immigrants*, (Cambridge, Massachusetts, 1956; London, 1972)

11 The Immigrant Heritage

Bowers, David F., ed., *Foreign Influences in American Life*, (Princeton, 1944; London, 1967)

Gerson, Louis L., *The Hyphenate in Recent American Politics and Diplomacy*, (Lawrence, Kansas, 1964)

Glazer, Nathan, and Moynihan, Daniel P., *Beyond the Melting Pot*, 2nd edn, (Cambridge, Massachusetts and London, 1970)

Handlin, Oscar, *Race and Nationality in American Life*, (Boston, 1957)

Rose, Peter, ed., *Nation of Nations: The Ethnic Experience and the Racial Crisis*, (New York, 1972)

Weed, Perry L., *The White Ethnic Movement and Ethnic Politics*, (New York and London, 1973)

ACKNOWLEDGMENTS

The illustrations in this book are from the following sources:

Associated Press Ltd: 236–7, 237, 244–5, 245 (bottom)

Baltimore and Ohio Railroad Company: 118–19

Brown Brothers: 152

Chicago Historical Society: 145, 147, 150 (top and bottom), 151, back jacket (bottom left and centre)

Children's Aid Society of New York: 156

Cincinnati Historical Society: 135 (bottom)

Flavio Constantini: 224

Culver Pictures: 72

George Eastman House: 19, 56, 105, 143, 199, 203 (top and bottom), 204, 205, 208 (Lewis Hine Collection)

Gleason's Pictorial Drawing Room Companion: 84

The Graphic: 36

Harper's Weekly: 41, 52, 53, 55, 74, 80, 83, 88, 128, 138, 166, 223, 229, 240

Harvard Social Ethics Collection: 61, 62

Illustrated London News: 27 (top), 28, 31, 51, 68

Frank Leslie's Illustrated Weekly Newspaper: 8–9

Maldwyn A. Jones: 219

Keystone Press Agency Ltd: 154, 217, 245 (top)

Library of Congress: 20 (photo by R. F. Turnbull), 22–3 (photo by Edwin Levick), 108, 109 (photo by Lewis Hine), 131 (photo by J. N. Templeman), 174 (Detroit Collection), 180 (photo by Bain), 49, 57, 60 (top), 194, 207, back jacket (top left and centre)

Life: 189

Edith LaFrance: 115

Liverpool Museum: 27 (bottom)

Mary Evans Picture Library: 71

Museum of the City of New York: 43, 175 (top), 178 (top) (Byron Collection), 157, 177, 184, 185, 192, 200, 202 back jacket (bottom right) (Jacob A. Riis), 77, 201

The National Archives: 110 (photo by S. J. Morrow), 218 (photo by Townsend), 46, 46–7, 47, 60 (bottom), 60–1, 121

National Library of Ireland: 66–7

National Park Service: 93, 96 (Sherman Collection), 79

National Committee on Employment of Youth: 174 (bottom) (photo by Lewis Hine)

New York Historical Society: 86

New York Public Library: 59, 65, 163, 197 back jacket (top right) (photo by Lewis Hine), 58 (William Williams Collection), 175 (bottom), 187

North American Civic League for Immigrants: 159

Parker Picture Gallery, London: 134 (top)

Paul Popper Ltd: 112 (right), 238, 242, (left and right), 246

Radio Times Hulton Picture Library: 112 (left), 241

Neal Squadrito: 210 (left, right and bottom)

State Historical Society of Wisconsin: 126, 137 (Dahl Collection), 134 (bottom) (Schildhauer Collection)

Touring Club Italiano, Milan: 194

University College, Dublin: 66

University of Liverpool: 39 (Cunard Steamship Company Collection)

Watertown Historical Society: 135 (top)

Wiener Library, London: 170

YIVO Institute for Jewish Research: 233 (HIAS Collection), 182, 183

Thames Television and the publishers would like to thank all those who have given them permission to reproduce material in this book. All possible care has been taken in tracing the ownership of copyright material used in this book and in making acknowledgment for its use. If any owner has not been acknowledged Thames Television and the publishers apologize and will be glad of the opportunity to rectify the error.

Maps drawn by Edward MacAndrew Purcell
Photographic work for front jacket by Derek Witty

INDEX

TO IMMIGRANTS

The State of California Commission of Immigration and Housing is created to protect and aid immigrants in California

PER GLI EMIGRANTI

צו די אימיגראנטען

КЪ ЭММИГРАНТАМЪ

A LOS INMIGRANTES | DO EMIRGRACJI

PARA EMIGRANTES | DOSELJENICIMA

A BEVÁNDORLÓKHOZ | PRISTĚHOVALCŮM

ΠΡΟΣ ΤΟΥΣ ΜΕΤΑΝΑΣΤΑΣ

TO IMMIGRANTS — **PER GLI EMIGRANTI** (Italian) — **КЪ ЭММИГРАНТАМЪ** (Russian) — (Yiddish)

A LOS INMIGRANTES (Spanish) — **PARA EMIGRANTES** (Portuguese) — **DO EMIRGRACJI** (Polish) — **DOSELJENICIMA** (Croatian)

A BEVÁNDORLÓKHOZ (Magyar) — **ΠΡΟΣ ΤΟΥΣ ΜΕΤΑΝΑΣΤΑΣ** (Greek) — **PRISTĚHOVALCŮM** (Bohemian) — **AUX IMMIGRANTS** (French)

Underwood Building, 525 Market Street
San Francisco, California

COMMISSION OF IMMIGRATION AND HOUSING
OF CALIFORNIA